MW01631322

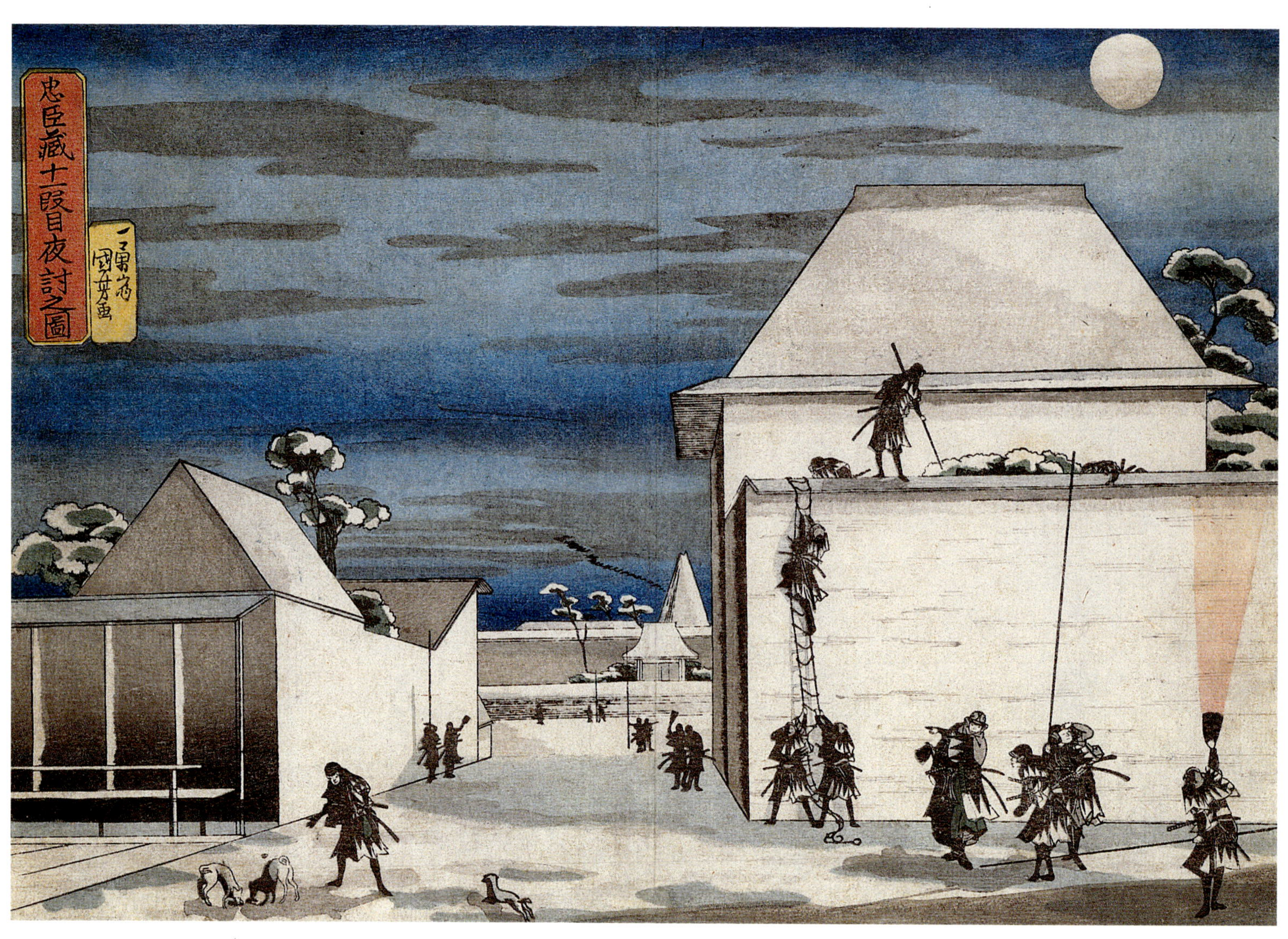
忠臣蔵十一段目夜討之圖
一勇斎國芳画

Kuniyoshi

The faithful samurai

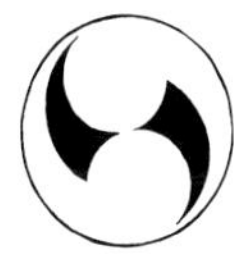

David R. Weinberg

Foreword
B.W. Robinson
Translations and essay
Alfred H. Marks

Hotei Publishing -Leiden

Colophon

Publisher
Hotei Publishing
Zoeterwoudsesingel 56
2313 EK Leiden
The Netherlands
Website: www.hotei-publishing.com

Copyright

ISBN 90-74822-17-7
NUGI 921

Design
Robert Schaap, Bergeyk
The Netherlands

Editing
Mark Poysden, Amsterdam
The Netherlands

Printing
Snoeck-Ducaju & Zoon
Ghent, Belgium

Notes to the Reader

The plates in this volume, except those acknowledged below, are from the author's collection (photography Dirk Bakker).

Plates II.9 and the frontispiece are courtesy of the Board of Trustees of the Victoria & Albert Museum, London (photography Ian Thomas).
Plate II.10 is courtesy of Museum of Fine Arts, Springfield, Massachusetts, Raymond A. Bidwell Collection.
Plates I.4, I.8, I.12, I.13, I.18, I.22, I.26, I.35-I.39, I.46, II.3, II.14, and II.15 are courtesy of B.W. Robinson (photography Ferdinand Carabott).
Figure 3, 'photograph 1996, the Art Institute of Chicago. All rights reserved'.
Figures 4, 5, 6, and 7 are courtesy of the National Museum of Ethnology, Leiden.

Photographs, unless otherwise acknowledged, were taken by the author.

References to the translations appear as I.1, I.2, etc.
References to the prints appear as plate I.1, I.2, etc.

***Mon* on title page**
The *tomo-e* feudal badge of Ōboshi Yuranosuke Yoshio, leader of the forty-seven *rōnin*

Frontispiece
Chūshingura, act XI, Night attack of the forty-seven *rōnin*
Courtesy V&A Picture Library, London

For
Effi and Nadia

Contents

HOKKAIDO
HONSHU
KANTŌ
Sumida
River
Tokyo
(Edo)
Kamakura
Tōkaidō Road
Hakone
KANSAI
Kyoto
Akō
(Akao)
Osaka
SHIKOKU
KYUSHU

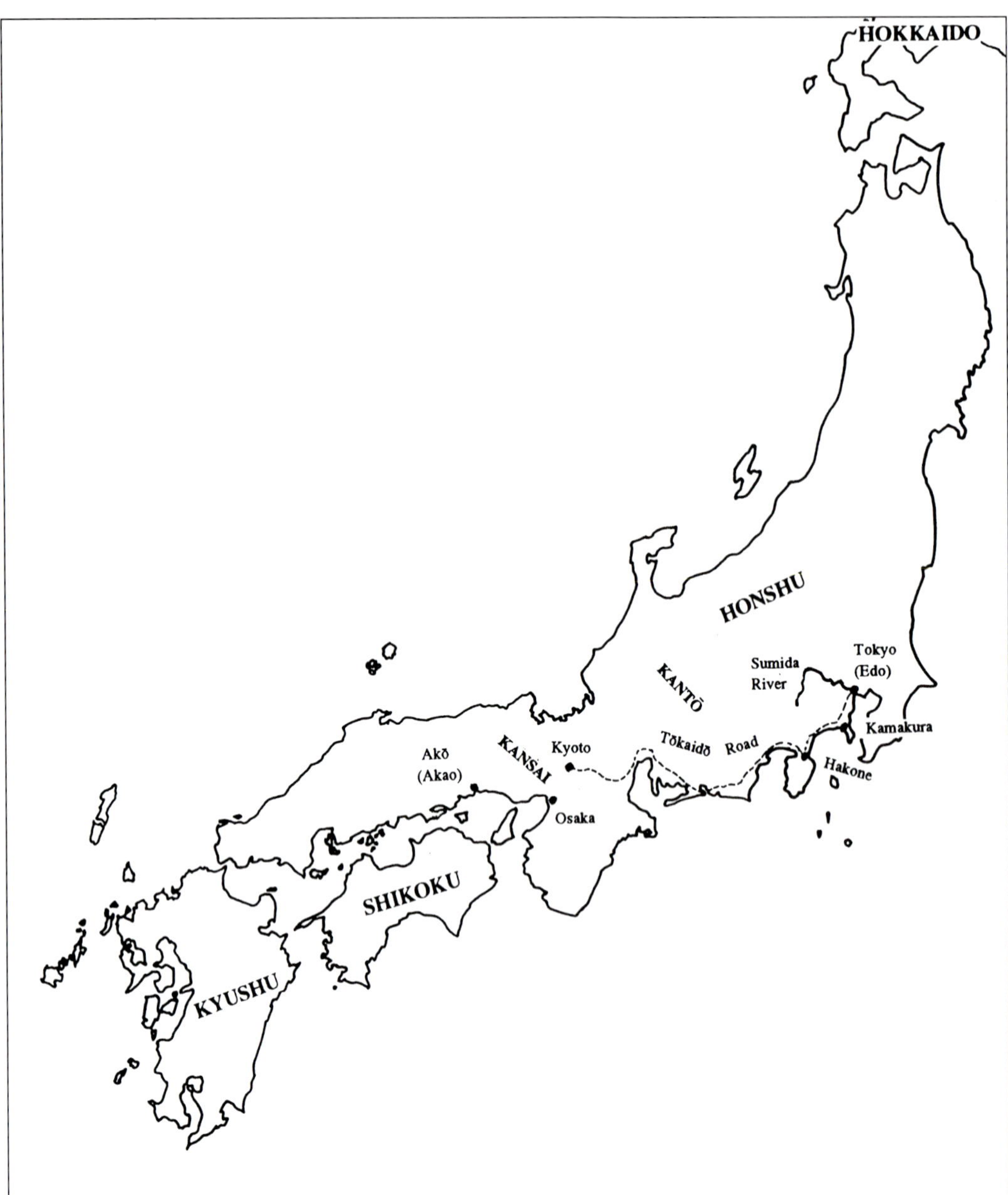

Map of Japan

Foreword

'A terrible picture of fierce heroism which it is impossible not to admire.' So A.B. Mitford (later Lord Redesdale) summed up the first story in his immortal *Tales of old Japan*, 'The Forty-seven rōnins.' It is noteworthy that this is the first story in the first European book of its kind, and rightly so. Although throughout their long history the Japanese have a brilliant range of heroic episodes to look back upon - the exploits of Raikō and his four retainers and the rebellion of Masakado in the tenth century, the bitter wars of the Taira and Minamoto clans in the twelfth, the gallant struggle of the Nitta and Kusunoki families in the cause of the Emperor against the Ashikaga war-lords in the fourteenth, and the ten-year feud of the Takeda and Uyesugi fought out at Kawanakajima in the sixteenth - it is to this comparatively minor episode of the years 1700-1703 that they invariably turn as the supreme example of the samurai ideals of cool courage and fidelity in revenge.

Within a very short period after the actual events, they were embodied in theatrical dramas which became firm favourites in the repertory of the Kabuki, or popular theatre. Hardly a year has since gone by without at least one dramatic production founded on the revenge of the forty-seven retainers left masterless *(rōnin)* by the death of their beloved lord, which had been brought about by the villainous nobleman Kira Kōtzuke no Suke, or Kō no Moronao as he appears on the stage. Dramatists were not permitted to put such recent events on the stage without altering the names of the characters and moving the events back to a comparatively remote period, so for theatrical purposes the whole story was transposed into the early fourteenth century.

The Kabuki theatre was the favourite form of relaxation for the great mass of urban Japanese in the pre-restoration period; in Edo (Tokyo) three theatres were in almost continuous operation, each staging two or three plays at a time, and changing their programmes every two or three months. Closely connected with the theatre and of equal popularity were the colour-prints, from which we derive most of our knowledge of old Japan. Most of this vast output was inspired by the Kabuki plays and the stories behind them, so there is no lack of prints depicting the stirring tale of the forty-seven *rōnin*. Among these by far the most popular is the series described in this book, a series of fifty-one prints, one for each of the forty-seven plus one each for their lord En'ya, the villain Moronao, a loyal friend of the clan Teraoka Hei-emon Nobuyuki, and the retainer Jinzaburō. (These are the names used in the plays and on the prints; the actual historical names will be found in Mitford's version of the story.) The series was published between August 1847 and January 1848.

The designer of this series of prints was Utagawa Kuniyoshi (1797-1861) who devoted much of his working life of 45 years to the celebration of his country's heroic past. His productions comprise both single-sheet prints in series and triptychs - sets of three prints of standard size placed side by side to accommodate a wide and spacious composition such as a panoramic battle-scene or sea-fight. This was due to the official restriction on the permitted size of the sheets of paper used for popular prints. In all, Kuniyoshi produced more than 1600 single-sheet prints and 360 triptychs of this kind. Of these at least twelve series and twenty triptychs are devoted to the *Chūshingura ('Treasury of loyal retainers')*, the name by which the story of the forty-seven *rōnin* is always known in Japan. Of all these prints, *Seichū gishi den,* the series to which this book is devoted, remained the most popular. It was printed and reprinted till the blocks were worn out, it was endlessly imitated by Kuniyoshi's pupils, and it even served for a set of matchbox covers or cigarette cards not so very long ago.

As we have seen, Mitford's *Tales of old Japan*, a classic that has been reprinted many times, remains the best source for the strict historical account of the episode. For the popular or dramatic version, F.V. Dickins, *Chūshingura, or the Loyal league*, Glasgow 1930 (original edition Yokohama 1876) is recommended. The prints in this series, however, are each provided with a biographical text by the noted writer Ippitsu-an, which amply expands on the basic narrative related by Mitford and Dickins. This seems to be the first occasion when a whole series of such biographies (which are a feature of most of Kuniyoshi's historical series) has been made available in an English translation, and so will prove to be of the greatest interest to all who are attracted to Japanese history and drama, as well as a valuable work of reference for collectors.

B.W. Robinson
London, March 1996

Preface

This book is the result of a twenty year love affair with Japanese prints of the 'floating world' or *ukiyo-e*. It all started in a bookshop during an interval of aimless browsing. My eye spied the spine of a book in a rather shabby cardboard slipcase high up on a shelf: Michener - *Japanese prints* - Tuttle. I reached up, probably because of author recognition, for I hadn't the slightest interest in Asian art.

Slipping it out of its cardboard case, I found myself holding a gorgeous silk-covered volume. It opened to the first colour illustration: *Harunobu: Girl with cranes* and immediately, the second: *Harunobu: Girl with ox*. By that time, whatever happened to me had already occurred. To this day I wish I knew how long I stood transfixed in the middle of that bookstore.

Years later, and by then an *ukiyo-e* collector, I came across an article by the eminent psychologist Abraham Maslow which explained, at least to my satisfaction, what had transpired in the bookshop. It concerned *peak experiences*, which he defined as 'moments of highest happiness and fulfillment.' These result from 'the parental experience, the mystic or oceanic, or nature experience, the aesthetic perception, the creative moment, the therapeutic or intellectual insight, the orgasmic experience, certain forms of athletic fulfillment [...]. It is felt to be so valuable an experience, so great a revelation, that even to attempt to justify it takes away from its dignity and worth.'[1]

Thus I had joined, with lifetime membership, that special fraternity of Japanese print lovers who share the same metaphor, vocabulary, literature, and joy.

While I have embraced the entire spectrum of *ukiyo-e* from *bijin-e*, or 'beautiful women pictures,' to landscape, sumo, actor, ghost, and legend prints, I developed a special affinity for those related to the story of the band of masterless samurai, the forty-seven *rōnin*.

That affinity came about through the acquisition of the magnificent Kuniyoshi triptych (fig. 9) at the end of Series I of this book. Each of the forty-seven illustrated figures is named in a small cartouche, making me realize that their characters and exploits are of historical as well as artistic importance.

My next finds were two Kuniyoshi single-sheet *rōnin* prints, full-action portraits surrounded by Japanese inscription. Though I loved the prints for themselves, I was sure that an awareness of what was written there would add another dimension to my aesthetic appreciation.

Then came the acquisition of B.W. Robinson's book *Kuniyoshi: The warrior-prints*, in which Kuniyoshi's dazzling output of Japanese historical and legendary heroes is catalogued and described. In it I discovered that Kuniyoshi produced series after series of the *rōnin:* single-sheets, diptychs, and triptychs of full-portraits, bust-portraits, and battle scenes.

What fascinated me most, however, was the list of some seventy prints in the series I had begun to collect: the *Seichū gishi den* or *Stories of the true loyalty of the faithful samurai,* and its sequel the *Seichū gishin den* or *Stories of the faithful hearts and true loyalty.*

What I longed for was a book in which the complete sets of prints of *The faithful samurai* and *The faithful hearts* would be illustrated along with translations of the calligraphy.

But I never found one. So I wrote one. And here it is.

Acknowledgements

In a project of this kind it is the sincere advice, assistance and moral support of others that brings it to fruition. I am grateful and indebted to many: my wife, Effi, for her endless patience and encouragement; Nancy Hauri, my assistant, who guided the project and shared in its development every step of the way; Joan Levine, for her camaraderie; Dennis Vasilopoulos, for his wise counsel; Tatsuo Takei and Roberta MacMullan Takei for the generous sharing of their knowledge of Japanese history, language and culture, and for their *rōnin* research; Chief Priest Kuwashi Iio, Ōishi Shinto Shrine, Akō for his hours of recorded interview, photographs of the Ōishi Shinto Shrine *rōnin* collection, and gracious tour; Rumiko Nishioka, Yokohama for her resourceful assistance; Yoshino Moriyama, Hiraki Ukiyo-e Museum, Yokohama for her research; Gene Seidman and Ana Rogers, New York for their friendship and professional advice; Robin Kennedy, London for his help and hospitality; Dirk Bakker, Detroit for the photography of the author's *rōnin* collection; George Dzahristos, Detroit for his graphics; and Douglas Bulka, Detroit for his archival work.

I am deeply grateful to Basil W. Robinson who originally inspired this book with his print lists in *Kuniyoshi: The warrior-prints*. He then saved the project by generously providing a number of transparencies of prints from his private collection. More importantly, he gave his blessing to the concept of this book and offered to examine the text. It is a privilege to know him and work with him. He radiates that wonderful but rare intellect which has ripened and matured with age. His eyes sparkle with wisdom and a touch of humour, and his first impulse is to help and assist. He is a credit to the world of scholarship.

The collaboration with Alfred H. Marks has been a joy from beginning to end, and I thank him for taking on the awesome task of translating the calligraphy and poems in these prints as well as preparing the appendices. His passion for this subject matched my own, and what he did in great measure was translate the original vision of this book into reality.

For the delightful time I spent in Holland at the National Museum of Ethnology, Leiden searching in the archives for the *rōnin* drawings by Kuniyoshi, I wish to thank Matthi Forrer. His enthusiasm, expertise and generous time was coupled with warmth, sincerity and friendship.

My gratitude to Chris Uhlenbeck for welcoming this volume into his 'family' of Kuniyoshi publications, and having Robert Schaap design the book further fulfilled my hopes for its final form. The generous cooperation and expertise of Arlette Kouwenhoven, Frank Vermeer and Mark Poysden of Hotei Publishing are also gratefully acknowledged.

There are others around the world who assisted in myriad ways to whom I am grateful: Athena Zonars at Christie's, New York; Toshihiko Isao in Japan; Floyd Beckford at the British Museum; and Bill Stein in Chicago.

There are those close to home whom I also wish to thank: Steve Myers and Izumi Suzuki of Novi; Kaethe Stella and Amanda Allen of Detroit; and Lova Khoram of Bloomfield Hills.

And finally, my appreciation to The Art Institute of Chicago, Clarence Buckingham Collection; Museum of Fine Arts, Springfield, Massachusetts, Raymond A. Bidwell Collection; National Museum of Ethnology, Leiden; and Victoria & Albert Museum, London for their loan of colour transparencies for reproduction.

David R. Weinberg

I have benefited from the determination of the author, David R. Weinberg, to emphasize translation in this project and have been assisted in implementing that emphasis by well-prepared scholars and linguists on both sides of the Pacific.

Early in the process Roberta and Tatsuo Takei of Royal Oak, Michigan prepared summaries of the texts that were of great use. Mr. Takei also assisted in the interpretation of the grammar of certain passages in this language of a century and a half ago. His great familiarity with the story in its myriad forms was also helpful and made available whenever needed.

My friend and one-time collaborator Professor Takashi Kodaira of Yokohama City University, sought out, as he always has, materials from Japan. My colleague Professor Alexander Young of SUNY, New Paltz, provided much historical information. Valuable scholarly advice on certain fine points of Japanese and Korean history came from a completely unexpected source in the person of Professor Benjamin Hazard of San Jose State College, University of California. Ben studied Japanese language with me in Military Intelligence schools over fifty years ago, but I have never had occasion to call upon his skills in the intervening years.

With such assistance, my task in translating these difficult texts has been greatly simplified. I hope the joy I have experienced has not interfered with my concentration.

Alfred H. Marks

Introduction

I. Background

Most events of history, regardless of their magnitude, flow so swiftly into that ocean of the unconscious that often the same generation that experienced them, and certainly the next generation, has little memory or feeling for the trauma or triumphs of the past. Mankind struggles to remember, raising statues, cenotaphs, and monuments.

Occasionally, though very rarely, an *event* occurs in the history of a people, of a race, of a nation, which so indelibly engraves itself on its psyche that the event is absorbed by the culture, and the culture is forever changed by the event. The result is a kind of crystallization which expresses and defines the soul of a people for those people, and for the rest of the world as well. It gives a permanence to the culture and provides a reservoir for expression in art, music, literature, mythology, philosophy, and religion.

Among the Hebrews, for example, the exodus from Egypt and the crossing of the Red Sea is still retold at the Seder table centuries and centuries after it occurred, despite even more shattering events in the history of that people. The Passover is a commemoration of shared identity.

Another such event is the Trojan War. From the gathering of the ships at Aulis to the return of Odysseus to Ithaca, events which spanned a mere twenty years, a crystallization took place in Greece called 'Hellenism' which nourished not only the Golden Age of fifth-century Athens but also laid the foundation for Western civilization, which it continues to enrich to the present day.

Similarly in Japan, an event occurred in Edo at the beginning of the eighteenth century which epitomized and crystallized Japanese culture before it could disappear in the tidal wave of change to the modern era. Forty-six[1] *rōnin,* or 'masterless samurai', in a ceremony prescribed by custom, willingly and proudly committed judicially-ordered *seppuku,*[2] or ritual suicide by disembowelment, for having avenged the death of their lord. It happened at a time when the samurai had lost their social and economic position in society to a rising merchant class, but had still retained their code of honour.

This event stirred the very core of the nation. It was enacted by men who violated a civil code to obey their higher code of *Bushido* - 'the way of the samurai.'[3] It initiated an outpouring of affection, reverence, and artistic expression that has continued to this day.

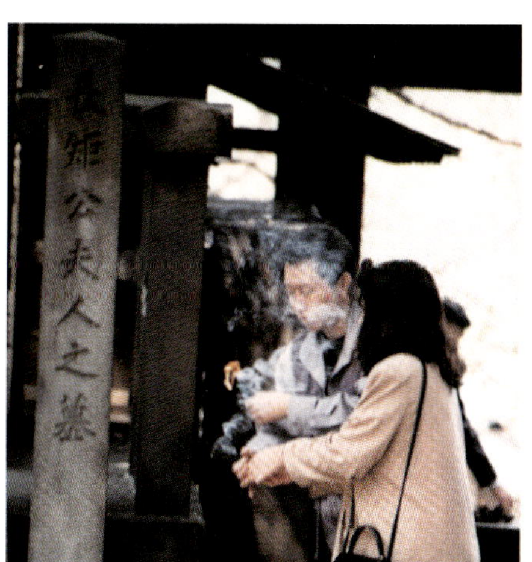

Pilgrims at the cemetery of the forty-seven rōnin *lighting incense at the grave of Lady Naganori, wife of Lord Asano Takumi-no-Kami Naganori.*

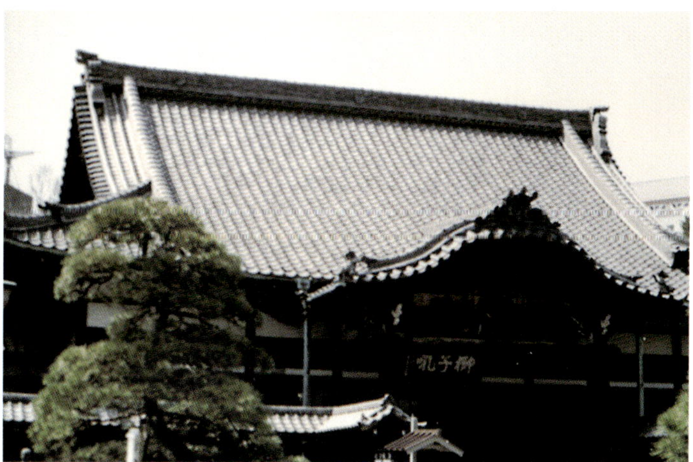

Sengakuji Temple, Tokyo where the graves of the forty-seven rōnin *have been tended for almost 300 years. A museum of historical artifacts, relics, and documents is maintained on the grounds.*

2. The event

It was customary in feudal times for the Japanese shoguns to call upon feudal lords, whose fiefs and castles were scattered throughout the country, to come to the shogunate in Edo (present-day Tokyo) to participate in various ceremonies, official dedications, or holiday celebrations. These compusary visits were a form of supervised homage and political control called *sankin kōtai,* meaning 'alternating in attendance.' This system was established by the Tokugawa rulers to maintain control over the *daimyō*, or 'feudal lord(s)', in order to reduce the possibility of the internecine squabbling and rebellions which had plagued Japan prior to the Tokugawa era.

The processions to Edo by the *daimyō* with his retinue, while very colourful and grandiose, were extremely expensive. These and other expenditures were purposely imposed on feudal lords by the shogunate to weaken them economically and militarily. *Sankin kōtai* also required the *daimyō* to maintain a residence in Edo throughout the year and to leave family members there indefinitely, literally as hostages.

In March of 1701, Lord Asano Takumi-no-Kami Naganori of Akō was called upon with another *daimyō* to participate in an official ceremony. The protocol and ceremonial details of the event required frequent rehearsals. These were to be taught them by the shogun's chief chamberlain, Kira Kōzuke-no-Suke. Chroniclers tell us that he was either dissatisfied with the gifts brought by the *daimyō* or was insisting on bribes from these noble gentlemen which were not forthcoming.[1] As the days passed, his insults and humiliating behavior towards them became less and less tolerable.

The exalted *daimyō* had little tolerance for insult or humiliation. Yet, inside the palace grounds, violent acts or the drawing of swords was so forbidden that to do so brought forfeiture of one's life, confiscation of the fief, ruin to one's family, and dispersion of vassals and attendants.

Apparently, after a particularly stinging insult and despite all efforts at self-control, Lord AsanoTakumi-no-Kami drew his dagger in a fit of uncontrollable rage and struck Kira Kōzuke-no-Suke.[2] He was not fatally wounded, but Lord Asano was immediately arrested and forced to commit ceremonial *seppuku* on the same day.

Two runners, vassals of the Asano household, were dispatched to carry word of the disaster to Akō. They ran the 700 kilometers along the Tōkaidō road which was the traditional route between Edo and the imperial capital Kyoto. Four days later they arrived at Akō and announced the news to Ōishi Kuranosuke, Lord Asano's chief councillor. He took command of all subsequent events.

In the days and months that followed, Ōishi Kuranosuke relocated the Asano family, dissolved the household, and surrendered the castle to the authorities. Then, in great secrecy, he recruited a band of fifty-plus Akō samurai, now cast adrift as *rōnin,* and had them swear an oath to avenge their lord. Revenge had also been outlawed, and all the conspirators had full knowledge that such a plan, if successful, would probably lead to their committing *seppuku.*

After a four day journey from Edo, the exhausted messengers stopped at this well to quench their thirst upon arriving in Akō with news of the disaster to the Asano household.
Photo courtesy Ōishi Shinto Shrine, Akō, Japan.

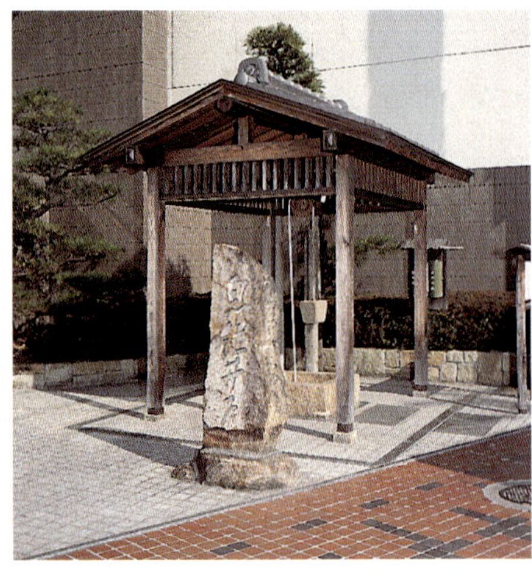

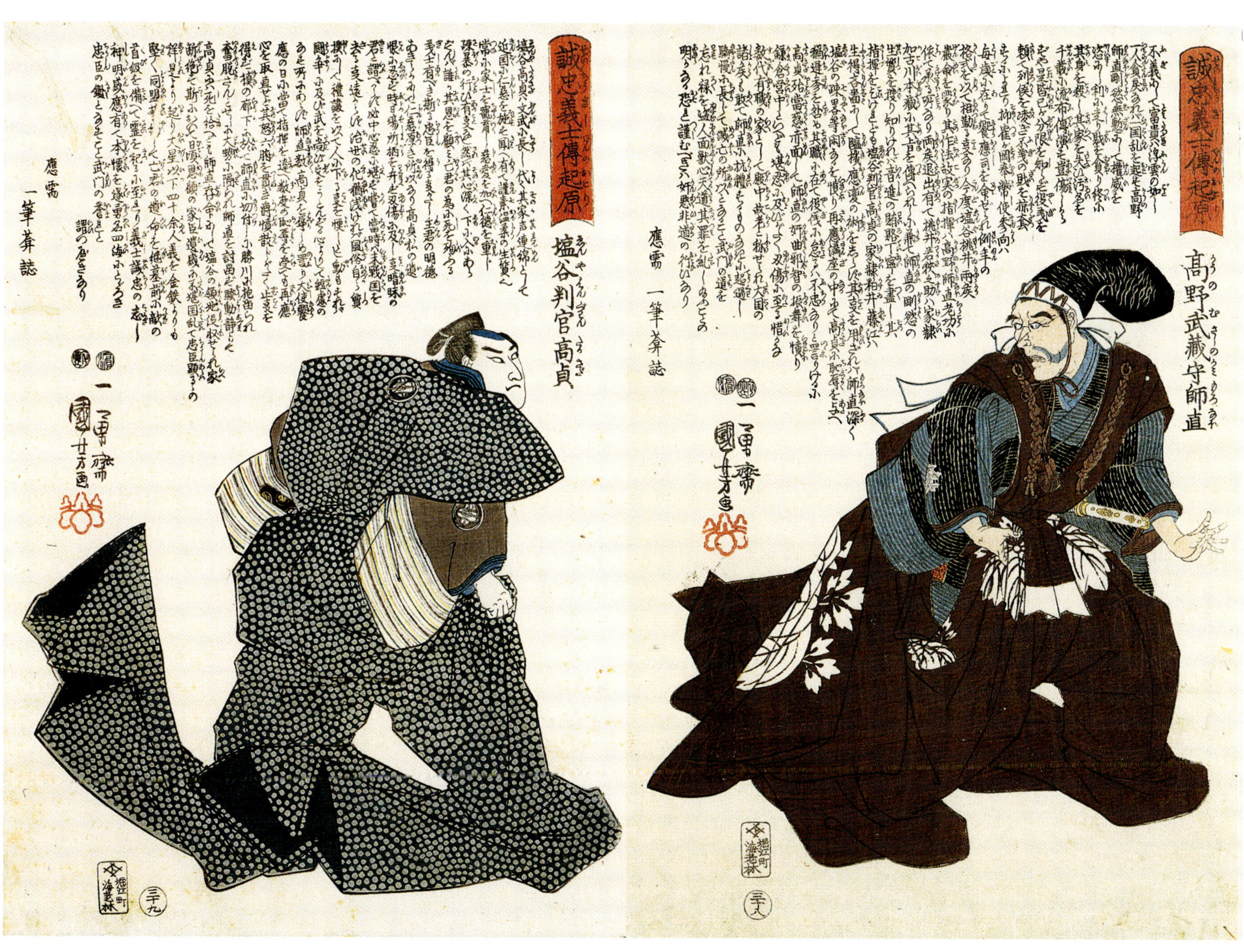

Fig. 1

Plates I.39 and I.38 placed as a diptych depict the moment of attack.

Their resolve, however, was reinforced by adherence to the samurai code, which emphasized teachings such as: 'Thou shalt not live under the same heaven nor tread the same earth with the enemy of thy father or lord.'[3]

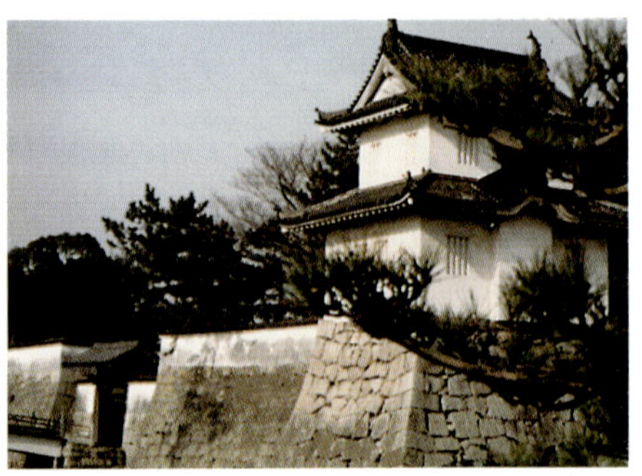

Ancient walls, moat, and gate at the site of the Akō Castle by the Sea of Harima, Akō, Japan.

Kira Kōzuke-no-Suke and his household anticipated an attempt at revenge. They fortified the family residence and hired spies to check on the activities of the Akō clan. The Akō *rōnin*, however, used every possible subterfuge to keep them off guard. It is said that Ōishi Kuranosuke even divorced his wife, took up with a courtesan, and feigned a life of careless, drunken dissipation.

After a time it appeared to all observers, especially to Kira's spies, that Lord Asano's *rōnin* had forsworn their samurai vows and begun new lives following the dissolution of the fief and the abandonment of the castle. In fact, their loyalty and resolve had never wavered. They secretly gathered arms, transported them at great risk to Edo, hired spies of their own to gather information on the layout of the Kira mansion, and monitored their enemy's daily routine.

Finally, after a year of planning, they all gathered in Edo and renewed their oaths. Then, on the snow-laden night of December 14 1702, they crossed the bridge over the Sumida River and marched toward the mansion in the Honjō district. When they arrived, Ōishi Kuranosuke divided his men into groups which stormed the front and rear of the guarded gates and scaled the walls (see the frontispiece of this book).

The feigning and subterfuge seemed to have worked, for Kira's defenders were taken by surprise. While fighting raged throughout the mansion, Kira apparently fled from his bed in panic to an charcoal shed on his grounds, where he was soon discovered. It is said he was given the opportunity to commit suicide, which through cowardice he refused. He was summarily beheaded.

The avenging band marched back with the head to Sengakuji Temple where their master was buried. They washed the head in a well on the temple grounds and placed it on Lord Asano's grave together with the manuscript of this speech:[4]

> *The 15th year of Genroku, the 12th month, and 15th day. We have come this day to do homage here, forty-seven men in all, from Oishi Kuranosuké down to the foot-soldier, Terasaka Kichiyémon, all cheerfully about to lay down our lives on your behalf. We reverently announce this to the honoured spirit of our dead master [...]. Every day that we waited seemed as three autumns to us. Verily, we have trodden the snow for one day, nay, for two days, and have tasted food but once. The old and decrepit, the sick and ailing, have come forth gladly to lay down their lives [...]. Having taken counsel together last night, we have escorted my Lord Kôtsuké no Suké hither to your tomb. This dirk, by which our honoured lord set great store last year, and entrusted to our care, we now bring back. If your noble spirit be now present before this tomb, we pray you, as a sign, to take the dirk, and, striking the head of your enemy with it a second time, to dispel your hatred for ever. This is the respectful statement of forty-seven men.*

The well at Sengakuji Temple in which the head of Kira Kōzuke-no-Suke was washed before it was placed on the tomb of Lord Asano Takumi-no-Kami Naganori.

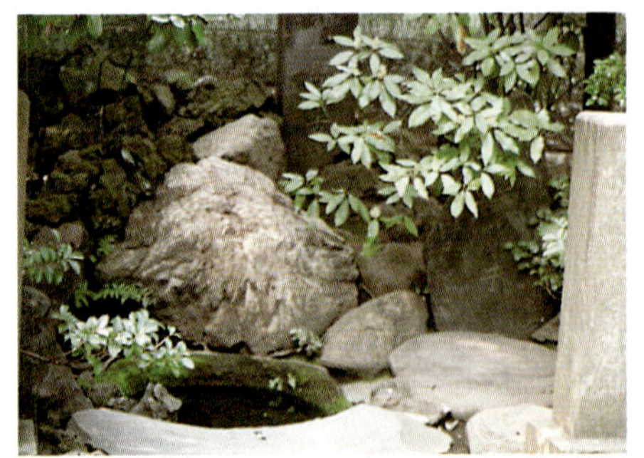

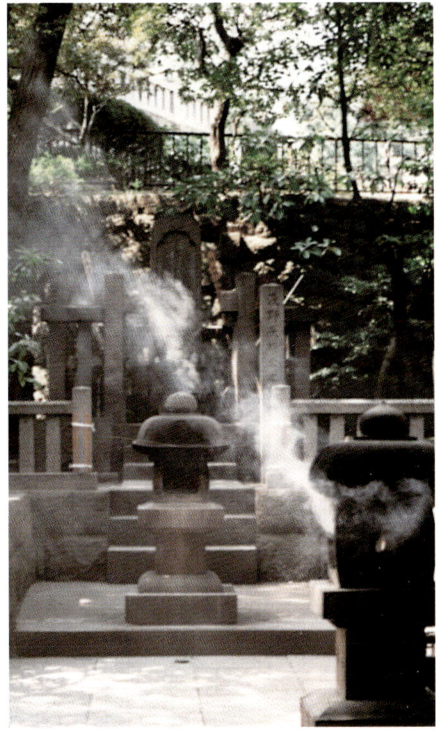

Grave of Lord Asano.
Sengakuji Temple, Tokyo.

Having accomplished their revenge, the men of Akō awaited arrest, which came soon. They were taken to various *daimyō* residences to await their fate.

In the meantime, the family of Kira Kōzuke-no-Suke sent two gentlemen to the priests of Sengakuji Temple to petition for the head, so the body of the chamberlain could be buried intact. The priests duly wrote a receipt which the messengers signed, to wit:

> Memorandum
> Item. One head
> Item. One paper parcel
>
> The above articles are acknowledged to have been received.
>
> Signed, Sayada Magobei
> Saitō Kunai
>
> To the priests deputed from Temple Sengakuji,
> His reverence Sekishi,
> His reverence Ichidon.[5]

Despite petitions by the populace to the shogun, the edict finally came down in February 1703 that all were to commit *seppuku*, from Ōishi's son of sixteen to the eldest man of seventy-seven. The condemned men were divided into four parties and placed in the custody of four *daimyō*. Shortly thereafter the sentences were carried out in solemn ceremonies with proper witnesses present. *Kaishaku*, or 'seconds', were there to strike off each samurai's head moments after his dirk pierced the skin of his abdomen. The bodies were taken to Sengakuji Temple and buried individually beside the tomb of Lord Asano Takumi-no-Kami Naganori, whose honour they had avenged.

The nation, stunned by the decision of the shogun to punish the *rōnin*, identified with their heroism. Something fundamental in the character and spirit of the culture had suddenly and dramatically been expressed by these warriors. An *event* occurred in the history of this people, and the result has been an endless stream of artistic and cultural re-enactment.

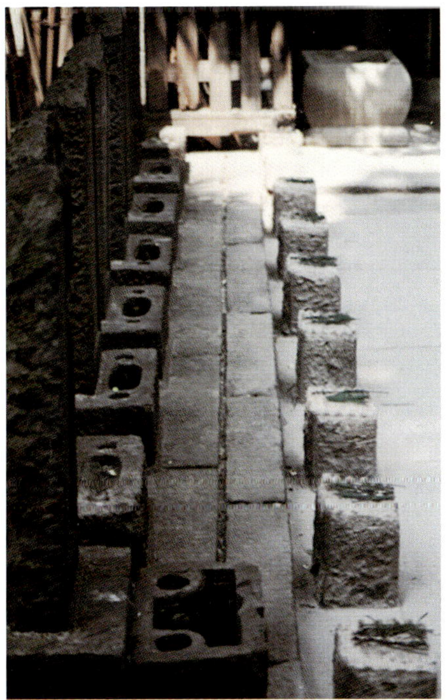

A section of the quadrangle of graves of the forty-seven rōnin.

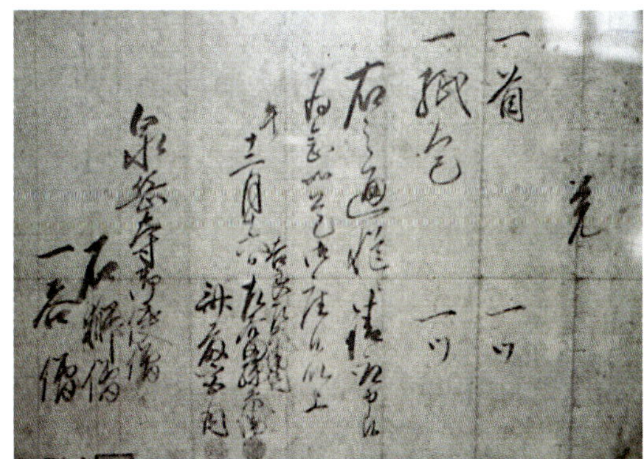

Receipt for the head of Kira Kōzuke-no-Suke.
Sengakuji Temple Museum, Tokyo.

3. The drama of the *Chūshingura* and its illustration

Almost immediately after the event, plays on the theme of the *rōnin* revenge appeared on the Japanese stage. Donald Keene tells us: 'Two weeks after the loyal *rōnin* were buried *Akebono Soga no Youchi (Night attack at dawn by the Soga)* was staged at the Nakamura Theater in Edo.'[1] Fearing embarrassment, the government closed the play after its third performance. But playwrights for the puppet and Kabuki theatres found the way around government censorship, especially in Osaka and Kyoto - a somewhat safer distance from the capital. Around 1710, the celebrated playwright Chikamatsu Monzaemon produced a play based on the *rōnin* story titled, *Goban Taiheiki*, with disguised time, place, and names of characters. Play after play followed for many years. Then, in 1748, the famous dramatist Takeda Izumo with two associates wrote the puppet play, *Kanadehon Chūshingura*, which was later adapted for the Kabuki stage.

In his essay 'Tokugawa plays on forbidden topics', Donald Shively states that by the time the *Kanadehon Chūshingura* appeared, 'there was little concern about censorship [...]. In fact, with its glorification of loyalty and samurai honour, it supports the ethical code in an age when samurai spirit was considered in decline.'[2] Indeed, this play, its name popularly shortened to *Chūshingura*, or *Treasury of loyal retainers*, has endured for 250 years as one of Japan's most popular Kabuki plays. It is said, 'any theatre which finds itself losing patronage has only to stage the *Chūshingura* to regain its audience.'[3] Every December, on the anniversary of the vendetta, the play or portions of the play are performed in Tokyo and other major cities.

When performed in its entirety, the drama has eleven acts. To satisfy the censors, the playwrights changed the action of the play from the eighteenth century to the fourteenth and moved the setting from Edo to Kamakura. The names of characters were also disguised: Lord Asano Takumi-no-Kami became Lord En'ya Hangan; Kira Kōzuke-no-Suke, his enemy, became Kōno Moronao; Ōishi Kuranosuke, leader of the vendetta, became Ōboshi Yuranosuke, and so on with all members of the dramatis personae.[4]

Humorous episodes were added, as were love stories and murders. Over the course of time, scenes and dialogue of the original play changed, but such alterations are the lifeblood of Kabuki theatre. Nevertheless, the essential structure of the story has remained intact.

Various *ukiyo-e* artists had long been employed producing advertisements for *kabuki-za*, the Kabuki theaters, especially in the form of woodblock prints picturing famous actors in stylized poses. Donald Jenkins in *The actor's image* tells us: 'It has been estimated that one-third to one-half of all the prints published during the Edo period depicted Kabuki actors. So large was the market for such prints that whole schools of artists specialized in designing them. The Torii school, which virtually monopolized the actor-print field through the 1750s, was one of these. The Katsukawa school, [...] was another.'[5] Kuniyoshi and others followed this tradition.

The *rōnin* story was a natural subject for them. Not only prints of individual *rōnin* on stage became popular, but also sets from each act of the play. Basil Stewart, in his book *Subjects portrayed in Japanese colour-prints*, devotes seven chapters to the history of the *Chūshingura* in *ukiyo-e* illustration. The list of artists of that period who produced sets of the drama, sometimes over and over again in various formats, reads like a who's who of Japanese print designers:

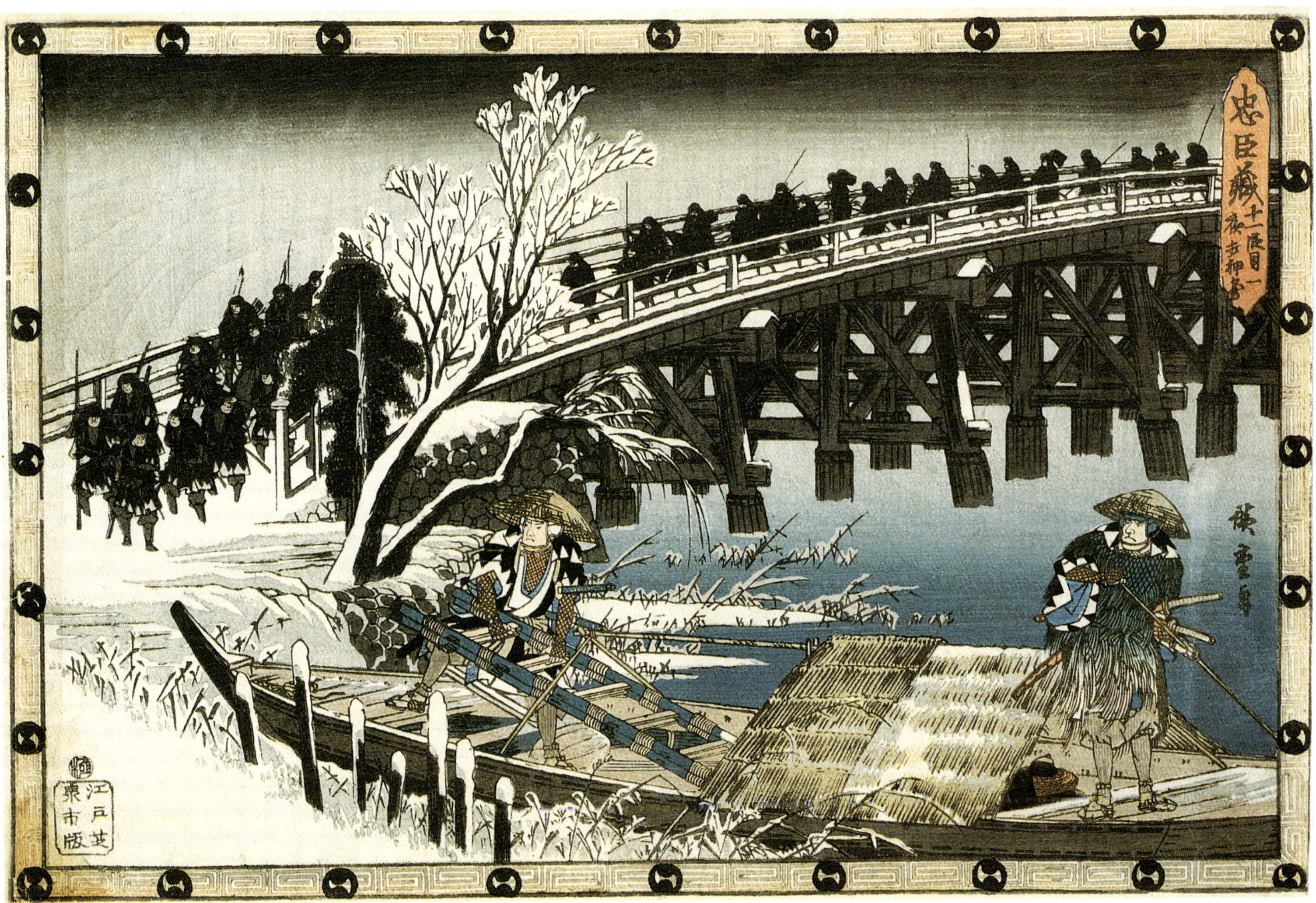

Fig. 2

Hiroshige: Chūshingura *act XI, scene 1* Night attack.

Masayoshi, Hokusai, Hiroshige, Shunsen, Shunei, Toyokuni, Eisen, Kunisada, Kuniyoshi, Sadahide, Utamaro, and Choki.

Many of these works have taken their place among those avidly sought by collectors. One of them is Hiroshige's *Night attack* from his *Senichi* series. Of this print Stewart writes, 'The first episode of the eleventh act, the *rōnin* crossing the bridge on their way to the attack, is so far and away the best plate in the series, that it is a real masterpiece' (fig. 2).[6]

A most interesting development in the depiction of scenes from the *Chūshingura*, led to the use of *mitate-e*, or 'parody print.' Recent scholarship on the nature of *mitate-e*, especially the summarizing work of Timothy Clark, helps those of us in the West to understand the content and structure of these prints, namely: their humour, their simultaneous presentation of past and present, the juxtaposition of the sacred and profane, and the demands on the imagination to comprehend intended metaphor.[7]

The artist most famous for *Chūshingura mitate-e* is Utamaro, who, as Stewart tells us, 'declined to paint actors or theatrical scenes as such, yet designed these 'brother-pictures' as a kind of compromise between his aversion to the theatre as a subject for his brush, and the public demand for dramatic prints.'[8]

These parodies or 'brother-pictures' as they were called, are scenes of everyday Edo life which substitute for the action of the play. To clearly communicate the parody, the artist usually placed an illustration of the real scene in an inset at the upper corner of the print. In fig. 3, the small upper left inset depicts a scene at Ichiriki tea-house from act VII of the *Chūshingura*. Ōboshi Yuranosuke is reading a letter about the enemy from Lady Kaoyo, wife of Lord En'ya Hangan. Okaru, her maid, using a mirror to shed more light on the text, is trying to read it too. Under the verandah, the spy Kudayu is also reading the letter.

Utamaro's parody of this scene substitutes a semi-nude young man on a balcony reading his fishmonger's bill for the formally dressed Yuranosuke. A woman, whose fan echoes Okaru's mirror, cools herself on the verandah. Meanwhile a dog below, parodying the spy, is sniffing at the fish list. The cricket cage above the young man's head even replicates the lantern.

Sometimes Utamaro substituted children for the warriors in his parodies of the *Chūshingura* prints. A famous series of his is titled *Chūshingura osana asobi* or *The faithful treasury of children's games*. One of the scenes in this series (act III) is of a boy holding back a baby brother armed with a drumstick who is trying to attack another boy sprawled on the floor. The inset in the top corner of the print depicts En'ya attacking Moronao.

Further variation of these parodies took the form of the *Chūshingura* 'analogue print' in which scenes of the play and the sentiments of famous poems are cleverly joined into a complex structure of literary and artistic transformation.

Such has been the effect of the *rōnin* event and the enormous thirst to witness its re-enactment. The success which the drama *Kanadehon Chūshingura* has enjoyed and the artistic output it has inspired are testament to the way in which this story fired the imagination of artists and gratified popular public demand.

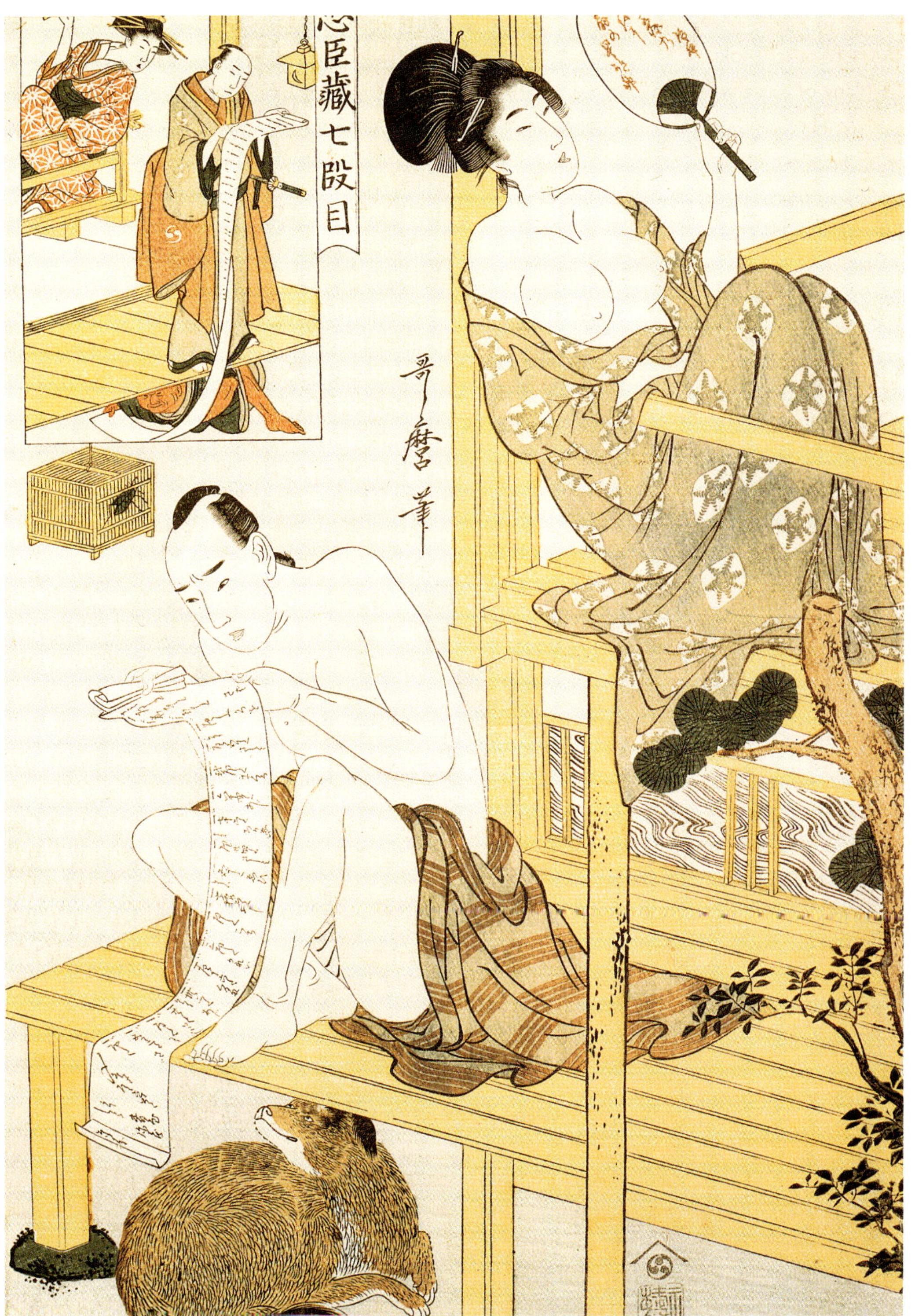

Fig. 3

Utamaro: act VII from the series Chūshingura *or* Treasury of the loyal retainers. Ōban *36.6 x 25.2 cm. Circa 1801-2. Signed: Utamaro hitsu. Publisher: Nishimuraya Yohachi. The Art Institute of Chicago, Clarence Buckingham Collection, 1925.3081*

4. Kuniyoshi and the forty-seven *rōnin* warrior prints

Utagawa Kuniyoshi (1797-1861) was born into the twilight years of the Tokugawa era of Japanese history. The peace produced by shogunate domination still reigned supreme throughout the land, and had also brought prosperity. As a result, urban life became pleasure-loving and was often characterized as the 'floating world.' In Western language one might refer to it as a *Belle Époque*. This 'floating world' is best described in George Sansom's *Japan: A short cultural history:*

> *The culture of the townspeople was essentially the culture of a prosperous bourgeoisie devoted to amusement. Their arts centered round what was called in the current language of the day* Ukiyo *or the 'Floating World.' This is the world of fugitive pleasures, of theatres and restaurants, wrestling-booths and houses of assignation, with their permanent population of actors, dancers, singers, story-tellers, jesters, courtesans, bath-girls and itinerant purveyors, among whom mingled the profligate sons of rich merchants, dissolute samurai and naughty apprentices. It is chiefly the life of these gay quarters and their denizens which is depicted in popular novels and paintings of the day, the* ukiyo-soshi *and the* ukiyo-e*, the sketch books and the pictures of the floating world.*[1]

Born and raised in Edo, the epicentre of the culture just described, Kuniyoshi was one of the last in the long history of 'floating world' artists. The artistic milieu which surrounded him, the world depicted by Masanobu, Toyonobu, Harunobu, Utamaro, Hokusai, and so many others, nourished the latent talent of the future artist.

By providence of birth, Kuniyoshi was the son of a silk-dyer, so that from a very early age, sensitivity to colour and design was his natural heritage. Moreover, his father was a friend of the renowned artist, Toyokuni I, to whom he apprenticed his son at about the age of twelve.[2]

From the beginning, Kuniyoshi's natural talent was directed toward historic and legendary themes. His earliest prints, book illustrations, and triptychs depicted the heroics of battle and scenes of legend. At first they were 'indistinguishable from hundreds of others being turned out by Toyokuni, Kunisada, and other members of the Utagawa school [...]'.[3] Soon however, Kuniyoshi's artistry took on an original, bold, and recognizable style of its own.

Indeed, Kuniyoshi's first real fame came from his illustrations of the *Suikoden*, or *Hundred and eight Chinese heroes*. Kuniyoshi completed seventy-four of them. Robinson tells us: 'Nothing like them had been seen before [...]'.[4] Therefore, it is not surprising, given its supreme heroic content, that Kuniyoshi lavished so much artistic energy on the story of the forty-seven *rōnin* and the details of the event which gave rise to the legend.

Toward the end of his Early period (1814-1830), Kuniyoshi produced the first five of his more than twenty *Chūshingura* triptychs, depicting scenes in the fighting for Moronao's head.[5,6] The characterizations of each member of the vendetta in single-sheet woodblock print format began in what is usually classified as Kuniyoshi's Mature period (1830-1842) and continued almost to the time of his death in 1861. The drawings for the first series (circa 1836) titled *Chūshingura gishi soroi*, or *Complete set of the loyal retainers* never reached the blockcutter's hands. Fortunately four *hanshita*, or 'final tracings', of this series survive (figures 4, 5, 6, and 7).[7] Perhaps Kuniyoshi was dissatisfied, for as finely drawn as they are, they lack the coiled 'kill or be killed' tension of battle so startlingly evident in the figures of *Seichū gishi den*, the series that followed twelve years later and which is the subject of this book.

The *Seichū gishi den* was begun in August of 1847 and completed in January of 1848. We know this because Kuniyoshi recorded it into the penultimate print of the series (plate I.50). This series, one of the most popular of his works of art based on the *rōnin* motif, began an 'extraordinary proliferation of series on the *Chūshingura* theme' which continued for a decade.[8]

Indeed, one could describe Kuniyoshi's concentration on the forty-seven *rōnin* legend at this time as 'feverish.' During this decade he produced eleven separate series (including one illustrating each act of the drama) and twelve triptychs, all on that subject, a total production of 266 known *hanshita* carved into woodblocks.[9] B.W. Robinson's comment about this in his *Kuniyoshi: The warrior-prints* is a mystified: 'Perhaps a Japanese scholar will be able to explain this phenomenon.'[10]

At the end of that decade, in 1857, just four years before his death, Kuniyoshi completed his final *rōnin* series, the *Seichū gishin meimei kagami* or *Mirror of the true loyalty of the faithful retainers, individually*. It is composed of fifty prints.[11]

Kuniyoshi siphoned a lifetime of artistic inspiration from the reservoir of Chinese and Japanese historical heroes. One might call his output encyclopedic in scope. But it is surely safe to assume, given the evidence that the *Chūshingura* theme held Kuniyoshi's artistic attention with so much passion and intensity throughout his life, that Robinson's hypothesized Japanese scholar might well answer: 'The *rōnin* event held a place of very special importance in the psyche of this artist'.

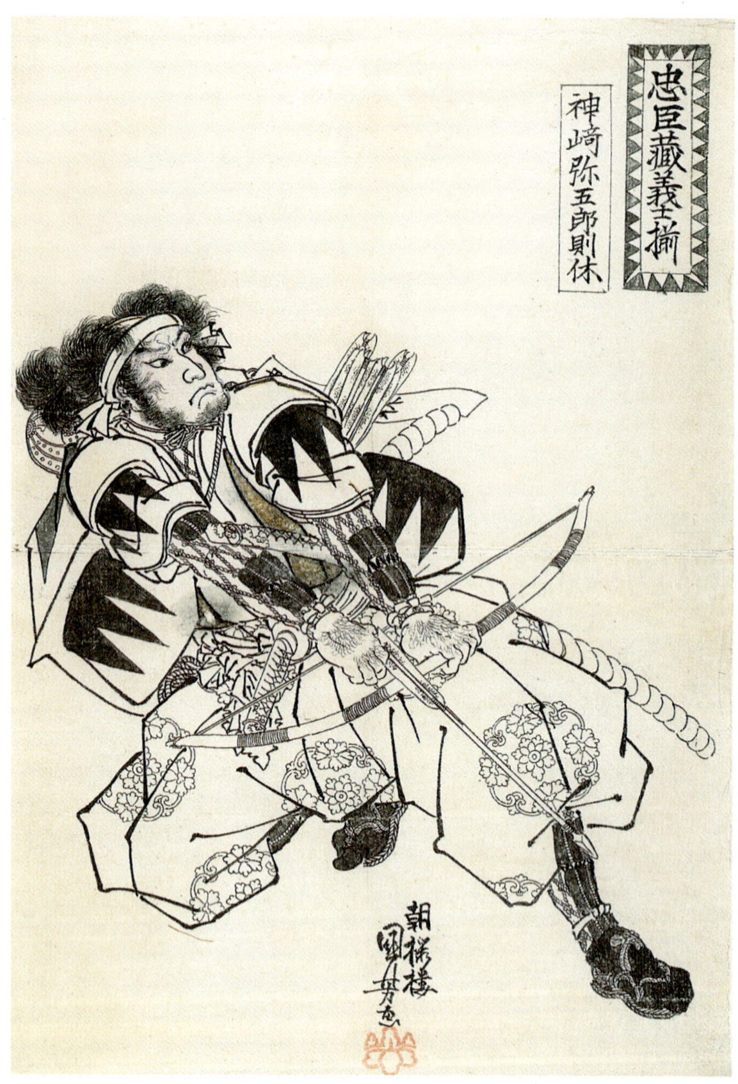

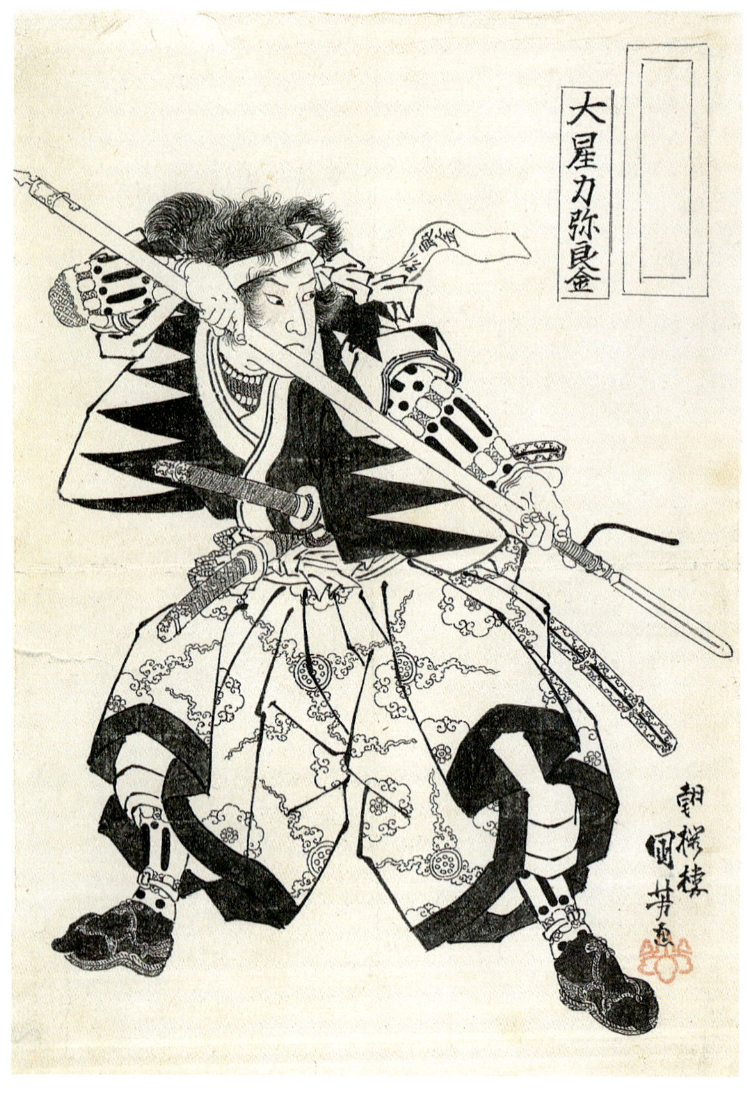

Fig. 4

Kanzaki Yagorō Noriyasu in Chūshingura *costume of black dog-tooth design. Series title* Chūshingura gishi soroi *in cartouche with dog-tooth design border upper right; cartouche with name of* rōnin *beside it.*

Drawing 39.0 x 25.9 cm. 1836. Signed.

Courtesy National Museum of Ethnology, Leiden.

Fig. 5

Ōboshi Rikiya Yoshikane in attack stance with long spear. His name appears in the cartouche and on a tanzaku *fluttering from his shoulder.*

Drawing 39.0 x 25.9 cm. Same series as fig. 4. 1836. Signed.

Courtesy National Museum of Ethnology, Leiden.

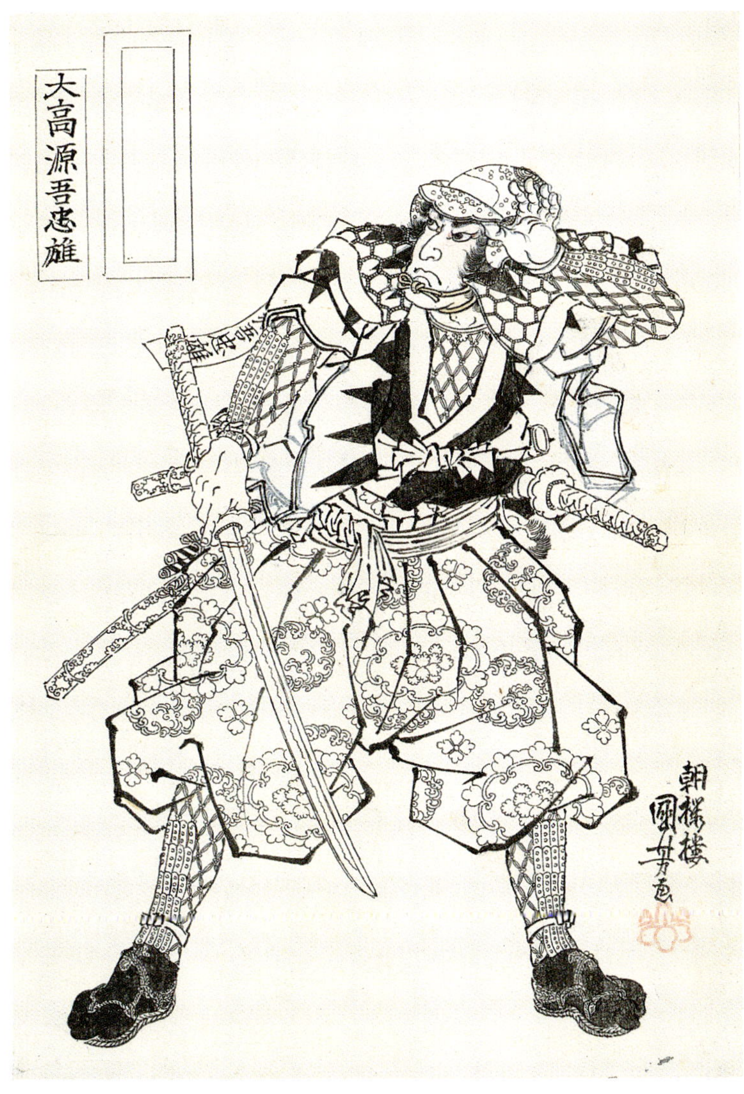

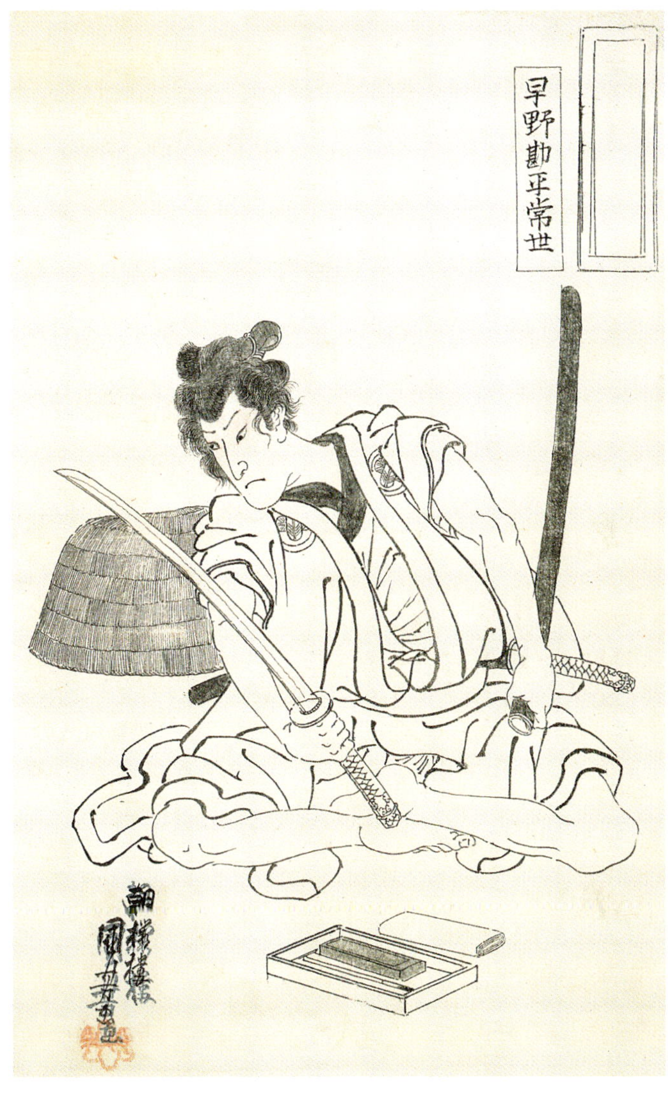

Fig. 6

Ōtaka Gengo Tadao holding a drawn sword; his name appears on a tanzaku *attached to the back of his uniform. Drawing 38.8 x 26.1 cm. Same series as fig 4. 1836. Signed.*

Courtesy National Museum of Ethnology, Leiden.

Fig. 7

Hayano Kampei Tsuneyo examining his sword; a sharpening stone on the floor in front of him. Drawing 39.0 x 25.3 cm. Same series as fig. 4. 1836. Signed.

Courtesy National Museum of Ethnology, Leiden.

5. Anatomy of the print

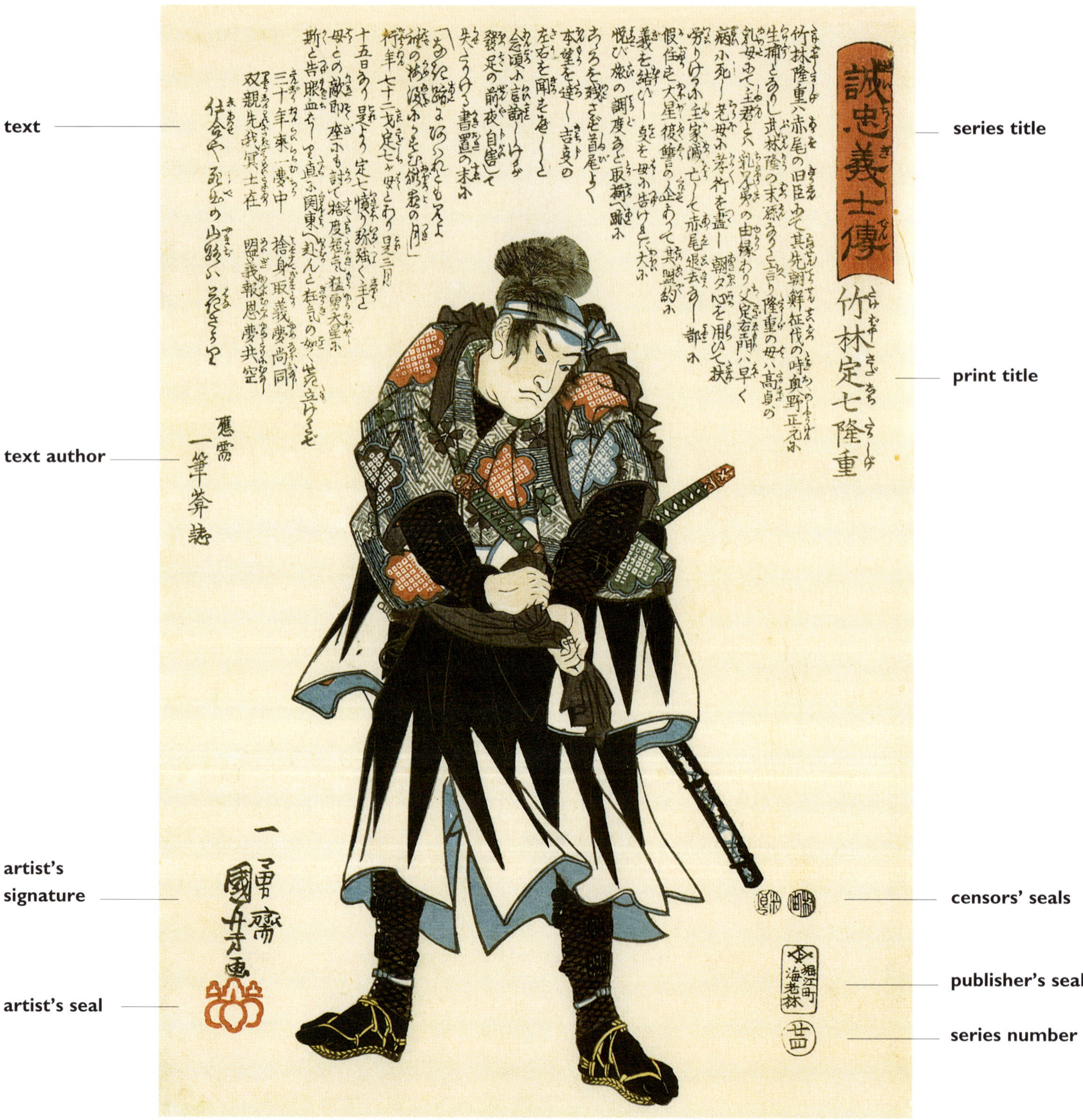

6. Technical details

Stories of the faithful samurai
Seichū gishi den

Series title

On each print the series title *Seichū gishi den* appears in an oblong red cartouche in the upper right corner. Its upper line is convex and its lower line concave. Plates I.38 and I.39 have *no okori*, 'origin of' added to the words of the title.

Print title

The print title appears below or beside the title cartouche with the name of the figure illustrated.

Text

Above each figure, usually partially surrounding it, is an inscription with biographical information on the *rōnin* being illustrated.

Text author

To the left of the text is written 'by brush of Ippitsu-an,' the name of the author of the inscriptions.

Artist's signature

The artist's signature *Ichiyusai Kuniyoshi ga* (*ga* means 'artist') appears on the mid- to lower extremes of each print on either the left or right side.

Artist's seal

The artist's signature is accompanied by a red seal known as the *Kiri* seal. It is a leaf of the *paulownia imperialis (kiri)* tree which appears on a Japanese imperial crest. Kuniyoshi used a variant of this crest for a time as his personal badge and that of his school. Plate I.50 uses a different signature seal. Kuniyoshi changed seals throughout his career.

Censors' seals

The period in which the *Seichū gishi den* was produced required two censors to approve the image. Thus this series has a pair of small round seals for censors of various names, placed near the artist's signature or publisher's seal.[1]

Publisher's seal

The trade mark (a lozenge) and the name of the publisher Ebiya Rinnosuke appears in a small rectangular cartouche at the lower extreme of the prints. Plates I.1, I.4, I.14, and I.19 carry only the lozenge trade mark.

Series number
Most prints of the *Seichū gishi den* are numbered in a small round circle. Plate I.51 is labeled *taibi*, 'the end'. In some editions, perhaps the earliest, the prints are not numbered. The plates listed above in 'Publisher's seal' and plate I.9 are not numbered.

The series dates between August 1847 and January 1848.
All prints are *ōban*, the standard print size of approximately 28 x 35cm.

Stories of the faithful hearts
Seichū gishin den

Technically, the series *Seichū gishin den* is identical in all details as the *Seichū gishi den*, except for one word in the title. It has the same red oblong title cartouche - convex at the top and concave at the bottom. There is the expected surround of calligraphy as well as the author's inscription, 'by brush of Ippitsu-an' (plates II.1 and II.2, however, have a writer's seal in red). The prints have the same publisher markings, 'Ebi-ya Rinnosuke'. For these reasons it is considered to be a sequel to the *Seichū gishi den*.

The series was published in 1848.
All prints are *ōban*.

7. The translations

All events of human history worth repeating suffer change over time in the retelling. Mythologizing is an old and very human phenomenon. Thus, the details of the *rōnin* vendetta have been elaborated upon over the centuries. The conventions of the Kabuki theatre further accelerated the process by visually substituting fiction for fact.

The texts of Kuniyoshi's prints translated in this book contain, no doubt, a mix of truth, tradition, and tale. To begin with, the names of the heroes and heroines themselves are Kabuki names, not true historical names. No doubt this was necessary so that the government censors would accept the prints for publication.

These stories of the exploits of each individual hero and the sacrifice and suffering of their loved ones are part of Japanese folklore. The combined presentation of text and figure has enhanced for the Japanese the aesthetic experience of viewing the print, an experience lost to anyone unable to read the text. This loss is felt particularly by all too many of us in the West who have become collectors or connoisseurs of these images.

The presentation of the English translation beside each reproduction in the series is an attempt to restore the total experience as originally intended. This total experience is characterized by the bonding of biographical detail to the delight of visual imagery. Suddenly these *rōnin*, their mothers and fathers, their sisters and brothers, their wives and loving courtesans take on perspective. We are drawn into their lives and participate in their heroics and personal tragedies.

Moreover, we arrive at a deeper understanding of the samurai culture and of *Bushido*, a code of conduct and order often horrifying but always elegant. Its feudal qualities are foreign to us, but therein lies much of its fascination.

As for the translations themselves, every effort has been made to retain the straightforward style and archaic quality of the original, while taking the necessary liberties to connect events and personages for the modern reader's understanding.

To avoid confusion in these translations, unless the character has a name that is repeated often in compound form, such as 'Senzaki Yagorō', or to distinguish one family member from another, we shall attempt to refer to each character only by the name used most frequently on the print (for assistance, refer to appendix b).

Transliteration of names from one writing system to another is filled with pitfalls, not easily bridged with devices like apostrophes and hyphens, foreign to the original language. The names of the women memorialized in plates II.1, II.2, and II.3 which have been rendered as O-Ishi, O-Take, and O-Hana, have been punctuated using the hyphen to convey some of the delicacy of their place in the scheme of the story. The 'O-' is an honorific, perhaps clumsily translated as 'honourable,' still alive in modern Japanese, as in addressing one's mother as 'O-kaasan' and one's father as 'O-toosan.' The 'O-' prefix before a woman's short name is not so common now. The *Ishi* of O-Ishi means 'stone;' the *Take* of O-Take means 'bamboo;' and the *Hana* of O-

Hana means 'flower', all precious objects in the Japanese scheme of things. The names are so carefully aligned in plates II.1, II.2, and II.3 in this series that one cannot help but conclude that the author Ippitsuan made them up as he went along.

In the titles of the prints, the names are treated more formally as Ishi-jo, Take-jo, and Hana-jo, as the rather personal prefix 'O-' gives way to the suffix *-jo*, meaning 'woman.' Even today, most Japanese women's names end with a similar suffix, *-ko*, meaning 'child.'

The hyphen has been used with all these names, in both forms, to avoid the assimilation of the sound - particularly the 'O-' - with the vowels around it.

Finally, many temple names conclude with the syllable *ji*, which means 'temple.' To avoid redundancy and to better reproduce what the Japanese call the place, we shall omit the word 'temple' after such names in these translations.

The calligraphy and the language

Alfred H. Marks

The narrations on the prints that make up these series are written in a very readable *kaisho* hand, the most readable style of Japanese calligraphy. This is evidence that the artist and his publisher wished to tell the story of each character in the *Forty-seven rōnin* saga with great clarity. The resultant treatment is almost reverential, as it is not uncommon for Japanese texts on religious subjects, whether Buddhist, Shintō, or Confucian, to use absolutely clear, correct characters. These *rōnin* are given treatment normally reserved for saints.

The adulation begins with the first words of the main series, the five characters in the cartouche with the red background, the title: *Sei-chū-gi-shi-den*. All five characters emphasize in their meanings the holiness of the exploit to be related on that page and those to come; a holiness related to the Taoist-Confucian political ethic as the Japanese practiced it, in which the feudal nation and each fief within it was looked at as a great hierarchical family. Virtue is judged by the enthusiasm with which one accepts one's place in that system, as stated in the text of print I.2, in a reference to the Taoist philosopher Lao Tzu: 'Showing loyalty and gratefulness to one's lord and reverence to one's parents were to Lao Tzu the highest of arts.'

Japanese titles are not always easy to read, but the calligraphy has informed us exactly how to pronounce this title, by placing little phonetic symbols beside each of the characters in the title. In fact, that phonetic glossing goes on all the way through every print in both series, making the readable *kaisho* calligraphy even more readable.

The first character, *sei*, means 'sincerity,' or 'truth;' the second, *chū*, means 'loyalty;' the third, *gi*, means 'duty;' the fourth, *shi*, means 'samurai;' and the fifth, *den*, means 'record,' or 'saga.' They combine into compounds to read *Seichū gishi den*, literally, 'The saga of the loyal, dutiful samurai.' The hero *rōnin* are referred to as *gishi* throughout both series.

The second series has the title *Seichū gishin den*, in which the character for 'samurai,' or *shi*, is replaced by *shin* for 'heart.' This series is concerned with the people who showed great depth of sympathy with one or more participants in the *rōnin* endeavour.

In a book much celebrated after World War II, entitled *The chrysanthemum and the sword*, Ruth Benedict devotes several chapters to discussion of the phenomena behind the first three words of these two titles, *sei*, *chū*, and *gi*, and their relationship to recent Japanese history.[1] Although she treats the forty-seven *rōnin* incident directly on only a few pages, it seems clear that the complex of stories and legends on the incident was a basic source to her in her theorizing. The entire book is a valuable source for anyone wishing to understand Japan, Japanese militarism, and the forty-seven *rōnin*.

Japanese calligraphy falls roughly into three major styles: *kaisho*, discussed above; *gyōsho*, or 'running hand'; and *sōsho*, or 'grass writing'. The *kaisho* is the standard. In it all the strokes are clearly represented. *Kaisho* is what children are taught throughout the period of their schooling in the language; the dictionaries are based on it, with characters analyzed and numbered part by part and placed in order by number of strokes. *Gyōsho* is much more abbreviated, with more personal expression. It is also simplified and more amenable to the needs of people in a hurry. *Sōsho* is even more abbreviated, by carefully codified rules, and in writing it the brush leaves the paper as little as possible, joining many words in one continuous line. *Sōsho* can serve some of the same purposes as *gyōsho*, but it generally goes beyond workaday utility and becomes elevated as one of the highest of arts, for both the writer and the reader.

The Japanese written language, as many are aware, is based on a wholesale adoption of the Chinese written language back in the sixth century A.D., a process of adaptation and combination that continues to this day. Each character thus adopted has one or more pronunciations in Chinese as the Japanese pronounce it, as well as one or more pronunciations that are Japanese translations of the Chinese. The character pronounced *sei* above, for instance, also has the reading *makoto* in historical Japanese, just as the character pronounced *shi* can also be pronounced 'samurai,' *mononofu*, and *masurao*. Figuring out how a character is pronounced at any given time - particularly if that character is used in a name - is one of the great adventures of reading Japanese. Countless languages and writing systems have come into use in Japan; however, the Chinese character (usually called *kanji*, or 'Han-dynasty character') variously modified, continues to be the medium most Japanese use to convey words of all languages in written form, whether the language be English, Russian, Greek, Korean or other.

The Chinese language, however, is monosyllabic, whereas the Japanese equivalents of language is historically polysyllabic. In order to use the Chinese monosyllables (*sei, chū, gi, shi* and *den*) in their polysyllabic structure, the Japanese had to invent a system of phonetics to express the extra syllables. That was not easy, and the process of arriving at a standardized set of sounds symbolized by unique abbreviations of *kanji* was not finally accomplished until about a century ago. That syllabary - generally called the 'Fifty sounds' but really only forty-seven - is known as *kana*, or 'temporary names,' and is used alternately with Chinese characters in the normal Japanese text. Incidentally, the syllabary symbols used in the texts of these prints, published a century and a half ago, are different from those which are now the standard.

The writing on the prints, therefore, is not all recognizable to literate Chinese, for the Japanese have made rather new characters of the *kana* to reduce the likelihood that the reader will take them as having a meaning apart from the sound. The Kabuki play that stands as the best known fictional production of the *rōnin* and on which most of the Kuniyoshi texts are based, uses the word *kana* advisedly in its full name, *Kanadehon Chūshingura*. Thus it plays on the coincidence of the number 47 in the phonetic alphabet and the number of the starring characters in its large cast. It might be freely translated as 'The alphabetized storehouse of loyalty.'

The basic Chinese characters are easy to recognize on the Kuniyoshi prints by their complex forms, each drafted in such a way that it can be enclosed in a square or tight rectangle. The five characters on the cartouche show this form most readily. The wispy writing on the right side of each of those characters is the *kana*, functioning here as the phonetic gloss.

This use of prompting characters is called *furigana*, and in these series only the signatures of the artist, of the author of the text, and of the various printing technicians escape the echoing busyness of the *furigana*. A quick examination of one of the full texts should enable the reader to distinguish the features of those vertical lines of Japanese running from top to bottom of each print. The lines are double, with the large Chinese character on the left and the light *furigana* on the right. The characters which have no *furigana* beside them are the *kana* used in the text.

The poetry in the texts can be recognized by the calligraphy as well as the format on the page. The viewer of the prints who has become accustomed to differentiating the complex square characters from the more cursive *kana* may be able to recognize the poems in the original, particularly in the text of print I.22, which ends with a poem in Chinese style of four lines of seven Chinese characters each, carefully arranged in blocks of two lines each, followed by a poem in lovely, flowing *sōsho*, the 31-syllable Japanese poem, the classical *tanka*.

Allegedly Chinese poems written by Japanese do not usually get accolades from Chinese readers, since they are often written with characters that have the right meaning but not necessarily the right tones, which Chinese poets consider essential. Thus the resultant poem can become for the Chinese an unpoetic jangle. The *furigana* used with the poems in Chinese form in this series have a completely different use than elsewhere, for here they show not the pronunciation of the character beside which each is written but the meaning of the entire line (the word order of Chinese is quite different from Japanese). With the Chinese poem in I.22, the *furigana* serves the purpose of simultaneous translation from Japanese-Chinese - also known as *kanbun* - into Japanese.

The narration taking place on the prints is part of a long history of narration of battles that goes back at least to the great epic *The tale of the Heike*, of the thirteenth century. Even before that period, itinerant lay Buddhist priests went about reciting tales to the accompaniment of great lutes called *biwa*, from which the men got the name *biwa hoshi*, or '*biwa* priests'. The emphasis on the number forty-seven and its association with loyal warriors is, in fact, an echo of the title of the series of Chinese tales known to Japanese as the *Nijūshi kō*, or *Twenty-four paragons of filial piety*. The *Forty-seven rōnin* are familiar to the Japanese under the term *Shijūshichi Gishi*, using the number forty-seven with the word *Gishi* that is used so often in the Kuniyoshi text.

A strong flavour of Kabuki and *Bunraku* narration, carried out to the side of the stage by men called *utai*, is also present in the texts, particularly in the passages in which the text refers to people shedding tears. One can almost hear the voice of the *utai* breaking as those words come off the print. The dialogue seems also to be highly attuned to oral presentation, as with the aristocratic message of Lord Takasada's widow as delivered by the Lady Toda in II.5 and the plebeian words of the servant Katsusuke in II.18.

This is only one of the features that makes the text of the second series so marvellous, as the reader is treated to other striking encounters, like the conversation of Ōboshi with the widow of his lord, and the arrival of the Lady Toda no Tsubone at the Sengakuji in a palanquin, there to be treated to a viewing of the enemy's severed head.

The first series is not to be depreciated however, with its marvelous weapon-play, chiming so well with the visual effects on the prints, which at times deal in hyperbole and even humour, as the warriors tramp about the enemy mansion in full regalia, lighting their way with delicate lanterns commandeered as they charged in. The blow-by-blow accounts of the battles even seem to have much in common with the narrations of sumo wrestling available on Japanese television several times a year.

The warrior names that head each print also reflect strongly the culture of feudal Japan: the social stratification, the serious Confucian morality, and the ever-present military concern. Every samurai is identified by his surname and two given names. The possession of a surname alone establishes each as a member of a respected class, in contrast to the servants, who have no surname and are referred to by only a single given name.

The given names, which were attached to men in coming-of-age ceremonies, are filled with words for virtue: 'faith,' and 'rectitude,' and goodness of all kinds. Such names are still common today. There are also the suffixes to those words, particularly *-emon*, *-zaemon*, as with Tōemon and Sozaemon, and also *-suke*, as with Zensuke and Wasuke. Thus *-suke* posits the man bearing the name as an 'assistant' to his lord and *-emon* and *-zaemon* place him in a 'guard' position beside the lord, either on the left (the place of honour) or on the right (still a place of consequence). Not so complicated are the suffixes *-tarō*, given to the first son, and *-jirō*, for the second son, and so on, with names ending in *-rō*, up to the limits of one man's fathering.

Thus the short illustrated biographies that are part of the series *Seichū gishi den* and *Seichū gishin den* are in many ways tales of saintly accomplishments, of military iconography, and the names, the vocabulary, and the calligraphy reverberate with martial, familial and political hope, concern, and devotion.

Notes

Preface

1. Maslow, pp. 44-49.

Introduction

1. Background

1. Hayano Kampei (plate I.47) committed suicide prior to the night attack. He was declared an honorary member and thus the forty-seventh *rōnin*.

2. The penalty of *seppuku* is best known internationally as *hara-kiri* meaning 'cutting of the stomach.' The Japanese, however, prefer the word '*seppuku*' which has the same denotation. For a detailed account of *seppuku* and the ceremonial traditions associated with it, see A.B. Mitford, *Tales of old Japan*, Appendix a. See also Jack Seward, *Hara-kiri: Japanese ritual suicide*.

3. For an understanding of this tradition and its historical perspective see Richard Storry, *The way of the samurai*, p. 83.

2. The event

1. An event of this kind immediately becomes subject to elaboration in its retelling. For the English reader, the best chronicle is still 'The forty-seven *rōnins*' in A.B. Mitford's *Tales of old Japan*, though it must be remembered that it was first published in 1871 - 170 years after the event.

2. For a novelized depiction of this moment see John Allyn, *The forty-seven ronin story*, pp. 37-38.

3. See Mitford's quotation of Dr. Legge, *Life and teachings of Confucius*, p. 39 for an explanation of this doctrine.

4. Mitford, p. 39.

5. Mitford, p. 38.

3. The drama of the *Chūshingura* and its illustration

1. See Keene, p. 3.

2. See Brandon, p. 44, essay by Donald H. Shively, 'Tokugawa plays on forbidden topics.'

3. Stewart, p. 230.

4. See Stewart, p. 233 for a comparison of names.

5. See Clark & Ueda, p. 12, essay by Donald Jenkins, 'Actor prints: Shunshō, Bunchō, and the Katsukawa School.'

6. Stewart, p. 250.

7. See Clark '*Mitate-e*: some thoughts, and a summary of recent writings,' *Impressions*, no. 19, 1997.

8. Stewart, p. 284.

4. Kuniyoshi and the forty-seven *rōnin* warrior prints

1. Sansom, p. 477.

2. For a detailed biography of Kuniyoshi, see Robinson (1961), pp. 5-24.

3. Robinson (1961), p. 6.

4. Robinson (1961), p. 7.

5. Period dates are taken from Robinson (1961).

6. For triptychs relating to the *Chūshingura*, see Robinson (1982), 'Catalogue part II: Triptychs and diptychs,' pp. 169-184.

7. Robinson tells us that figures 4 and 5 were found in an 'Album bound in printed cotton and labelled Kuniyoshi no Kusa ('Kuniyoshi miscellany'), containing eleven full-sized drawings and sketches for prints of heroic and theatrical subjects.' See Robinson (1953), *Summary catalogue of drawings by Utagawa Kuniyoshi in the collection of Ferd. Lieftinck*, p. 40. The Lieftinck collection is now in the National Museum of Ethnology, Leiden.

8. Robinson (1982), p. 14.

9. See Robinson (1982) for complete list of Kuniyoshi's *rōnin* series.

10. Robinson (1982), p. 14.

11. See fig. 8 (I.27) for an illustration from this series.

6. Technical details

1. For censors' names see Robinson (1982) series S54 and S56, pp. 139-141.

The calligraphy and the language

1. Benedict, *The chrysanthemum and the sword: patterns of Japanese culture*, 1946.

Stories of the faithful samurai
Seichū gishi den

Series I

The prints of the *Seichū gishi den* or *Stories of the true loyalty of the faithful samurai* are prints of heroes. They do not depict scenes from the *Chūshingura* Kabuki drama. Nor are they those ubiquitous actor prints of the Kabuki theatre which pay homage to famous thespians in specific roles. They belong to the genre of the 'warrior print' which takes its material from the vast treasure-trove of personalities and idols of Chinese and Japanese history.

Yet, because the *rōnin* story was popularly associated with the Kabuki theatre, as we have seen, these *rōnin* warrior prints are Kabuki in feeling and presentation. This may be seen in the proper names. Each *rōnin's* Kabuki name is announced next to or below the title cartouche.[1] Indeed, the Kabuki name of each *rōnin* is also emblazoned on the lapel of their uniforms.

The costumes of the *rōnin* are also reminiscent of the Kabuki stage. The warriors are drawn wearing the traditional *Chūshingura* black uniform with white dog-tooth pattern over their colourful clothes. Their dress, similarly, is sometimes tailored to a specific role or exploit as is, for example, Tokuda Sadaemon's straw cape (plate I.20). It was he who would accompany and safeguard the journey of the severed head by boat, if it became necessary. We can see the same straw cape in Hiroshige's *Chūshingura* act XI, scene 1, *Night attack* (fig. 1).

But the most striking characteristic of the genre is the warrior in action. Perhaps in no other series by any artist is the warrior more dazzling in the variety of his actions than in the *Seichū gishi den*. Kuniyoshi's genius for movement in combat has never been surpassed, even by his most brilliant student, Tsukioka Yoshitoshi (1839-1892). In this series the movement is athletic, taut, and tense from the top of the head to the tip of the toes, but never exaggerated no matter how contorted.

Kuniyoshi's drawings also relate the story. He intensifies the drama not only by his representation of a particular action but also through his depiction of the emotions of his subjects. Note the warrior's face in plate I.45 as he presses his left hand under Moronao's *futon* and the aptness of the description: 'He gnashed his teeth when he ran his hand under the quilts and found the bed still warm.' Note also the facial expression in plate I.25, and the realization: 'It was a secret door into the garden!' Both prints reproduce what Kabuki-goers call a *mie*, defined by Masakatsu Gunji as 'one of the exaggeratedly theatrical poses that are used to mark moments of emotional climax.'[2] Audiences are familiar with the *mie* in plays they attend, watch each *mie* critically when it is enacted, and often demand that a particular *mie* be repeated before they let the play go on.

The vitality and strength of this famous series is the synthesis of all these elements: colour and calligraphy; motion and emotion; tradition and text. In this series, the warrior print gains clearest definition.

When viewing the plates, it should be remembered that all the fighting in the *Seichū gishi den* takes place in the Kōno mansion as it is being stormed by the forty-seven *rōnin*. The night attack,

1. See 'Anatomy of the print.'

2. Gunji, *Kabuki*, p. 16.

memorialized in Kuniyoshi's celebrated masterpiece, the frontispiece of this book, was the prelude. The series *Seichū gishi den* consists of fifty-one prints as listed in B.W. Robinson's *Kuniyoshi: The warrior-prints*. In his unpublished *Supplement to Kuniyoshi: The warrior-prints*, an alternate print for Rikiya is cited which is included in this book (plate I.2a).

One might ask why there are fifty-one prints in the series. Kuniyoshi chose to include their lord, En'ya (plate I.39); their enemy, Moronao (plate I.38); and Teraoka Hei-emon Nobuyuki (plate I.18) who, though not a noble samurai, was allowed to fight in the night attack because of his loyalty to the clan. He was not counted among the forty-seven, nor was he allowed to commit *seppuku* afterwards. One man included in the forty-seven, Hayano Kampei Tsuneyo (plate I.47), participated in spirit only, since he committed *seppuku* prior to the night attack. Finally, Kuniyoshi concluded the series with one *rōnin's* faithful retainer, Jinzaburō (plate I.51), who served refreshments to his comrades after the fighting was over.

Series I

Stories of the faithful samurai
Seichū gishi den

The plates

Ōboshi Yuranosuke Yoshio

The 'Yuranosuke' in Yoshio's name came from his father.[1] His mother was the daughter of a family named Ikeda, of Bizen. Through his mother, Yuranosuke became a chief councillor of the Akao clan, in Banshū, and managed the clan's lands with such concern for the farmers that they accorded him all the respect of a parent.

After the unforeseen disaster to the central family and the dispersal of all the retainers, Yoshio watched the repose of their enemy with ever-increasing resentment. He then took charge and laid plans, swearing forty-some faithful samurai into an iron confederation.[2]

They then swept in one night and attacked the enemy's mansion, took the head of the enemy lord, and offered it up at the grave of their departed master.

Their craft, courage and self-sacrificing loyalty has gone beyond anything known to man, past or present.

Yoshio excelled in all the martial arts of the Kōshū school and was a favoured student of Yamaga Jingoemon Motoyuki. Under conditions of complete secrecy, he handled his subordinates with great skill. His son, Yoshikane, age sixteen, followed his father and never looked back, as did the boy's mother, faithful even to death, the epitome of heroism.

One's lord's life is heavier than ten thousand mountains.
One's own life is lighter than a hair.[3]

I.I

Ōboshi Yuranosuke Yoshio seated on a campstool beating a drum

1. His historical name was Oishi Kuranosuke Yoshio (1659-1703). He is referred to in this series mostly by his surname, Ōboshi. The names of the warriors are varied subtly, and not so subtly, in the countless retellings of this story.

2. Forty-six *rōnin* actually participated. The pennant on Ōboshi's spear reads: 'Hayano Kampei, killed in battle.' He was the honorary forty-seventh *rōnin*.

3. This is a two-line poem written in what the Japanese call *kanbun* or 'Chinese text.' It has seven characters to the line, an example of what the Japanese call a *shichi-gon sekku*, or 'seven-character stanza form.' The inscription on the drum, is an abbreviated variation on the proverb cited in the poem: 'Life is lighter than duty.'

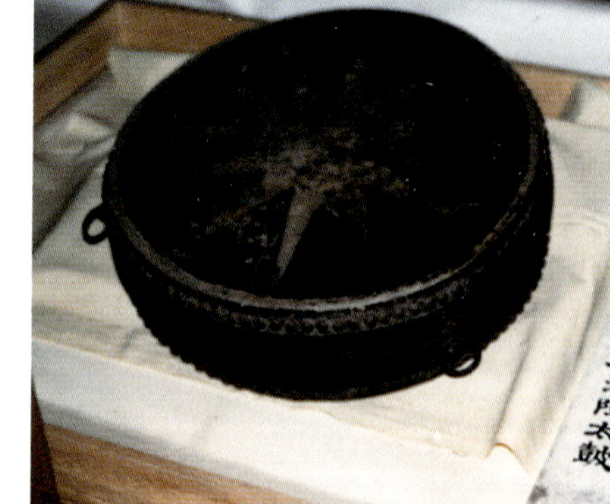

Military drum.
Sengakuji Temple Collection.

▼▼▼▼▼▼▼▼

'Having thus laid all his plans and posted his men, Kuranosuké with his own hand beat the drum and gave the signal for attack [...] and Kuranosuké sitting on a camp-stool, gave his orders and directed the rōnins.' Mitford p. 29.

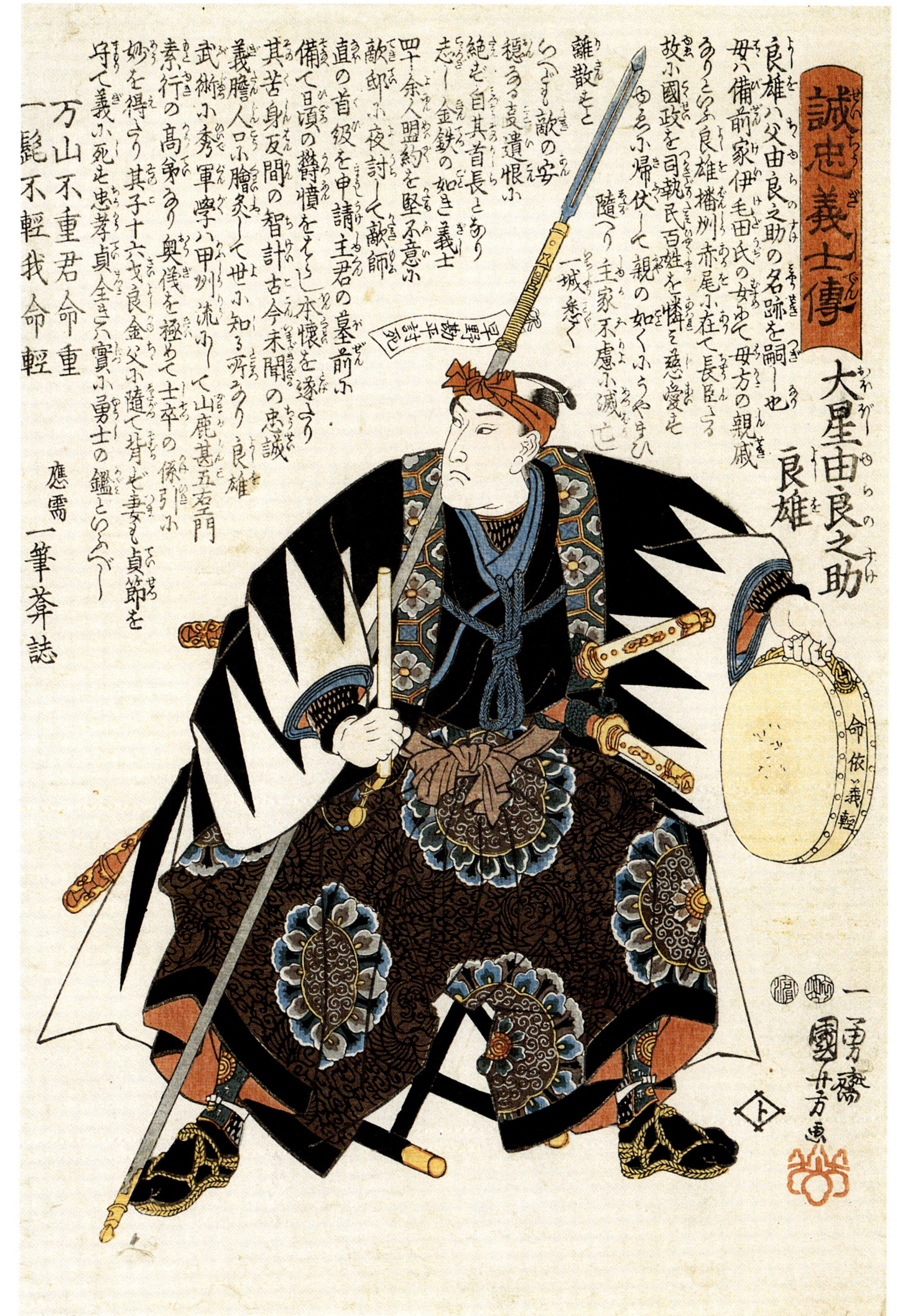
誠忠義士傳
大星由良之助
良雄
一勇斎國芳画

Ōboshi Rikiya Yoshikane

Although Ōboshi Yoshio's son Rikiya was a youth of only sixteen years, he was taller and stronger than most and expert in the martial arts.[1] When the house of Akao fell and the determined confederates gathered at Kagakuji to take the vendetta oath, his father left him off the roll.

Hara Gōemon turned to Ōboshi and said: 'Your son is truly courageous and could even be given command responsibilities. How can you leave him out?'

Ōboshi answered: 'He is very young, and so conscious of his mother's love that at some time he may have serious doubts. So I left him off to spare him possible embarrassment.'

When Rikiya heard this, he turned quite red, went to the sanctuary, stripped off his upper garments, and gave every indication of preparing to commit *seppuku*. His comrades, however, rushed to stop him. Yoshio was pleased to see Rikiya's determination, as were the other members of the band, and he then administered the blood oath. The father was so deeply pleased that he shed tears without realizing he was doing so.

So, afterward, Rikiya made his way to Azuma and quietly took up residence in the village of Hirama, in Bushū. On the night of the attack on the enemy mansion, he performed with distinction and inflicted much pain on the enemy. Showing loyalty and gratefulness to one's lord and reverence to one's parents were to Lao Tzu the highest of arts. Both of these Yoshikane exhibited.

If it comes to that
sacrifice even your life
see the fallen snow![2]

(Izakereba inochi wo sutete yukimi kana)

I.2

Ōboshi Rikiya Yoshikane seated, helmet and cape attached to his spear

I.2a[1]

Ōboshi Rikiya Yoshikane standing, holding a spear

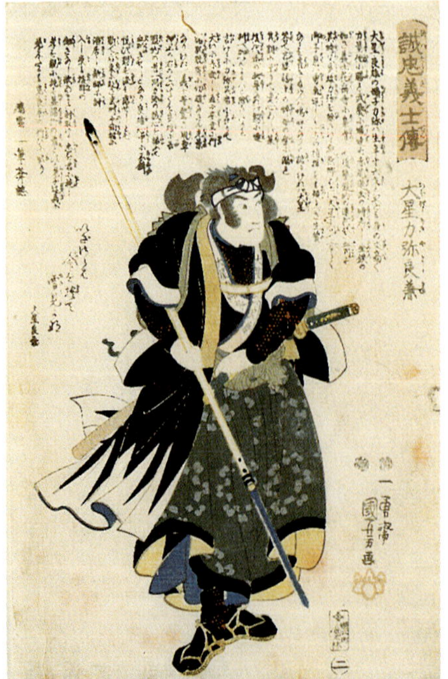

1. Attached to Rikiya's long spear in the print is the *rōnin* headgear and dog-tooth pattern cape.

2. An allusion to the Bashō *haiku:*

Let us say farewell
until we tumble about
viewing fallen snow

(Iza saraba yukimi ni korobu tokoro made)

1. This rare print of Rikiya standing is an alternate design to the opposite print of Rikiya seated. The text of plate I.2a is the same as plate I.2.

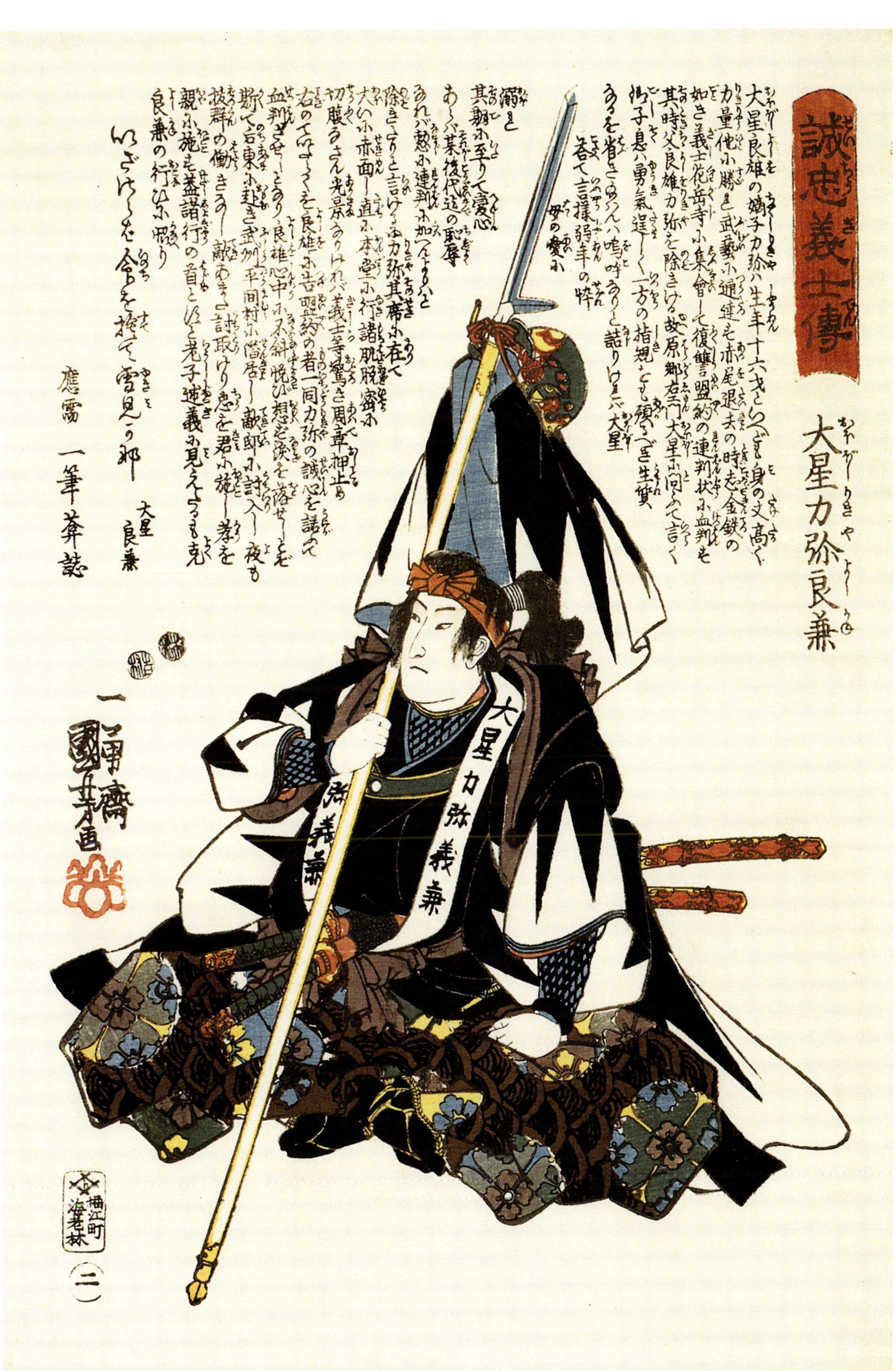
誠忠義士傳
大星力弥良兼
大星力弥義兼
應需 一筆菴誌
一勇齋國芳画
海老林
二

Yatō Yomoshichi Norikane

1.3

Yatō Yomoshichi Norikane drinking from a decorated cup

Yomoshichi's father, Yatō Chōsuke, came from a family that had been Akao retainers for generations. After Seki Castle was confiscated, he wandered about Naniwa supporting himself by teaching Noh recitation.[1] He also joined company with the loyal retainers, even though he was not well.

Before long he felt his end was near and called his son, Yomoshichi, to his bedside. There he told him: 'The vendetta I swore to with Ōboshi Yoshio is going to mobilize soon, but my illness will prevent me from achieving what I have set my heart on. You are very young, but I would like you to carry out my wishes and join Ōboshi on his trip to the Kantō to avenge the death of our lord and relieve him of his torment in his grave.[2] I regret this much, but ...' and with that he said no more.

Yomoshichi did not grieve long, and after his father's funeral went with his mother to Yamashina to see Ōboshi. There she tearfully described her late husband's dying wish and begged that this very young man be part of the vendetta, or at least be taken to the Kantō as a servant.

Ōboshi was impressed by the mother's sincerity. Here was this woman who had never learned how to compromise with love, standing there like a cow licking its calf, offering her beloved son to face death for loyalty's sake. This was an extremely rare expression of human wishes in this world. He then accepted the boy into the band.

At sixteen, Yomoshichi was the same age as Ōboshi Rikiya. He was adept with sword and spear, and courageous with a heroic quality even greater than that of his father.[3] He enjoyed *haikai* and wrote under the name Chihō.

His mother lived very long and died in Mayabashi, in Jōshū, at the age of eighty-seven. Her gravestone is still there.

A snowy morning
and on this spot someone's life
will come to an end.

Chihō

1. The first character of the name Akao has two pronunciations. One is *aka*, the other is *seki*. The name of the castle used the reading *Seki*.

2. The area around Edo, or present-day Tokyo, is known as the Kantō region, meaning 'east of the barrier gate at Ausaka.' This is in contrast to the name Kansai ('west of the barrier') for the Kyoto, Osaka, Kobe area.

3. All the samurai in this series wear the two swords that are the regulation accoutrements of their trade as well as the symbols of their status. The longer sword was sometimes too long for the occasion, at which time the other was drawn. Most of the prints carefully show which sword is in play. The spear, or javelin, which is being carried in many of the prints, could be hurled before the sword is drawn or used as a weapon of choice.

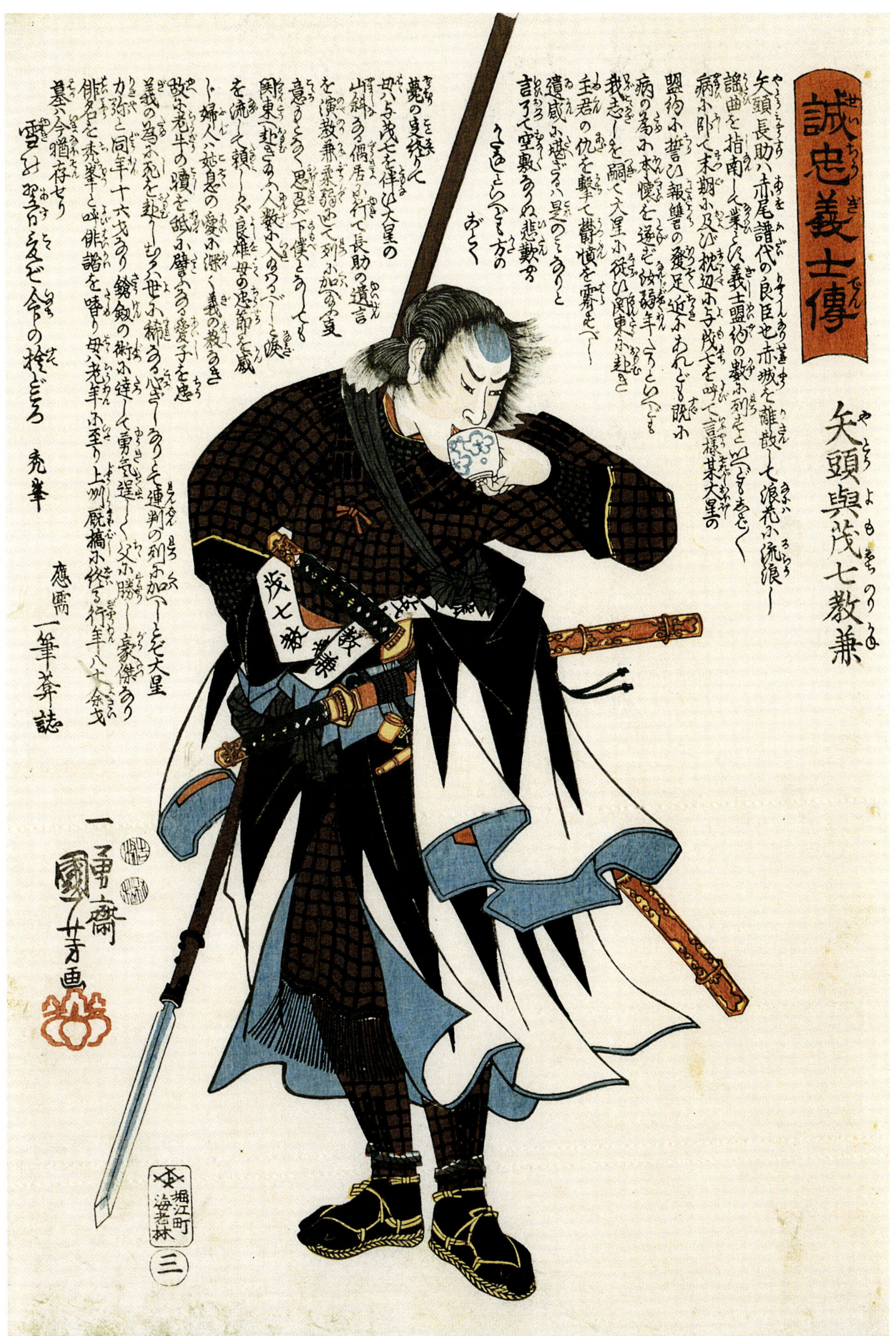
誠忠義士傳
矢頭與茂七教兼
應需 一筆菴誌
秀峯
一勇齋國芳画
堀江町 海老林
三

Fuwa Katsuemon Masatane

1.4

Fuwa Katsuemon Masatane examining the cutting edge of his sword

Masatane was over six feet tall, with a hot, quick temper - strong and a lover of the martial arts. He knew all the secrets of the Kurama Shindō school of swordsmanship.[1] He was also skilled at *suemono-giri* - now known as *tameshi giri* - meaning the art of cutting a body in two.

There was a paper merchant in town whose wife died suddenly of a venereal disease. She had been a promiscuous woman, whose adulteries and liaisons were an open scandal. Masatane had a new blade that he wanted to test and, aware that she was big-boned and corpulent, decided to test it on her. So he went to the cemetery, dug up the corpse, and cut to his heart's content.

The merchant was shocked and complained to the authorities, and the lord, saying that what Masatane had done was unworthy of a samurai, regretfully discharged him. He wandered about under the stigma of having displeased his lord.

When he heard about the catastrophe involving the Akao, he rushed back to the castle with his weapons, ready to join them in any uprising. Ōboshi, however, said he had no use for someone with the disfavour of his lord upon him. So Masatane swore that he would apologize at the grave of his lord and swear allegiance to him to the death. Ōboshi then told him of the plot.

When they got to the Kantō his heroism was unmatched.

1. Masatane examining the blade of his sword is an appropriate illustration of a 'lover of the martial arts who knew all the secrets of the Kurama Shindō school of swordsmanship.'

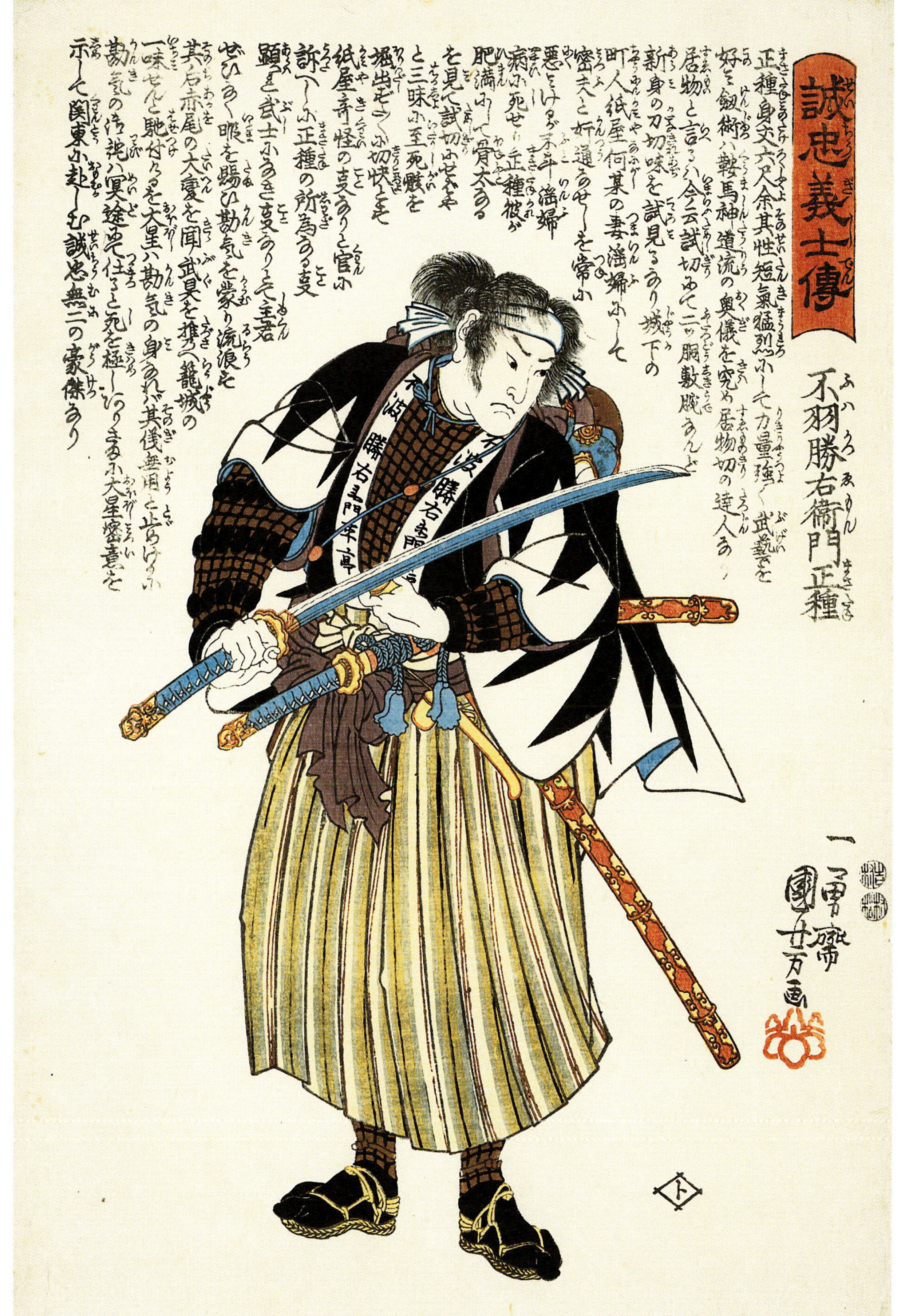
誠忠義士傳
不破勝右衛門正種
一勇齋國芳画

Shikamatsu Kanroku Yukishige

1.5

Shikamatsu Kanroku Yukishige wringing water from his sleeve

Kanroku's family had been faithful Akao retainers for generations. He was proficient in all the military arts, was particularly skilled in archery, and could even kill birds in flight.

He was a good son to his aged mother, almost seventy, and never talked back to her or neglected her in any way. He was a splendid person.

When fate intervened and their lord was executed and the Akao estates were confiscated, he went to stay with friends in the village of Yoko-o, in Banshū. That was when over 360 men signed in blood a compact with Ōboshi to defend the castle and die martyr's deaths.[1]

After the castle was surrendered peacefully, more than 150 men gathered again in the sanctuary of Kagakuji and swore to die together. Fifty of them, however, considering their oath to be iron-clad, followed the counsel of Ōboshi and his advisers and worked out plans for a more secret vendetta. With that they made their separate preparations to move to the Kantō, where they could vent their burning indignation.

At that time, Kanroku was busy taking care of his mother and informed Ōboshi that she was unable to travel with him. Ōboshi told him that, although he was going to the Kantō at this time, Kanroku could follow later at his own pace. In fact, Ōboshi met with the mother and told her not to worry.

She then talked to Kanroku and told him that if he was so concerned about his mother he might do something of which he was not worthy, and with that she told him he must go. That night she hanged herself.

Those who heard the story were taken by the self-abnegation she showed and broke into tears.[2]

1. The text of this print shows four phases of the vendetta: 1. the aborted standoff at the castle, 2. the compact at Kagakuji, 3. the separate compact of the fifty retainers, 4. the march, in separate groups, to the Kantō. The last, the night attack, is not narrated.

2. Kanroku's sad expression and the echo of tears represented as water dripping from wringing out his sleeve is, no doubt, Kuniyoshi's way of illustrating this *rōnin's* grief at the suicide of his mother.

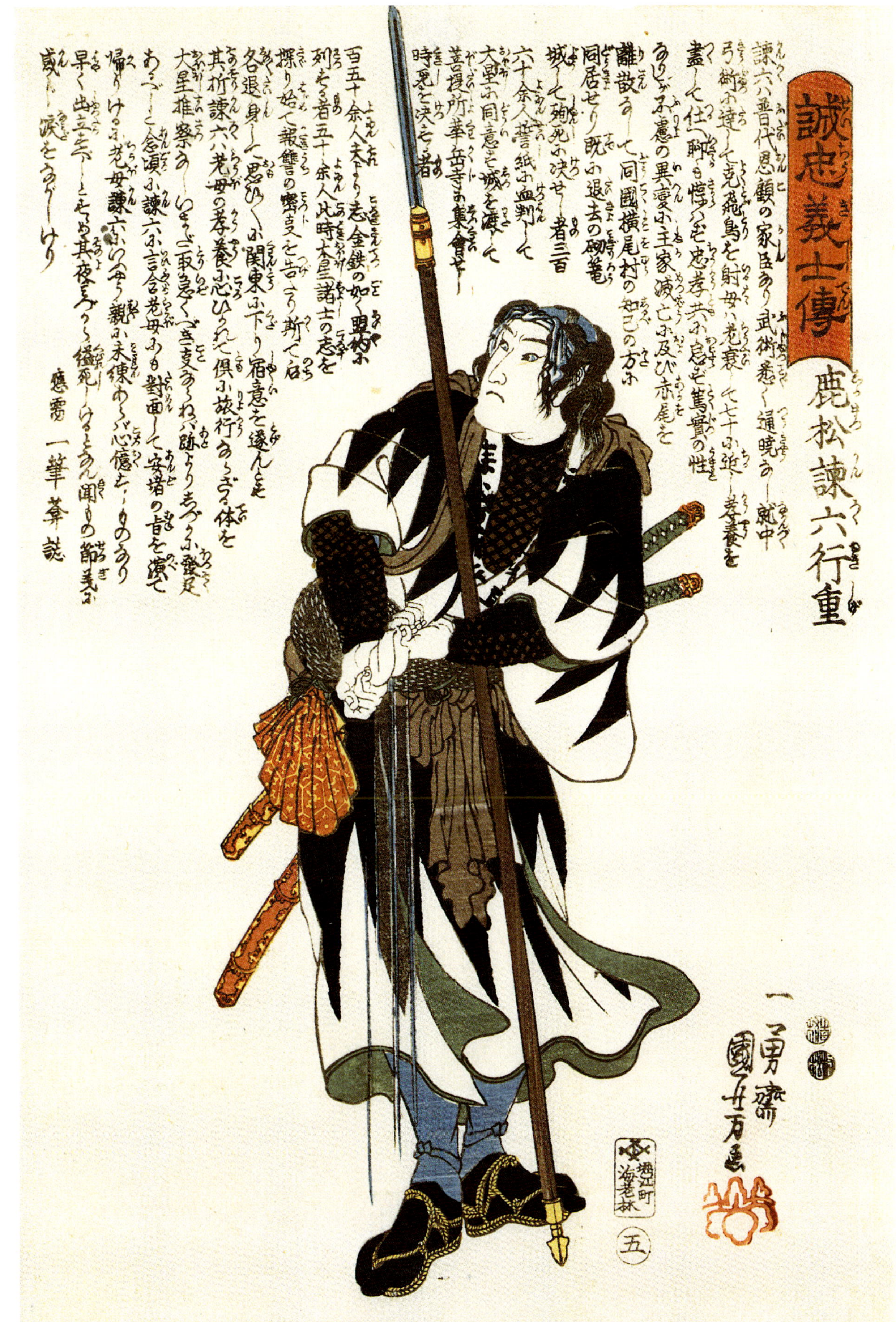
誠忠義士傳
鹿松謙六行重
一勇齋國芳画
五

Yoshida Sadaemon Kanesada

I.6

Yoshida Sadaemon Kanesada fending off arrows

Sadaemon was the son of Yoshida Chūemon Kanesuke. After he left Banshū, he went to Kyoto, where his brother Dennai was in service to another family. Then, after a time, he went to the Kantō and took up residence in Kōjimachi. There he saw much of his father, whom he treated dutifully and who taught him much.

After he joined the vendetta, he spent his time day after day in various disguises, roaming the streets of Honjō and inspecting the enemy mansion. He saw much of a comrade named Oyamada Shōemon.

As the time for them to carry out the attack drew near, Ōboshi called him and Shōemon in and said: 'Pretty soon there are going to be a lot of people around here who lent us money while we were unemployed. Now, after we are gone we don't want people to say that we acted improperly out of poverty. That would be a stain on our records as samurai. So let's take care of those things right now.' With that he gave each of them 200 *ryō*, and they hurried off.[1]

Shōemon, however, suddenly disappeared; he had changed his mind. Sadaemon stayed and was part of the victory. Shōemon was later killed by Shimobe Naotsuke during a robbery at Fuyuki mansion, leaving a bad name. His father, Jūbei, not quite eighty years old, committed suicide in shame.

1. See I.19, in which Uramatsu Handayu Takanao gave the swordsmith what he felt to be a handsome tip of one *bu*. Since the *ryō* was worth four *bu*, Ōboshi was paying these men sums worth 800 such handsome tips. See appendix d.

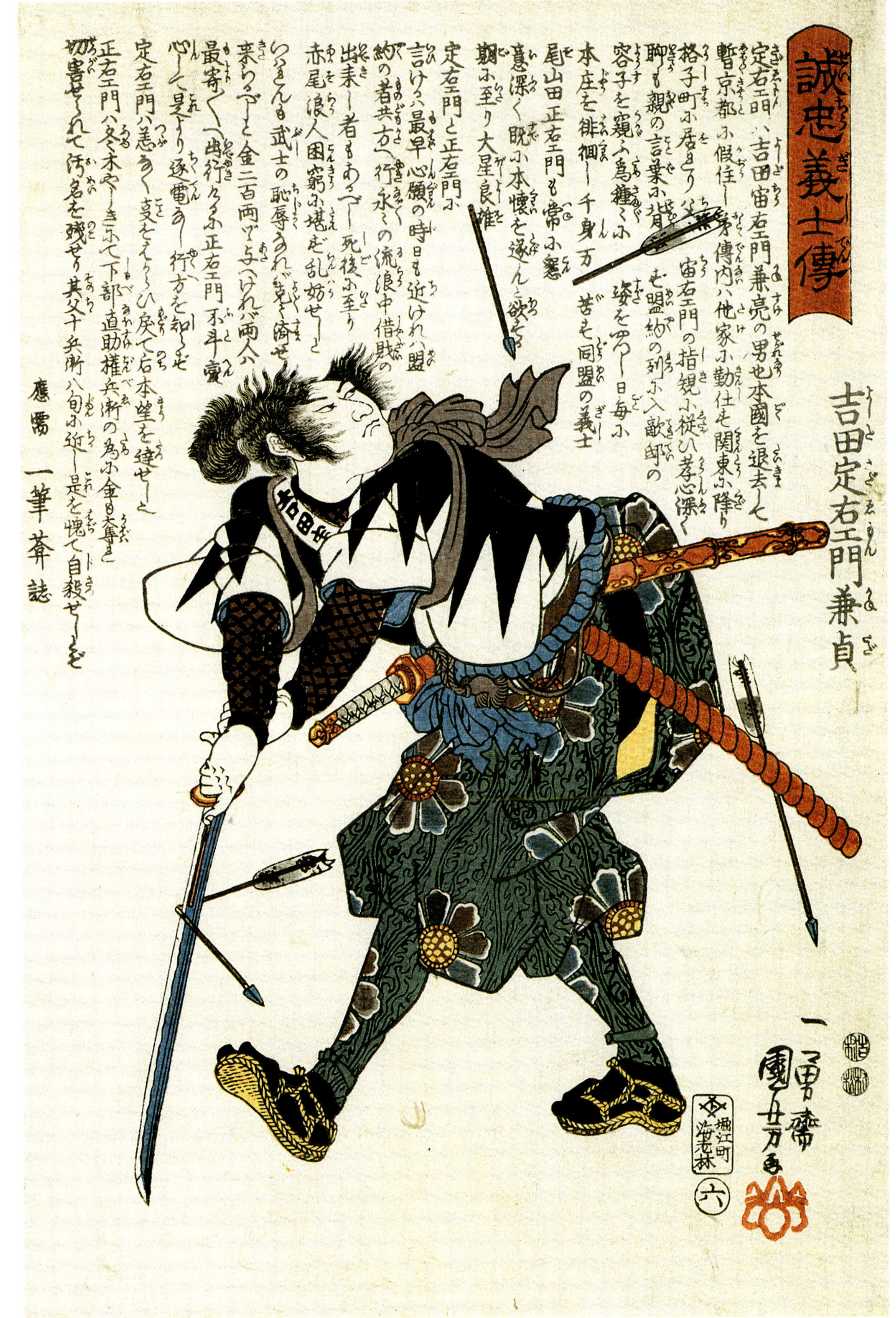
誠忠義士傳
吉田定右エ門兼貞
一勇斎國芳画
堀江町 海老林
六

Sakagaki Genzō Masakata

Genzō was superior with the spear but also an inordinate lover of sake, which he drank from morning to night. In fact, he tied a one-quart sake bottle to his spear and drank from it even as he moved about.[1]

He avoided fancy foods and hewed to a plain regimen. He also wore rough clothes, projecting, in this respect, an unassuming, abstemious character.

After the fall of Akao, he lived in Honjō Hayashida Chō, never forgetting his debt to his lord. On the day of that man's death, every month, he did not go near the sake he loved more than rice, and would spend the day sunk in inconsolable grief, a sad figure.

One day, Fuwa Katsuemon came to see him and suggested they go to the Kabuki, where a *kyōgen* about a lord who shed blood in the palace was a great success. They went and saw Takenojō play the part, but when it was over they were filled with indignation and vented it by beating up the producer, Hanai Saisaburō.

Ōboshi heard about it and let them know that men who have a supreme objective in mind do not get into altercations of this kind. This is what happens when one mixes uncompromising loyalty with a little too much sake.

1.7

Sakagaki Genzō Masakata seated on a broken slab

1. The little pitcher used to pour sake is known as a *tokuri*. Genzō is shown with his *tokuri* serving as a canteen.

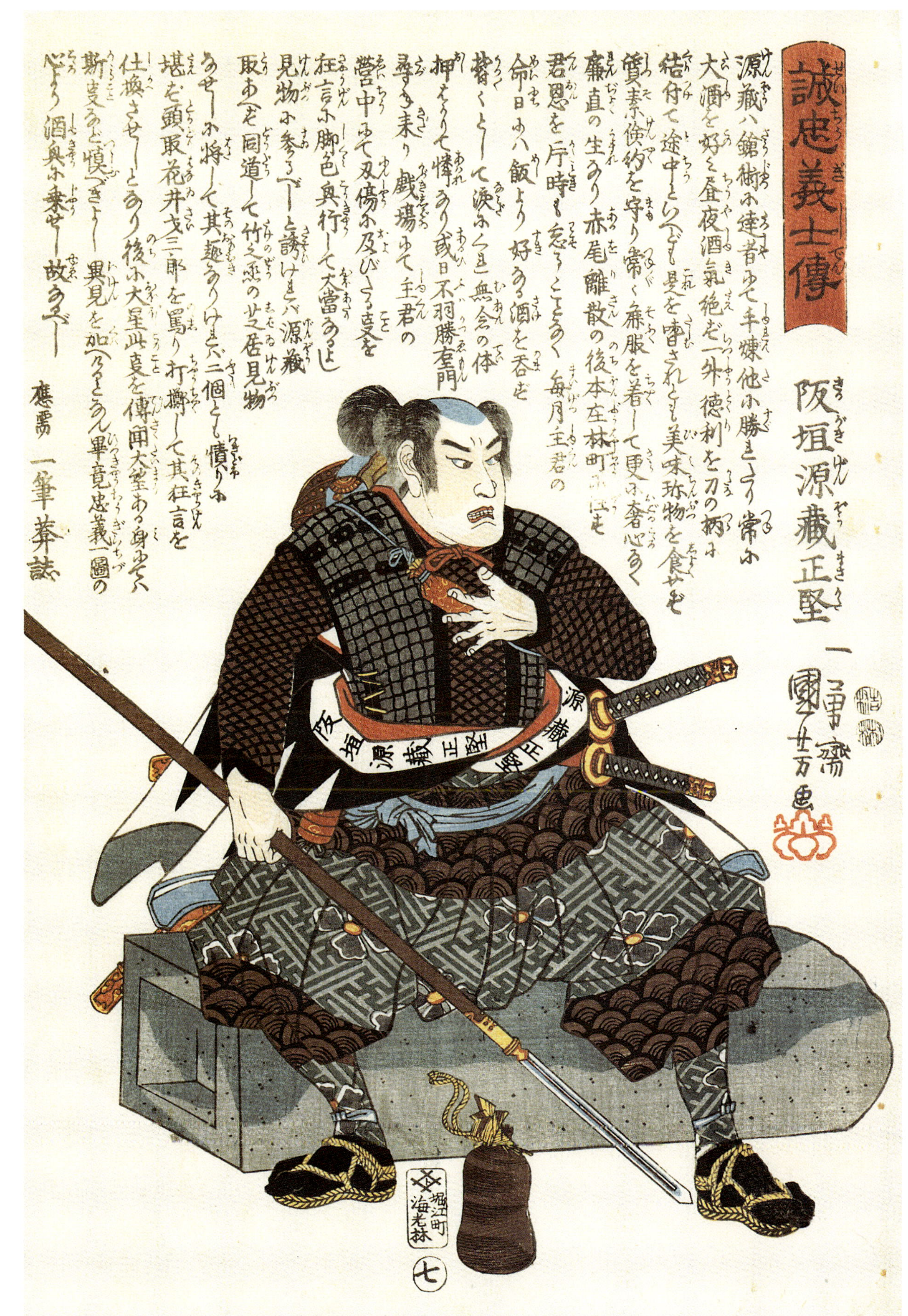

1.8

Yukukawa Sampei Munenori warding off a lantern with his sword

Yukukawa Sampei Munenori

A lord is a boat afloat,
his retainers water.[1]
Water is what makes the boat
float, but don't forget
it can also make the boat
sink beneath the waves.
There are lords and there are lords.
But don't forget retainers.[2]

Takasada loved his retainers as he did his children.[3] His retainers loved him as children love their parents. So the faithful band never forgot their lord's pain for a moment.[4] They endured hunger and thirst and worked to the limits of their endurance, single-mindedly, to achieve what they set out to do.

As a *rōnin*, Sampei stayed with an aunt in a samurai dwelling in the Shiba area. He was a very presentable man and a talented warrior, but he was also good with figures, and his aunt suggested he might find service with another family. He told her, however, he had other plans and accepted no other suggestions, but would leave before sunup and return at dusk each day. One day Sampei prepared a meal of fish and wine, then turned to his aunt and uncle and thanked them for all their kindness and care, and told them he had been successful in his applications and was going on a trip.

They drank a number of parting cups together. Then he gave them all the articles of his personal property he was not taking with him and, as night fell, departed. That was the night of the assault on the Kōno mansion, an exploit in which he performed valiantly. Showing all the arts of his training, he killed many of the enemy. Like all the other members of the band, he achieved what he had set out to do.

As they made their way to Sengakuji, with what triumphant joy he passed the gate of his aunt and uncle!

Last poem:

The long awaited
journey on the path of death
is not known to me,
so I set out before you
utter stranger to the road.

1. A useful statement on the power structure prevailing in the Japan of this period is given by Mikiso Hane in *Peasants, rebels and outcasts: The underside of modern Japan*, p. 5: 'Under the Tokugawa rulers, there were about 270 feudal lords *(daimyō)* with domains *(han)* of various sizes. These lords had autonomous authority over their *han*, but they were in effect vassals of the shogun [...] and their political conduct was strictly regulated by [him]. The shogun as well as the *daimyō* had their own retainers who, in most instances, were allotted a fixed stipend in return for their services. Unlike the vassals of medieval Europe, the warrior retainers of Tokugawa Japan were not granted fiefs and did not reside in manorial estates but in 'castle towns' where their feudal lords were ensconced. In this sense they were military bureaucrats.'

2. A folksong.

3. The *daimyō* En'ya Hangan Takasada will be referred to mostly as Takasada in these prints.

4. In Buddhism the soul transmigrates after forty-nine days. In Shinto, however, the soul remains sentient, even in the grave. The Japanese respond to both interpretations.

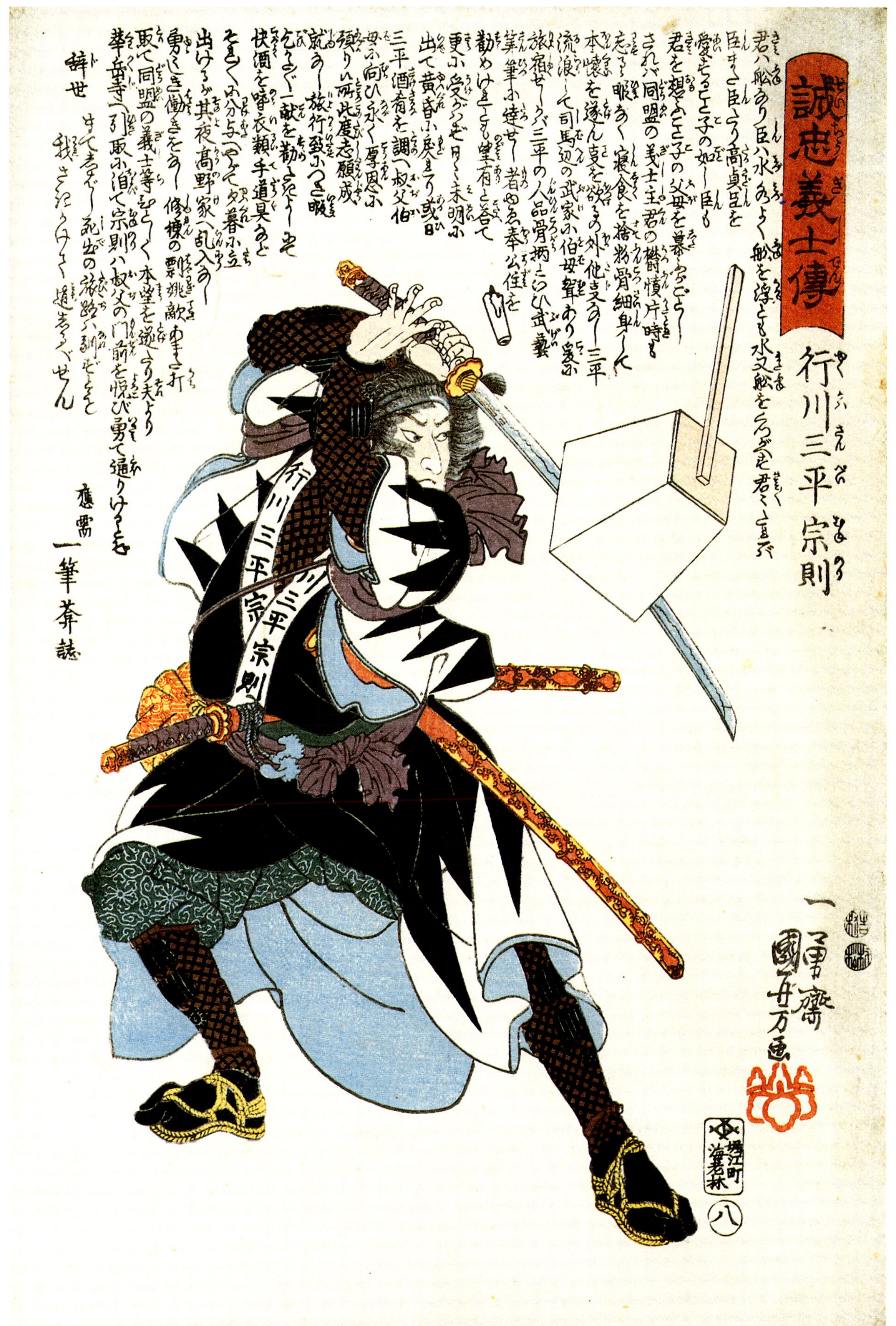
誠忠義士傳
行川三平宗則
一筆菴誌
一勇齋國芳画
堀江町
海老林
八

Onodera Jūnai Hidetomo

One's debt to his lord has the weight of Korea's Taisan mountain, but obeying one's lord's commands is as light as light can be. Loyalty is the highest of virtues, but living by it is far from easy.

The loyal retainer Onodera Jūnai joined with Ōboshi Yoshio and took the oath of vengeance with their co-conspirators.[1] Then, a while after the younger men had departed for the Kantō region, he followed, accompanied by Ōboshi Rikiya, along the Tōkaidō road. At Hakone, his fellow-conspirators Sugino and Yatō caught up with him, bearing a letter from his wife, her response to the letter he had left when he departed:

When I read the words
your pen left upon the page
a shower of tears fell
And now all the leaves are gone
That I might use to answer

Hidetomo then took a poem-card and wrote:

Limits there may be
on whether I shall return
but as I travel
My love goes along with me
Like a garment of nine folds

He then sent that back with a returning courier.

In Edo, he changed his name to Jūan and set up business as a physician. Though he was over sixty, he was in vigorous health, with courage inferior to none. He was deeply versed in all the martial arts and also a man of deep learning.

He assumed a leading role in the night attack, killed two of the enemy, and wounded many others. He did what he came to do and then lived for a time in a guest house. At the end of the year, he wrote:

As one grows older
one waits with anticipation
the day the flowers bloom;
How difficult to witness
The year coming to a close

Hidetomo

I.9

Onodera Jūnai Hidetomo on one knee, shading his eyes

'... beautiful hata-sashimono, *or 'war ornaments,' were designed to intimidate the enemy and inspire the samurai.'* Allen, p. 88.

1. The first four characters of Onodera Jūnai's name are visible above his sword hilt.

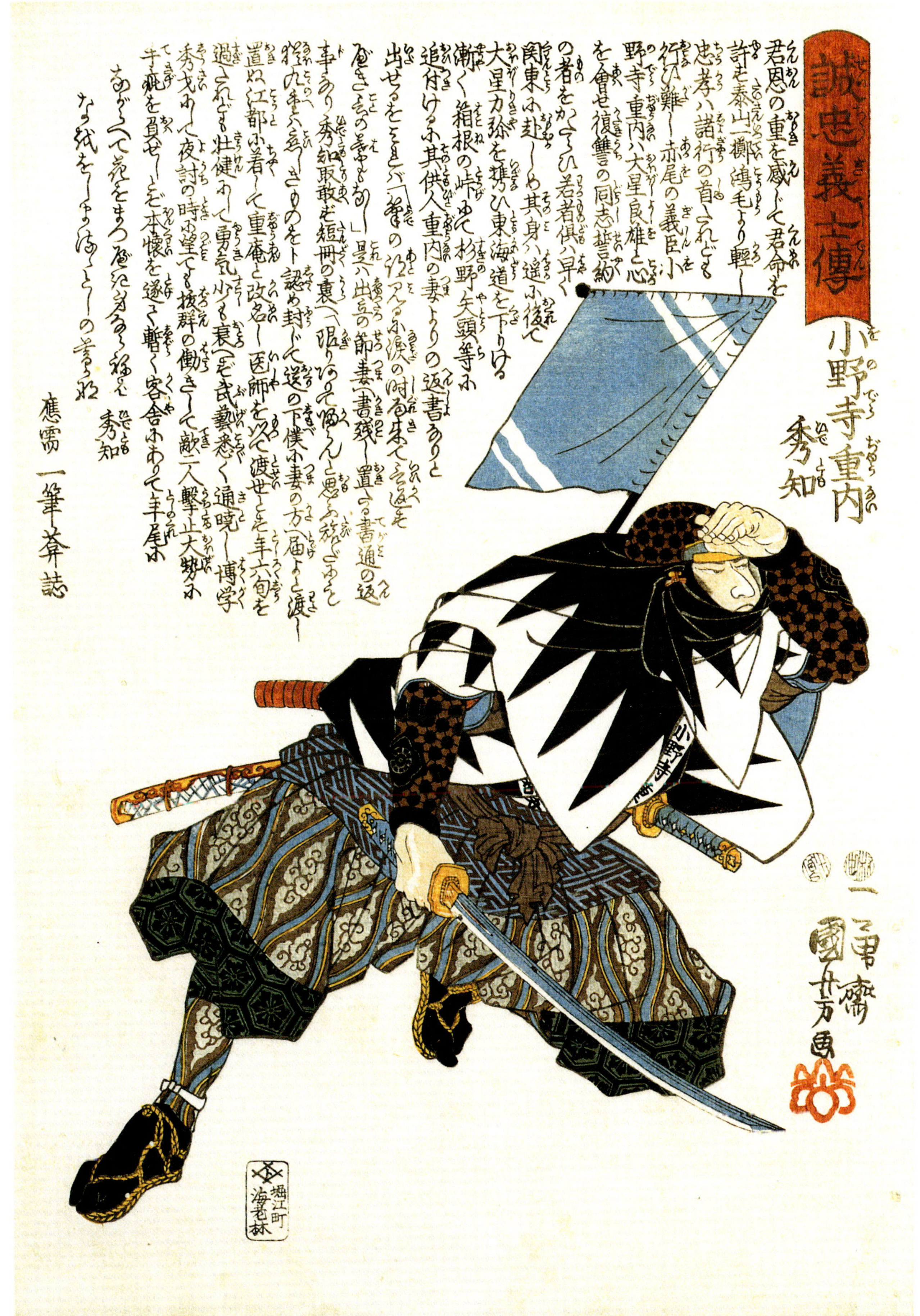
誠忠義士傳
小野寺重内秀知
一勇斎國芳画
堀江町 海老林

Isoai Jūroemon Masahisa

Masahisa was a graduate of the Atago Mountain Kyōgakuin, in Kyoto, a great reader and an expert in the Saga school of calligraphy.[1] He enjoyed the martial arts and was particularly adept in the use of the *naginata*, the glaive.[2]

He played the *koto* constantly and, in fact, had a *koto* plectrum in his pocket during the night attack. Everyone admired his elegance.

He worked closely with his lord and was a useful adviser at all times. When that lord died, he was preparing to martyr himself at Kagakuji when Kataoka Dengoemon informed him of Ōboshi's plot and stopped him.

When the fief was dissolved, he rented a house in the Shiba neighborhood and thus was on the scene to join with the other loyal samurai in their attack on the Kōno mansion.[3] He killed many of the enemy with his glaive. He served, everyone said, with great distinction.

It is true that it doesn't take a crossbow to kill a mouse, and it is also true that when the time comes to show one's mettle and stare down dragons and tigers, a gentle, respectful man can dig down and summon the effort necessary to strike fear into a host of enemies.

He was such a man.

I.10

Isoai Jūroemon Masahisa wielding his *naginata*

1. An educational institution, probably of what we would consider college-level.

2. The weapon is pictured on the print. Perhaps no further description is necessary.

3. The fictional surname given here has the same spelling in English as that of the historical record, and also that of the *Chūshingura*, but all use different Chinese characters.

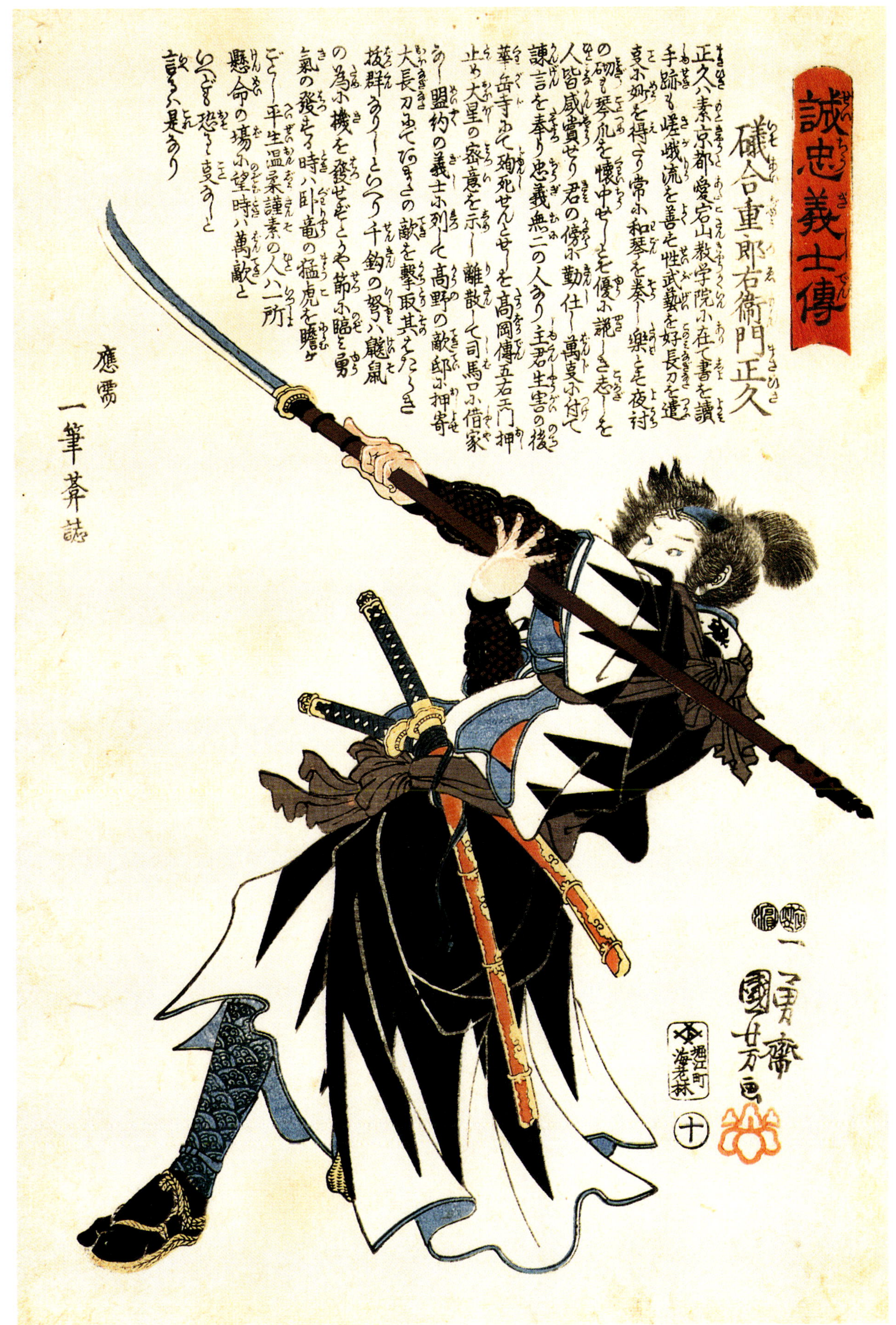
誠忠義士傳
礒合重郎右衛門正久
應需 一筆菴誌
一勇齋國芳画
堀江町 海老林
十

Okano Gin-emon Kanehide

Kanehide's childhood name was Kujūrō. When Akao was dissolved, his father took him along to Kyoto when he discussed plans for vengeance with Ōboshi Yuranosuke. The old man died suddenly, however, and the son took his name, Gin-emon.

Succeeding also to his father's vow, Gin-emon went to Kamakura, opened a store selling saké and general merchandise near the Konō mansion, and bided his time.[1]

There he made the acquaintance of a woman who had been wet-nurse for Torii Jiroemon, a retainer of Moronao, and obtained from her a floor plan of the enemy home, which he showed to his co-conspirators.

He distinguished himself in the night attack, and when he and his comrades went to the Senseiji afterward to pray and to have a last meal together, Ōboshi read a poem to him from the head seat:[2]

Oh, with what great joy
these feelings come together
to fall upon you.
No cloud now obscures the moon
Shining on the floating world.

And Okano chimed in:

Nothing so fragrant -
not even the plum that blooms
in tomorrow's snow.[3]

All joined together in praising his bravery.

I.11

Okano Gin-emon Kanehide, arm extended, holding a lantern

1. See also II.14, which recounts Gin-emon's story in much more detail, some not consistent with this text.

2. Another name for Sengakuji Temple.

3. Okano is reminding his comrades that New Year's Day is coming soon, but they will not live to see it. The flowering plum, thought of as the first blossom of the year, is still a standard New Year's decoration. January 1 in the lunar calendar fell on what we think of as February 16 in 1703.

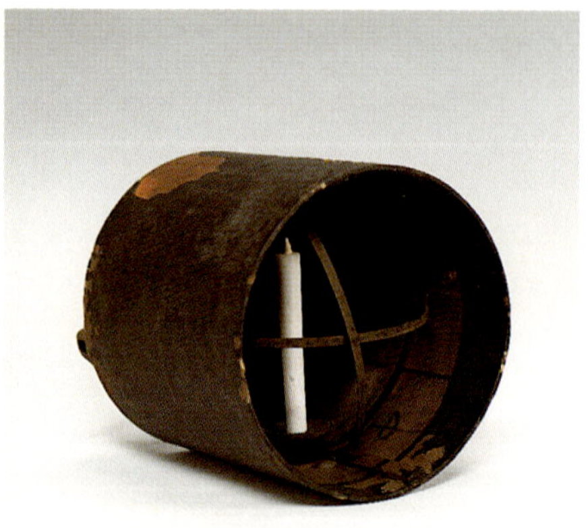

Rōnin *lantern.*
Ōishi Shinto Shrine Museum, Akō.

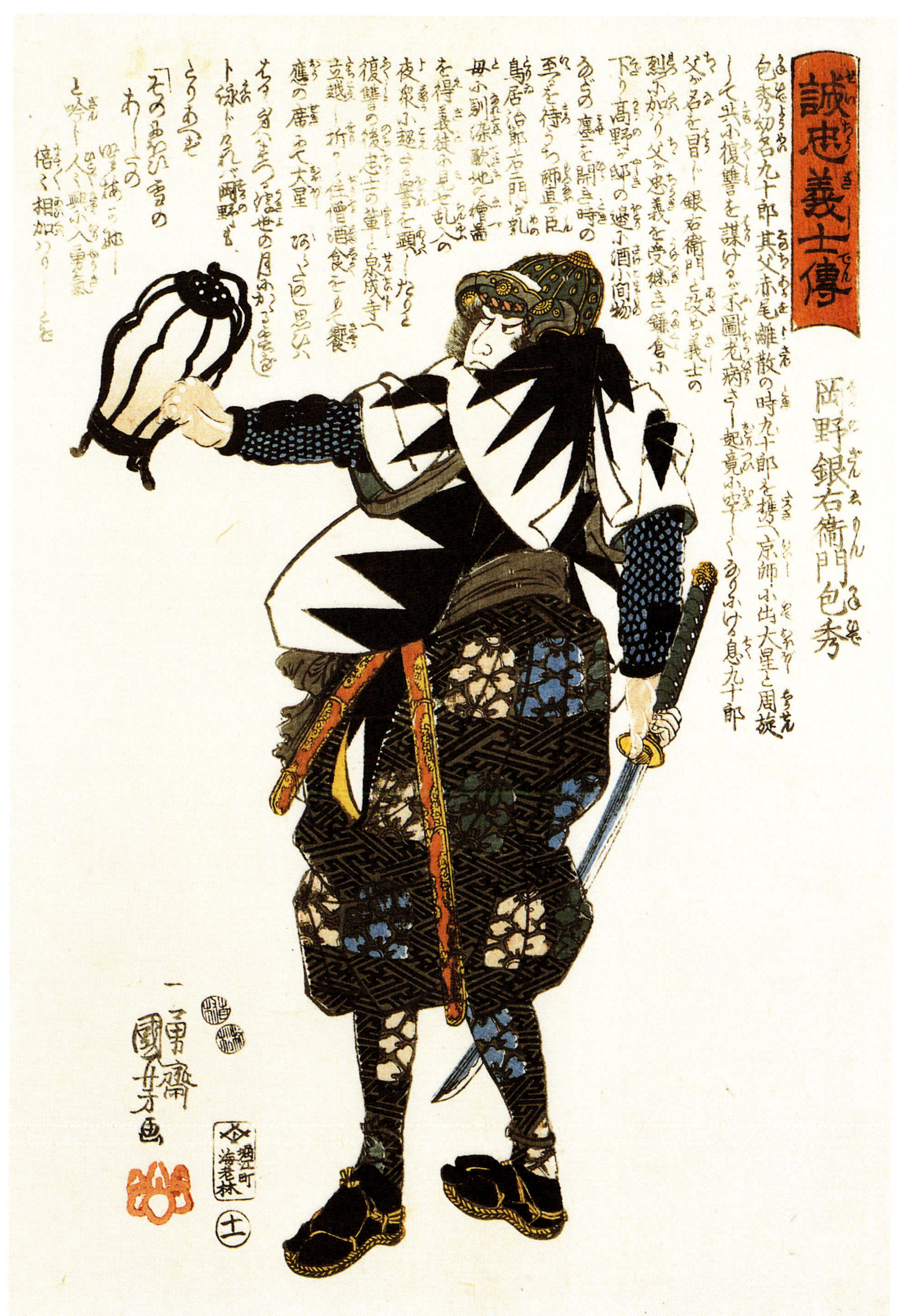
誠忠義士傳
岡野銀右衛門包秀
一勇斎國芳画
堀江町 海老林

Senzaki Yagorō Noriyasu

Senzaki Yagorō was a descendant of Sakazaki Suruga no Kami, who was a retainer of the Ukita family. He served the Mori family for a time but then became a retainer of Akao. It was said that as a child he had suddenly killed his cousin.

He was skilled in the martial arts but also enjoyed reading and the writing of *tanka* and *haikai*.

When Akao fell, he went to the Kantō and lived in Hayashi Chō under the assumed name of Mimasakaya Zenbei and walked about selling fans and watching the enemy. He had artistic pretensions and whenever he could, recorded the exploits of his loyal co-conspirators in a book he called the *Akao chronicle*. He would go over it with one of his comrades when his agitation became unbearable.

All he had in the world was an old mother, whom he told about his secret compact with Ōboshi when he left Banshū. She was very pleased and praised Ōboshi. Here were a mother and son locked in the same resolve.

Fortunately, he had neither wife or children, but his mother warned him that if he were too concerned about duty to his mother he might do something cowardly and bring dishonour on himself. That night she went to bed with good cheer and the next day committed suicide.

Yagorō was overcome with grief. Here he was avenging not only his lord but also his mother. It is reported that he set out with complete tranquillity coupled with unending indignation.

1.12

Senzaki Yagorō Noriyasu running with his weapons

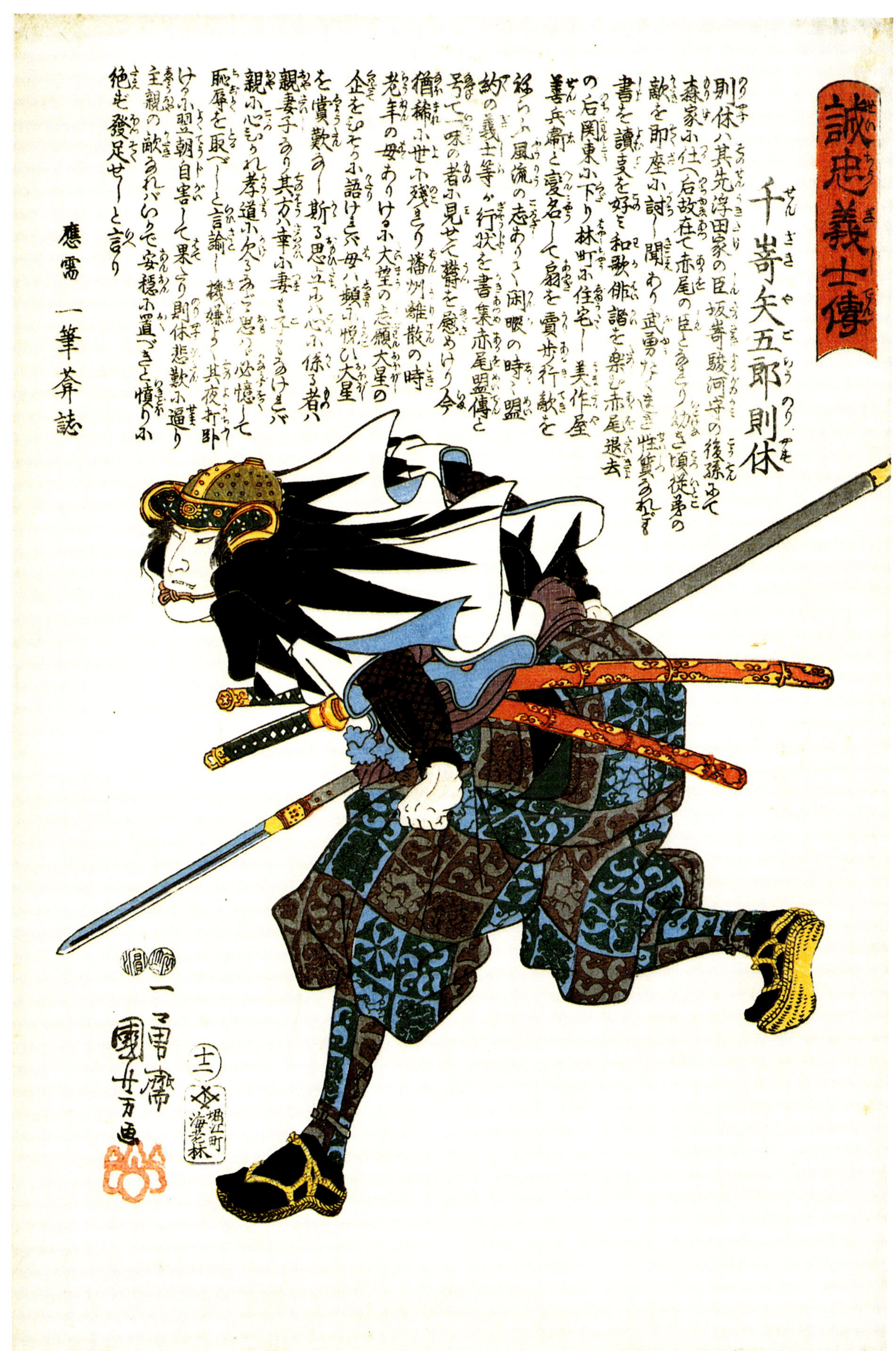
誠忠義士傳
千嵜矢五郎則休
應需 一筆菴誌
一勇斎國芳画

Yazama Jūjirō Moto-oki[1]

1.13

Yazama Jūjirō Moto-oki blowing a whistle

Moto-oki was the eldest son of Mitsunobu and a brother of Mitsukaze, all iron-willed, devoted, hereditary vassals of Akao. After the fall of Akao, they rented lodgings in Kōjimachi and sold incense. They were willing to expend every effort to avenge their master's death.

One day they happened to meet Senzaki Yagorō and tearfully told him of their unending indignation over the end of their lord and how they were making daily vows before Buddha and using their disguises as peddlers the better to prepare themselves for the time when they could take the head of their enemy, Moronao, and offer it at their master's grave.

Senzaki was amazed and told Ōboshi of the resolve of this father and his sons, and he enlisted them in the conspiracy.

In the night raid, they fought beside Takebayashi Sadashichi and discovered Moronao in a charcoal shed. They prodded him off a cabinet with a spear handle, cutting his forehead in the process, whereupon Sadashichi got a candle and confirmed that it was indeed Moronao.

Moto-oki then decapitated him and blew his whistle. The faithful warriors gathered together and raised a victory cheer.

After Moto-oki committed suicide, on February 7, his wife visited his grave and, as a farewell offering, left this poem written on a poem-card:

For love of your lord
you possessed only one heart,
so you threw away
your warrior's existence
and left us only your name.

Then she took her own life.

1. This name is given as Jūtarō in the prints devoted to this man's father and brother, a significant difference in a society based on primogeniture. The suffix *-jiro* is used in names to show the second son. See appendix c.

Rōnin *whistle.*
Ōishi Shinto Shrine Museum, Akō.

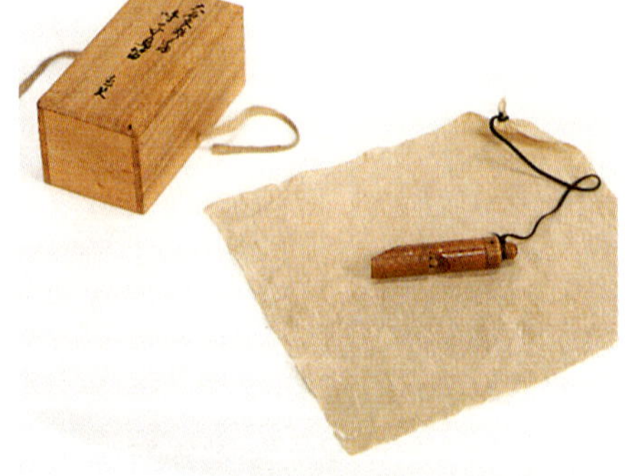

'... and that if anyone slew Kōsuke no Suke and cut off his head he should blow a shrill whistle, as a signal to his comrades, who would hurry to the spot.'
Mitford, p. 28.

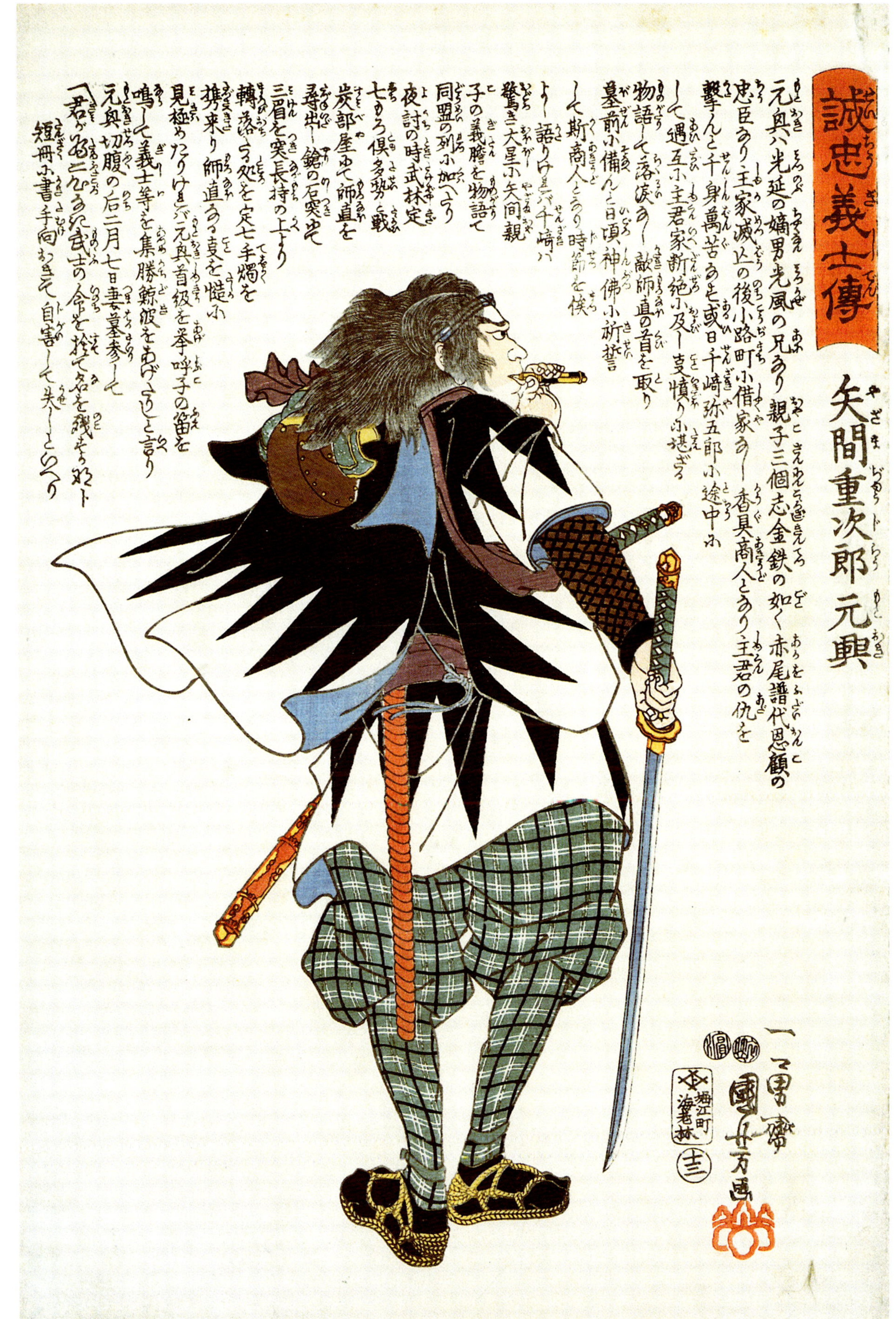
誠忠義士傳
矢間重次郎元興
一勇斎國芳画

Ōtaka Gengo Tadao

1.14

Ōtaka Gengo Tadao taking careful aim

Tadao was born a retainer of the Akao family, a man of unparalleled loyalty and an expert in military horsemanship. After the withdrawal from Banshū, he wandered aimlessly about Edo, plotting vengeance. On the surface, he was a stylish dilettante bearing the *haiku* pseudonym Shiyō, a disciple of Nendō Sentoku. He was also closely associated with Shinshi and Kikaku.[1]

His interest in the tea ceremony, of which he was a student of Yamada Sōhen, enabled him to inspect Moronao's home when he was not there.[2] Thus he was able to inform Ōboshi of the right day for the night attack.

He was in the business of selling bamboo housecleaning utensils and was aware that the Kōno mansion was cleaned on the 14th of the month. Thus he knew that everybody there would be tired and drunk, permitting his party to enter.

In the darkness, he did not know the man he fought against, but it must have been Kobayashi Heihachirō, a skilled opponent, who wounded Tadao before he died.

On the morning of the 15th, at the Kyūbei noodle shop, Tadao drew the stopper on a sake barrel, drank, attended to his wounded hand and wrote, on a piece of soiled tissue:

It has the power
to bend trees and fold mountains -
snow on pine branches

Then he threw down his purse and said: 'This is for the sake'.

When he joined the rush to get Moronao's head, he put in his purse a note that read: 'This is to certify that he who gets rid of the body of Ōtaka Tadao, retainer of the Akao family in Banshū, lost in combat, will be entitled to the enclosed sum of three *ryō* to buy some sake'.[3]

He also had a poem-card that read:

The first bonito
and the spices of Edo -
four seasons of sweat

1. Enomoto Kikaku (1661-1707), prominent *haiku* poet.

2. Also Moronao's tea ceremony teacher.

3. See appendix d.

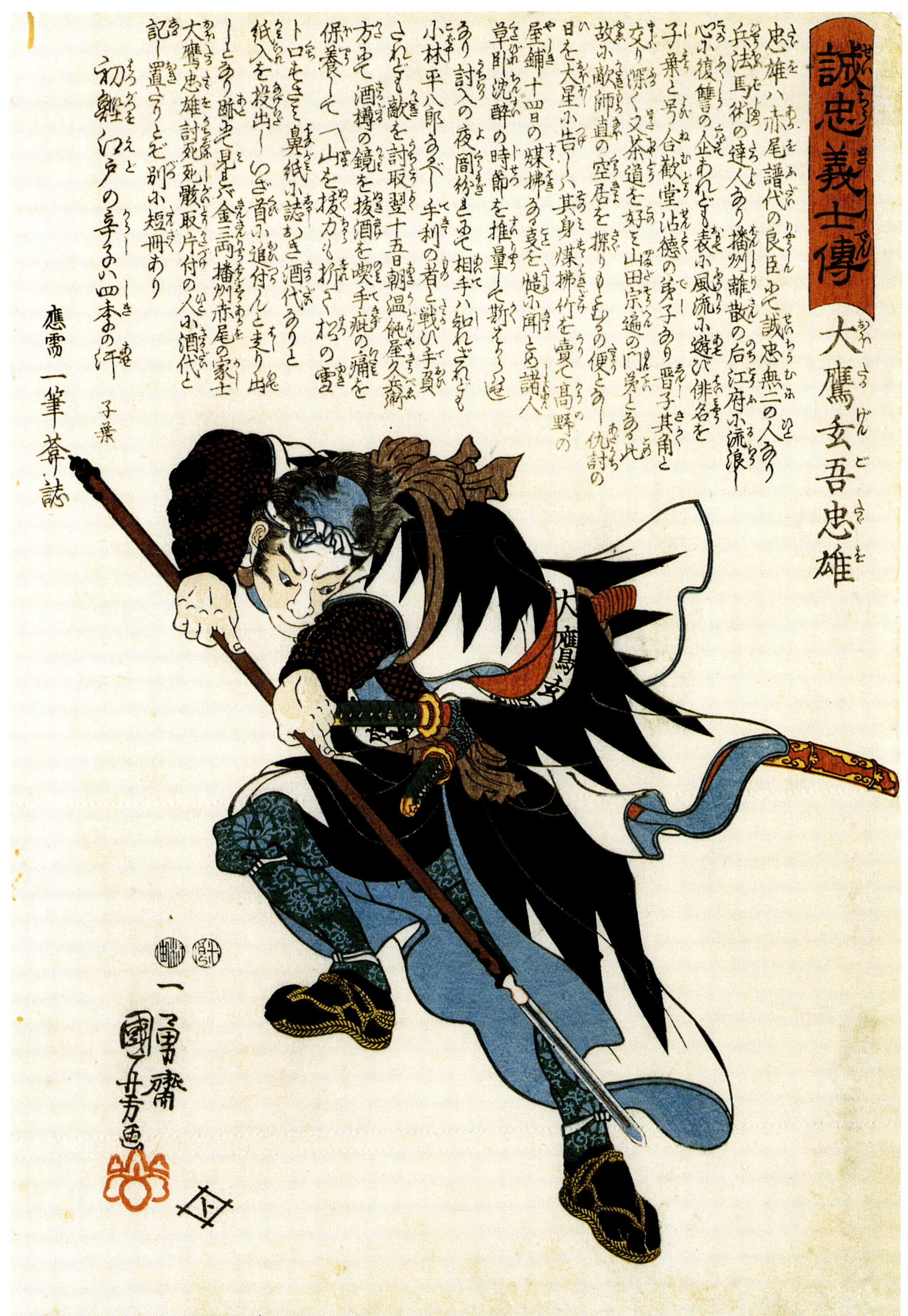
誠忠義士傳
大鷹玄吾忠雄
一勇齋國芳画

Kataoka Dengoemon Takafusa

1.15

Kataoka Dengoemon Takafusa leaning on his bloodstained spear

The *Shubokuden*, of the Later Han Dynasty, says:

Out of obligation to one's lord render affection.
When it comes to duty, life is light.

Kataoka Takafusa was a favourite vassal of En'ya Hangan. His regard for his lord differed from the regard shown by the others and was constantly manifested, never for a moment forgotten.

When he heard that Hangan had started a battle scene in the palace and drawn blood and then had to commit suicide, he was filled with indignation that the enemy was still alive. He acted before Ōboshi did, working out a plan with Isoai to ambush Moronao. Then he received word from Ōboshi and returned to Akao with alacrity to join the conspiracy.

Kataoka was a native of Owari, located nearby, and a grandson of Shiba Takatsune. He was thoroughly versed in the martial arts and a devotee of military strategy, in which he knew every detail of the school of Yamaga Sokō.

In the attack that cold night, he charged through the gate and into the entryway with his deadly spear, cut the bowstrings with his blade, entered into fierce combat with a multitude of foes, and led the loyal band in the search for Moronao.[1]

His last poem was:

A snowy morning -
when human life seems to be
lighter than goose-down

1. The print has a quietly graphic quality, showing the warrior leaning on his spear, grimacing as he fights for breath, blood on his spear blade and handle as well as his head and *hachimaki* or 'headband'.

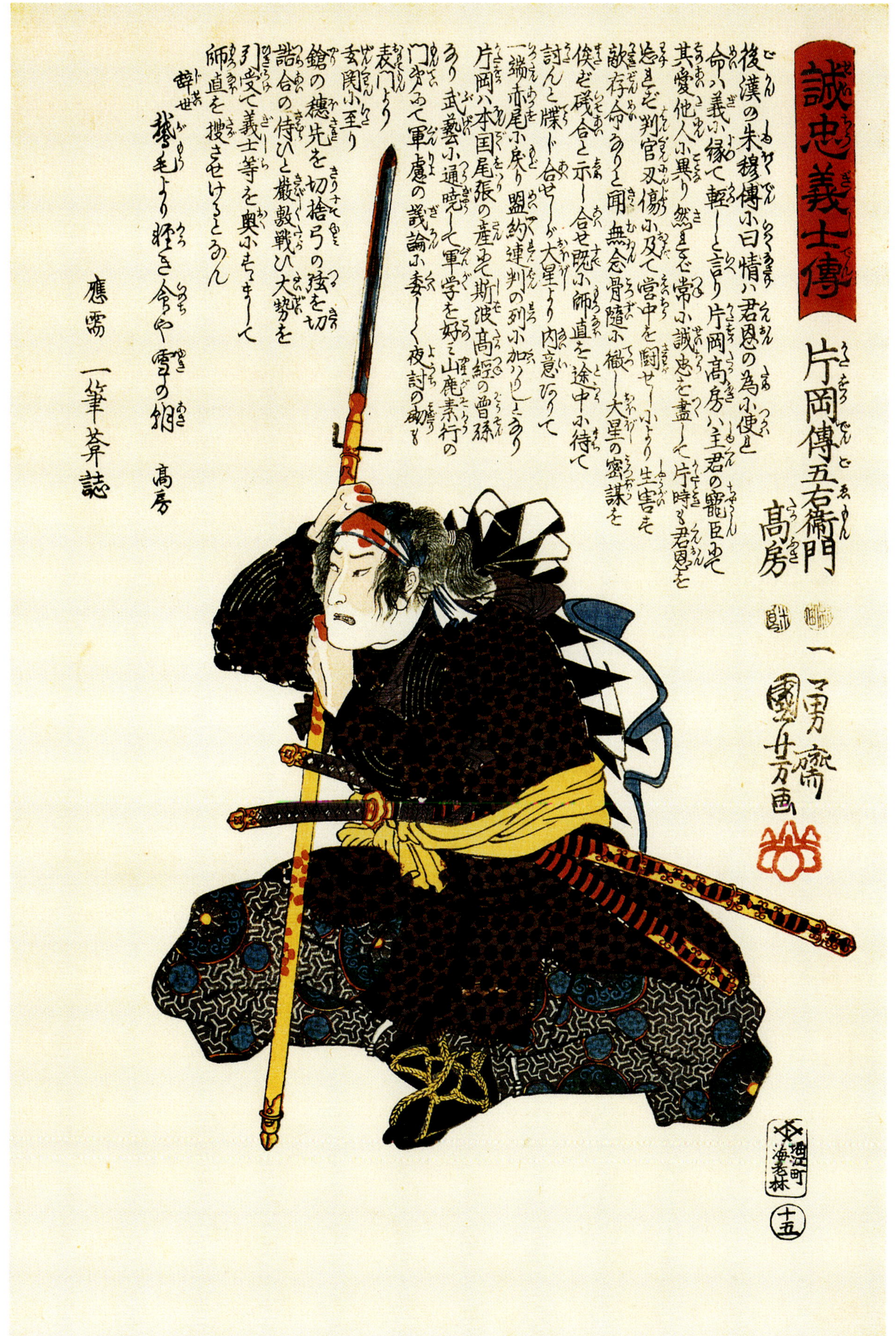
誠忠義士傳
片岡傳五右衛門
高房
一勇齋國芳画
應需 一筆菴誌

Nakamura Kansuke Tadatoki

I.16

Nakamura Kansuke Tadatoki dodging bundles of firewood

Kansuke Tadatoki was a hereditary retainer of Akao, thrifty but warm-hearted. He was an expert in martial arts but free of conceit. When his lord's house was confiscated and he and his family departed from Banshū, his oldest son, Kanjirō, was five years old, and his second son, Chūsaburō, was two.

In Kyoto, he and Ōboshi, not under house arrest, used their time planning vengeance. Tadatoki then used money he had laid aside to send his wife and children to her parent's home to be cared for and educated.

He met with his former comrades in Azuma (Edo), ostensibly to visit their master's grave and to see the sights, and without much ado settled in Honjō, where he became a member of the school of Shinshi and Kikaku and wrote under the pseudonym Hyōshu.

He saw much of Otaka Shiyō, Senzaki Chikuhei, and Tomomori Shunpo at Kikaku's Sentoku villa.[1] There they indulged in artistic pursuits and at the same time acquainted themselves with the enemy's quarters.

In the night break-in, Tadatoki performed brilliantly and powerfully and used his daytime research well in helping to make their plan of avenging their master's death a success.[2]

When they had achieved what they came for and left the main gate in a group, they took a guard with them. The guard carried a lantern, which Tadatoki told him to extinguish.[3] 'What's wrong with the lantern?' the man muttered. Tadatoki heard him and flew into a rage and said, 'You rotten low-life,' levelled his spear and, with a shout, ran the man through. Then he walked away laughing.

That is one of the stories that was told later.

1. Surnames of conspirators are each followed by the appropriate pen name. Thus Ōtaka Gengo Tadao (I.14) signed himself 'Shiyō', Senzaki Yagorō Noriyasu (I.12) was 'Chikuhei', and Tomomori Sukeyemon Masakata (I.27) composed under the name 'Shunpo.'

2. Tadatoki must be in the kitchen area at this time. He is resting his foot on a bundle of charcoal and defending himself against tied strips of kindling wood.

3. See quote regarding fires following the translation to I.18.

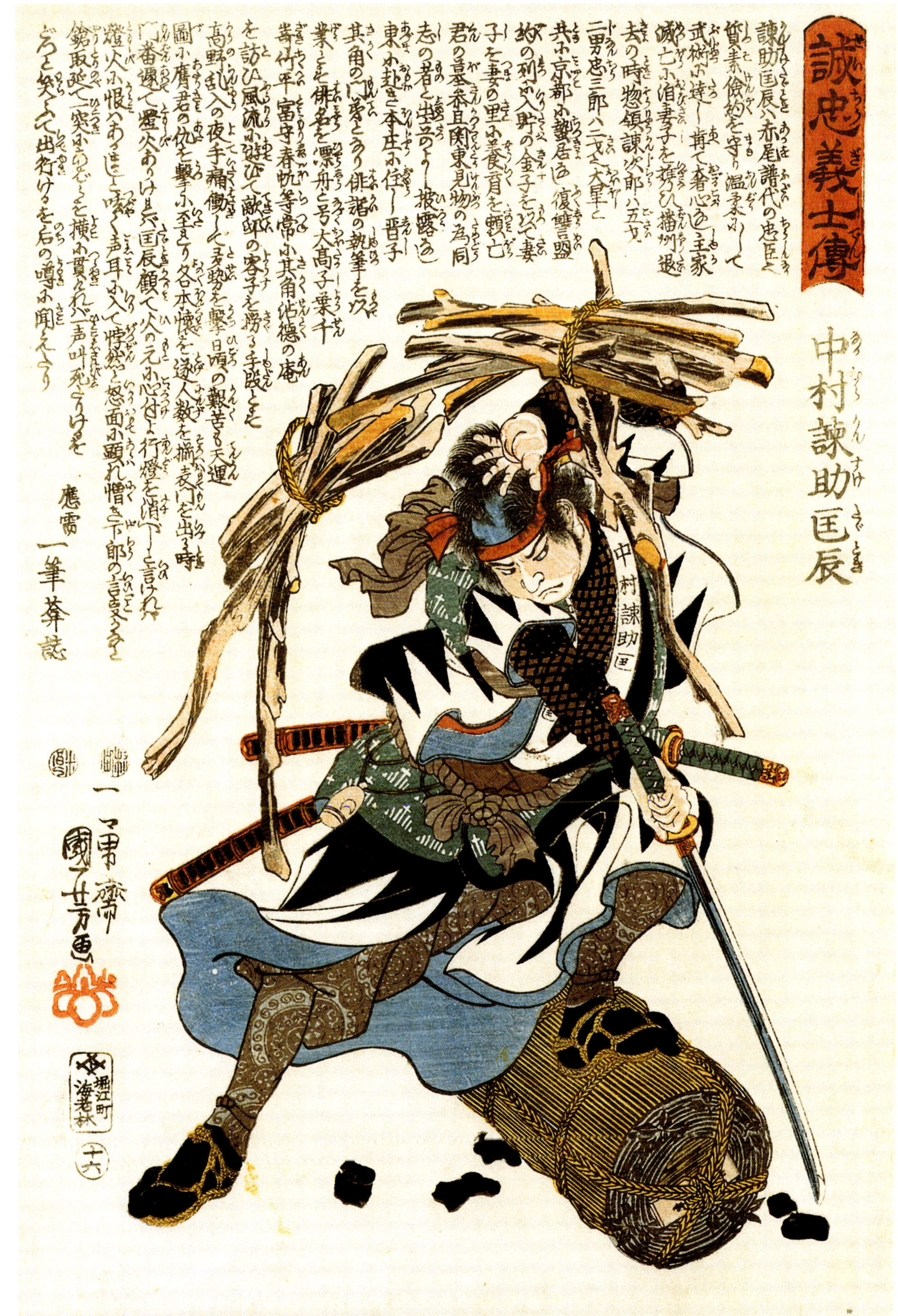
誠忠義士傳
中村諫助匡辰
一勇斎國芳画
堀江町 海老林
十六

Okashima Yasōemon Tsunetatsu

1.17

Okashima Yasōemon Tsunetatsu defending himself behind a fireplace cover

Okashima Tsunetatsu had two sons at the time the house of Akao fell. The older, Fujimatsu, was nine; and the younger, Gorōsuke, was six. With his wife and children, he journeyed to Shikabe, in Sesshū, and rented housing. There they lived simply and frugally. He saw to it, however, that his family had enough to eat.

While drilling in martial arts, he re-injured an old hip bruise, and went to the Arima hot springs to treat it. At the same time, he paid a visit to some relatives.

He was travelling alone on a mountain road when he had to draw his sword and defend himself against five thieves bent on stealing his money and his baggage. He wounded them all, then cut some wisteria vines and tied all five side-by-side to a pine tree. Then he took out his portable writing equipment, made some ink with spring water, and wrote in broad brush-strokes on a paper handkerchief: 'This evening, suddenly, I was set upon by five robbers who prey on travellers. Any travellers who have been robbed of money or luggage by these men, feel free to decide whether they shall live or die.'

He signed it 'Okashima Yasōemon' and tied it to the end of a pine branch. Then he struck fire and lit his pipe and smoked a leisurely pipeful. One can easily imagine how courageous he was.[1] The bandits were dumbfounded at the resourcefulness of this traveller.

1. Okashima is defending himself with a cover for an *idō*, or 'floor fireplace.'

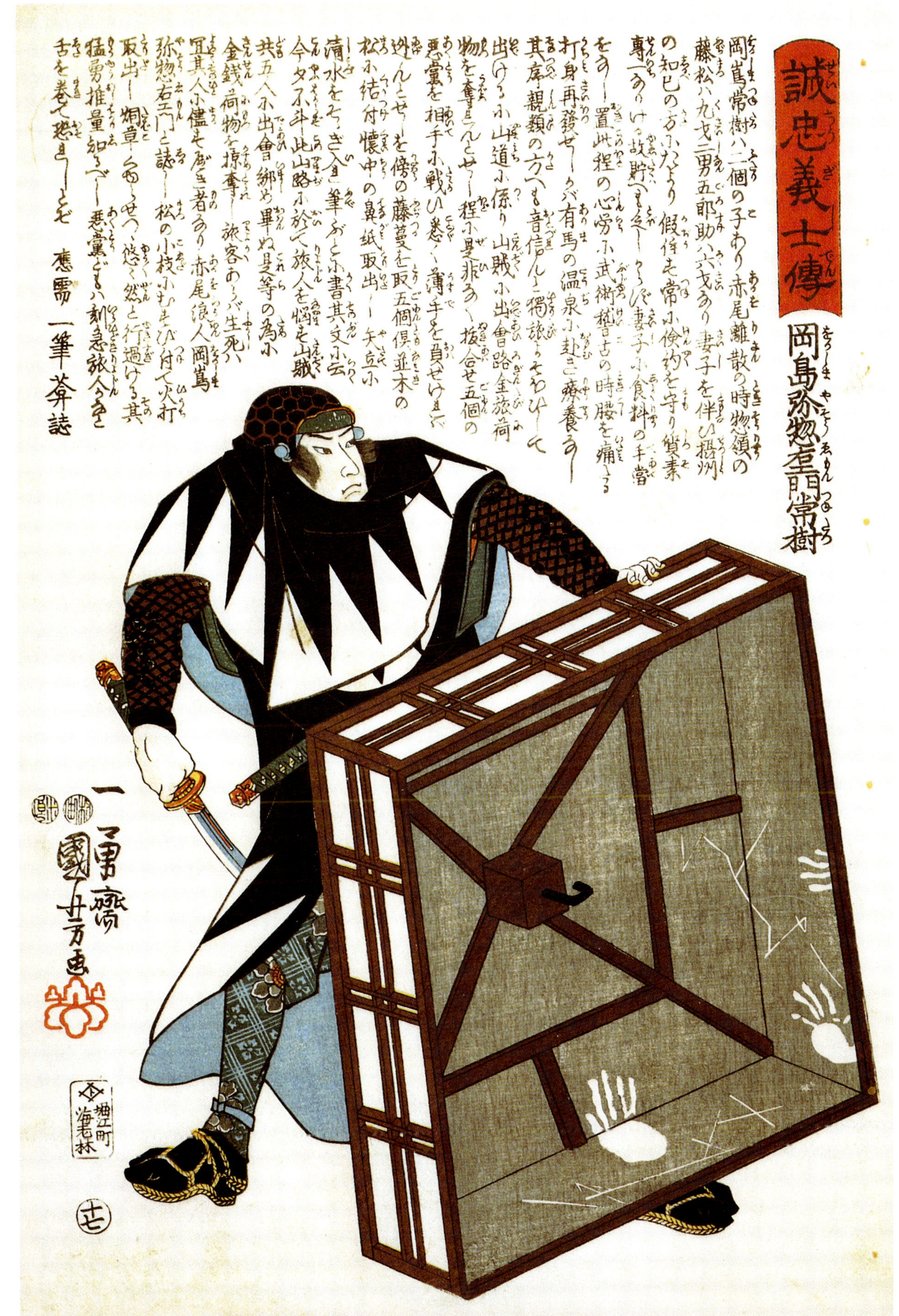

誠忠義士傳
岡島弥惣右衛門常樹
一勇齋國芳画

Teraoka Hei-emon Nobuyuki

1.18

Teraoka Hei-emon Nobuyuki extinguishing the fire in a brazier

Teraoka Hei-emon was the chief foot soldier of Yoshida Chūzaemon. His foster father, Hyō-emon, was a native of Gochōda village, in Hitachi province. One day, at the Chinju festival, Hyō-emon had come upon a child who was obviously abandoned and took him home and brought him up. The boy's childhood name was Sutekichi, meaning 'foundling.'[1]

When he came of age the boy's name was changed to Hei-emon. His heredity was undetermined, but he turned out to be a gentle young man, talented, nevertheless, in military pursuits.

When the lord's family fell, and Akao was sundered, he wandered at first, in the company of a comrade named Yano Isuke. They went together to Ōboshi and attempted to enlist in the conspiracy, but Ōboshi rejected them. Isuke did not apply again.

Ōboshi was spending much time in the pleasure quarters, and one day a spy of the Uesumi clan concealed himself in a doorway with the intention of assassinating him. Hei-emon saw the spy waiting, captured him and made him confess. Then he took him to Ōboshi, who beheaded him. After this proof of Hei-emon's loyalty, Ōboshi described the plan to him and administered the oath.

On the night of the attack, Hei-emon's fervent wishes were realized, but then Ōboshi sent him to Geishū in order to save his life.[2] After he carried out his mission there, however, he returned in great haste and petitioned the authorities to allow him to die with his comrades. They, however, refused.

He was rewarded financially, and honoured for his loyalty, but he took the tonsure and devoted the rest of his life to prayer for the *rōnins'* salvation. He died well past his eightieth year.

'Then the forty-seven comrades, elated at having accomplished their design, placed the head in a bucket and prepared to depart; but before leaving the house they carefully extinguished all the lights and fires in the place, lest by accident a fire should break out and the neighbours suffer.' Mitford, p. 33.

1. The figure in the print bears no name on his armour, an omission probably related to his foundling origins, which may have been another reason that he was not executed with the others. He is extinguishing the coals in an *hibachi*, using water from a convenient pail bearing a highly stylized rendering of the character *kyū*, meaning 'emergency.'

2. Also known as Akikuni, located in the area of present-day Hiroshima.

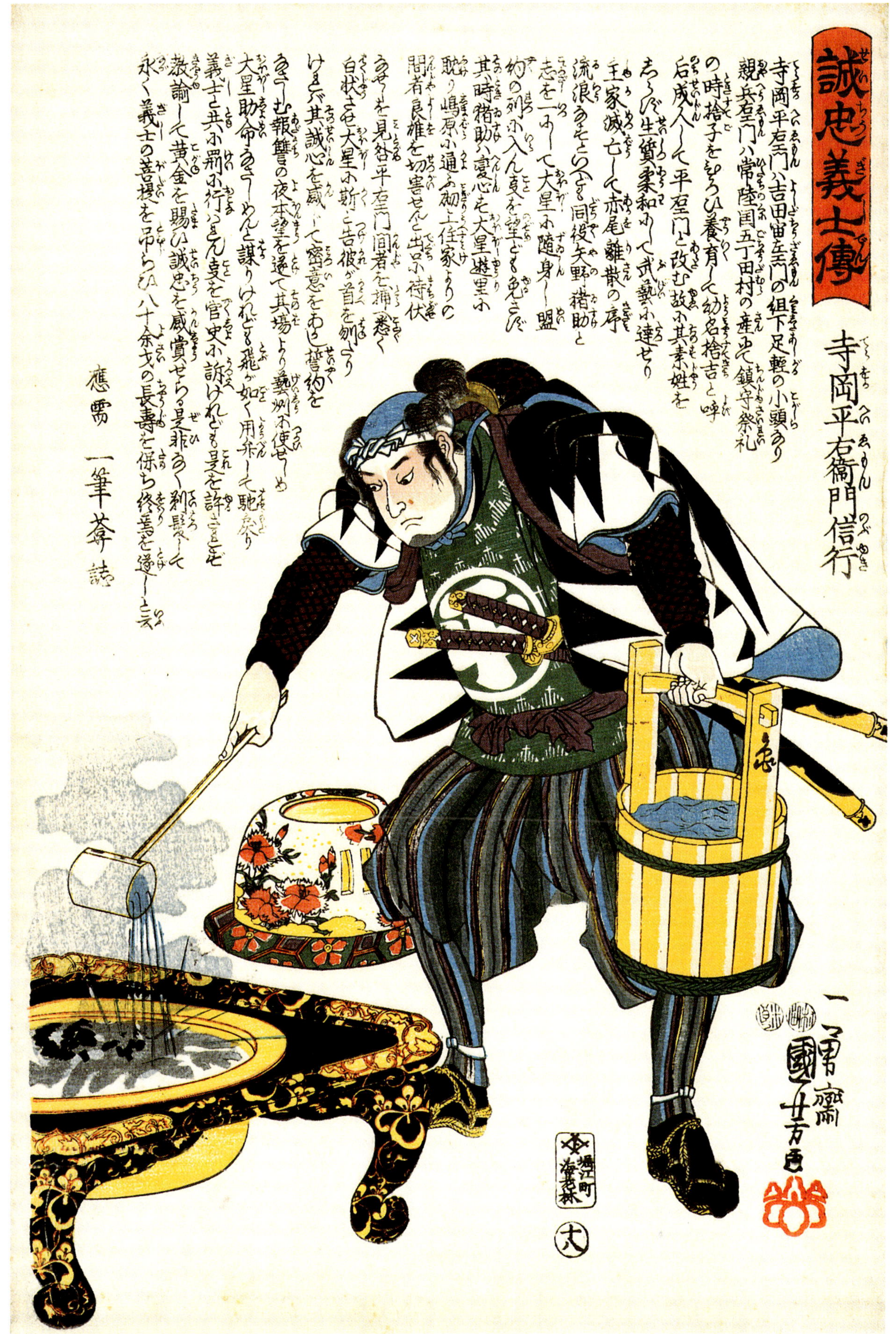
誠忠義士傳
寺岡平右衛門信行
應需 一筆菴誌
一勇齋國芳画

Uramatsu Handayū Takanao

1.19

Uramatsu Handayū Takanao falling backwards into the snow

Uramatsu Takanao was the eldest son of Uramatsu Kihei, six feet tall, strong, skilled in the martial arts, and a supremely powerful young man. His father, whose full name was Uramatsu Kihei Hidenao, became a priest and took the name Ryūen. The family lived in Hatchōbori and later moved to Honjō.

Takanao lived in Shiba Gensukechō with Naitō Jūrozaemon, and went out to work daily. Naitō had changed his name to Isogai.

Takanao took his sword to the sharpener, Tazaemon, to be honed and went to get it early in December. He was overjoyed at the work that had been done and added a tip of one *bu* when he paid the fee.[1]

Then he told Tazaemon that he was leaving for his home soon, and Tazaemon brought out a feast of fish and sake. Takanao got quite drunk and asked his host what he might test his sword against. Tazaemon saw that he had a determined man here and suggested that he should cut the pillar supporting the eaves. 'That's not hard. I'll do it,' said Takanao, and, with a shout, sliced the pillar off at an angle. The blade was made by Osafune Sukesada, and Takanao's technique was that of the Shinkage school. He might as well have been slicing a *daikon*. Off to the side, the host was amazed at the sharpness of the blade and let out a shout. When word of the night attack by the faithful band got around not long after that, stories were told of Tazaemon's pillar, and curiosity seekers came to look at it.

In the attack, Takanao came upon Kasahara Chōshichi in the garden and killed him.

When he practiced, his swing would bring down pine branches. One large one with snow on it knocked him on his backside. He laughed about that.

Afterward, he told his comrades the story.

1. See appendix d. See also 1.6 and its note.

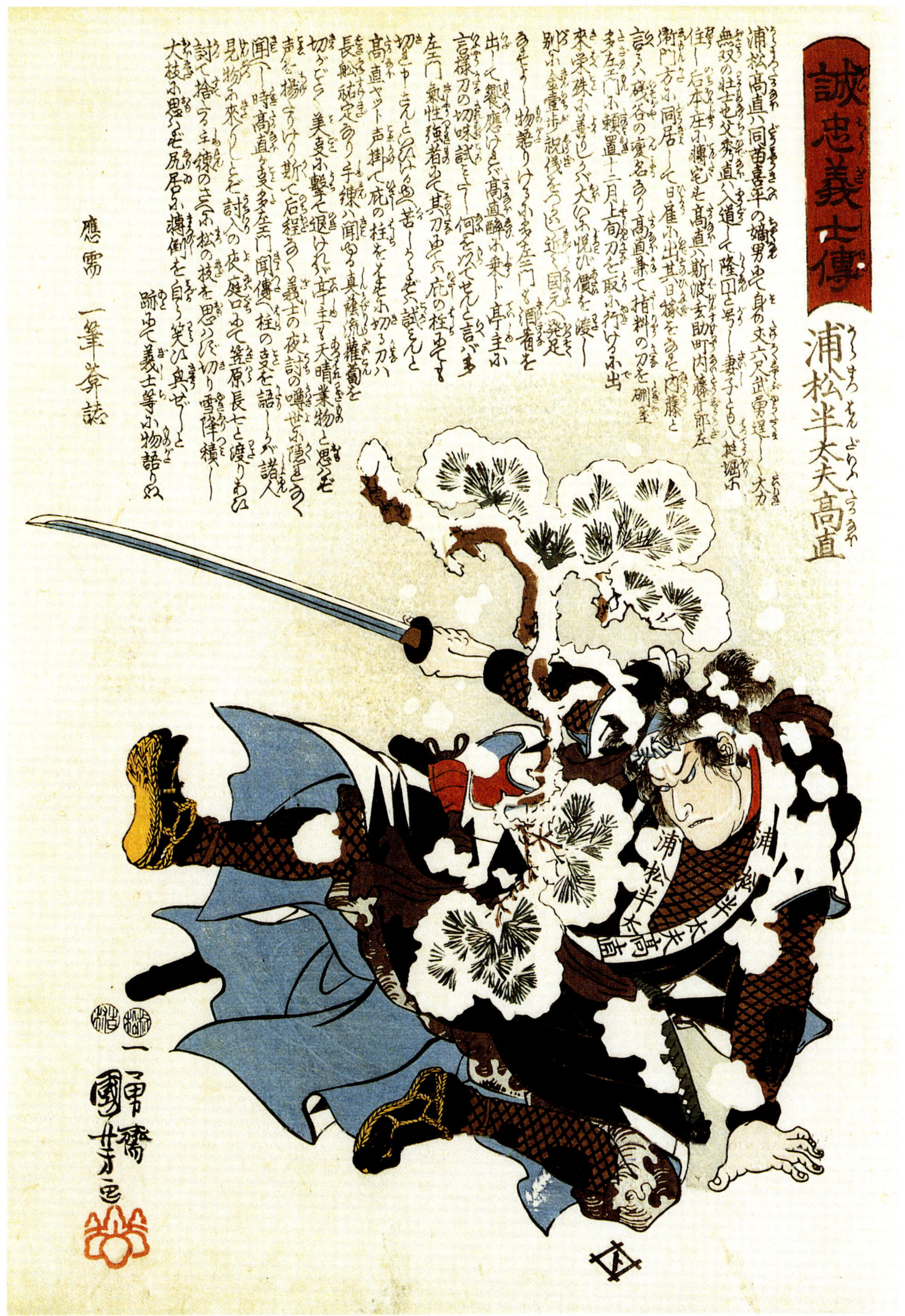
誠忠義士傳
浦松半太夫高直
應需 一筆菴誌
一勇齋國芳画

Tokuda Sadaemon Yukitaka

Tokuda Yukitaka was a fine swimmer. When they were carrying Moronao's head to Sengakuji, a messenger reached them at Ryōhoku Bridge and informed them that a party of the Uesumi clan was coming to attack them.[1, 2] So Yukitaka, Kataoka Dengoemon, and Senzaki Yagorō were sent on to Sengakuji in a small boat.[3]

The rest of the band, determined to stand their ground and treating death as a matter of no consequence, waited for a time outside the Nekoin Temple.

Everything was calm at the temple, and no attacking force appeared. So they gathered their forces, moved away from the temple in good order, and hurried through Tsukiji on the way to Sengakuji.

1.20

Tokuda Sadaemon Yukitaka in a straw rain mantle

1. This was really the famous Ryōgoku Bridge over the Sumida River. The name was changed to satisfy the censors.

2. Moronao's father-in-law was the head of the Uesumi clan.

3. Rain, which will be worse on the river journey, has turned the warrior here into a peasant for a time, as he dons a straw rain mantle and broad hat to protect his armour and equipment.

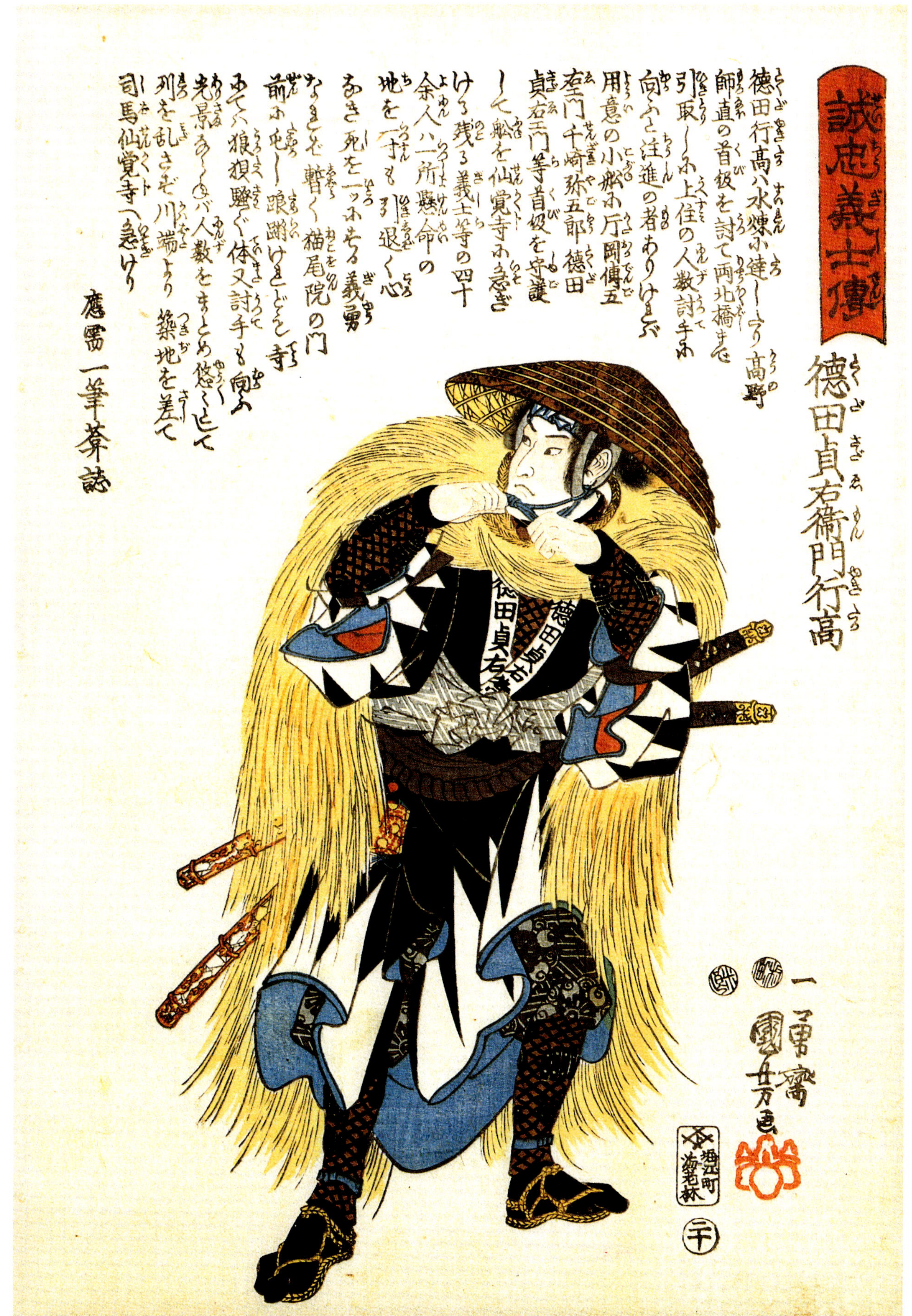
誠忠義士傳
徳田貞右衛門行高
一勇斎國芳画

Oribe Yahei Kanamaru

Oribe Kanamaru was seventy-eight years old when the vendetta was concluded.[1] He was more courageous than most younger men and had long experience with martial pursuits, in which he was a student of the Yamamoto school.

He had one daughter, whom he married to a man named Yasubei, famous for his part in a vendetta at Takata-no-Baba, in which he showed uncommon power. Kanamaru respected greatly his fierce disposition.

About this time, in Kaneyama, in Seishū province, the Ishii brothers were exacting vengeance on their father's enemy Akahori Mizuemon. Kanamaru loved to listen to the stories associated with that action, all the while emitting wild ejaculations of wonder, then would recount over and over the admirable exploits of Yasubei at Takata-no-Baba.

In this year, however, the news of their lord's death brought him considerable grief. He made the pledge with Ōboshi and waited impatiently for their day of reckoning.

He had always been good with the spear, and during the night attack the old man's battle cries struck terror into the multitude. His son, Yasubei, helped him when he could.[2] Father and son killed a number of the enemy. They avenged the dishonour visited on their departed lord but then had to pay the penalty for their lawless action.

Yahei's daughter, Kane-jo, sixteen years old, then donned charcoal-coloured robes to devote the rest of her life to prayer for the salvation of her husband and father. She took the name of Myōkai and lived at Kamedo opposite one of the six Amidas.[3] She lived, it is said, until she was ninety-three, in a hut she built herself at Sengakuji.

Attached to Yahei's spear was a poem that read:

Long as I have lived
and known all the pleasant things
long life can enjoy,
there is nothing to surpass
the victory we won today.

I.21

Oribe Yahei Kanamaru holding a banner emblazoned with name and clan membership

1. See II.3, concerning the same family. Not all details coincide. In the print Yahei carries a banner that gives his name and identifies him as an Akao retainer.

2. Yasubei had assumed the surname of his bride, and thus became Yahei's son and heir.

3. Meaning one of the six temples consecrated to Amida Buddha.

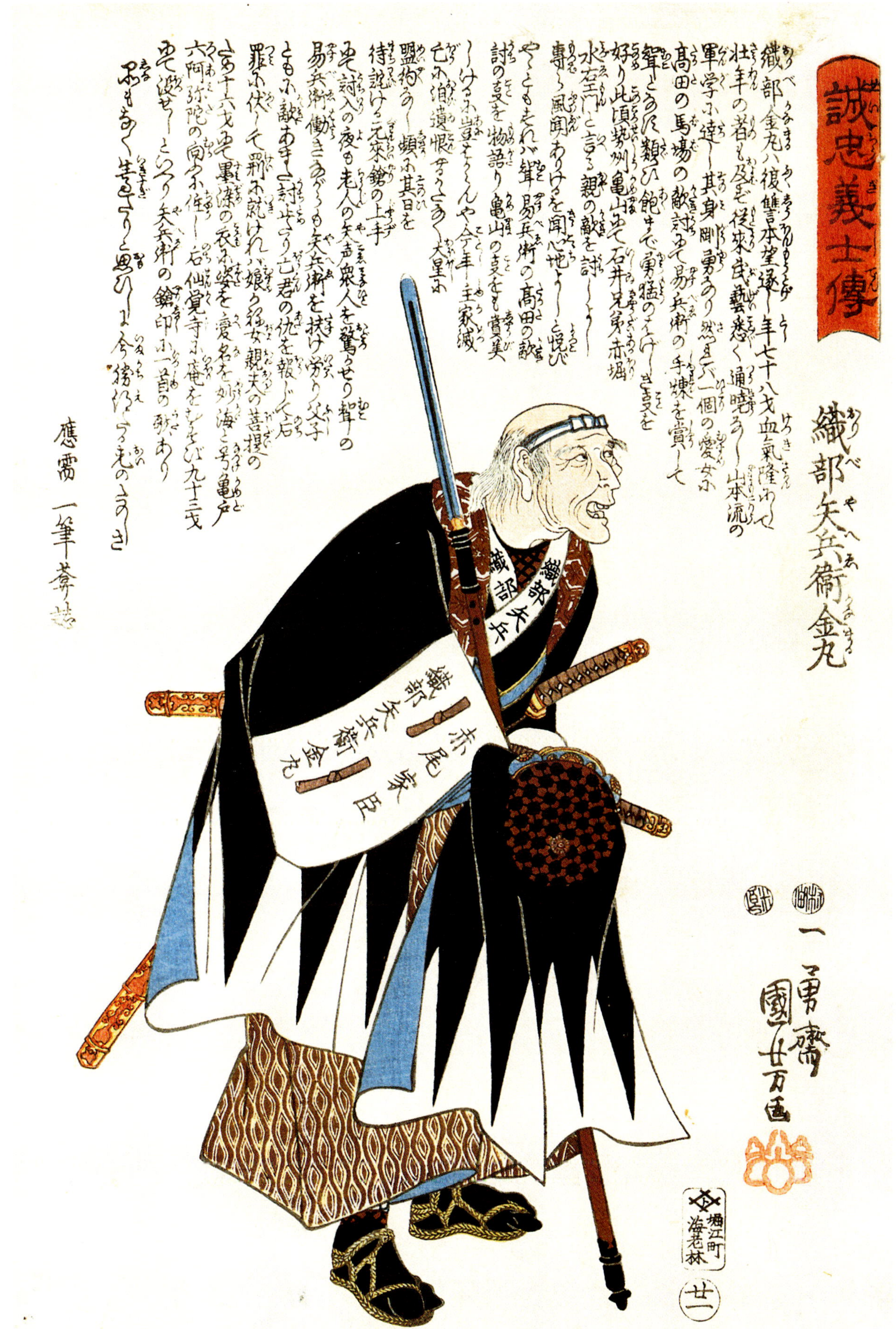
誠忠義士傳
織部矢兵衛金丸
赤尾家臣
織部矢兵衛金丸
應需 一筆菴誌
一勇斎國芳画
堀江町
海老林
廿一

Kiura Okaemon Sadayuki

1.22

Kiura Okaemon Sadayuki poised to strike

Kiura Sadayuki was from a family that had been retainers of Akao for generations. He was a skilled swordsman and tactician and was also tall, strong and of good appearance. In the night attack against the Kōno, he fought like a tiger, taking on all comers with a force suited to the destruction of mountains, wading in with a shower of sparks, panting and thirsty.

He saw, out of the corner of his eye, a boy who helped with the tea ceremony, cowering in a corner, trembling. 'Get me some water!' he shouted.

The boy was unable to move, even to save his life. He tried to stand, but his legs refused to function. All he could do was point, off to one side.

Sadayuki laughed and kicked down a partition enclosing what seemed to be the tearoom. In it was a platform supporting a brazier and a kettle of water. He drank from the kettle and then took the boy by the collar and said: 'Show me your master's room,' and pushed him, powerless, before him.

At that point, however, a large man jumped out and blocked his path. Sadayuki made smoke of that man's blood and, without more ado, fought his way further into the centre of the house.

He had two poems written in his sleeve:

Viewing flowers, drinking sake for a time
amid cold clouds from the eastern sea
and the obligations of the dusty world,
I greet dawn's snow, frost, and wind.[1]

How unexpected
to find the way I travelled
as a samurai
should lead me along the path
of the eternal law.

1. A poem in the Chinese form the Japanese call the *shichi-gon-sekku*, or 'poem of seven-character lines.'

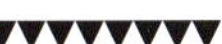

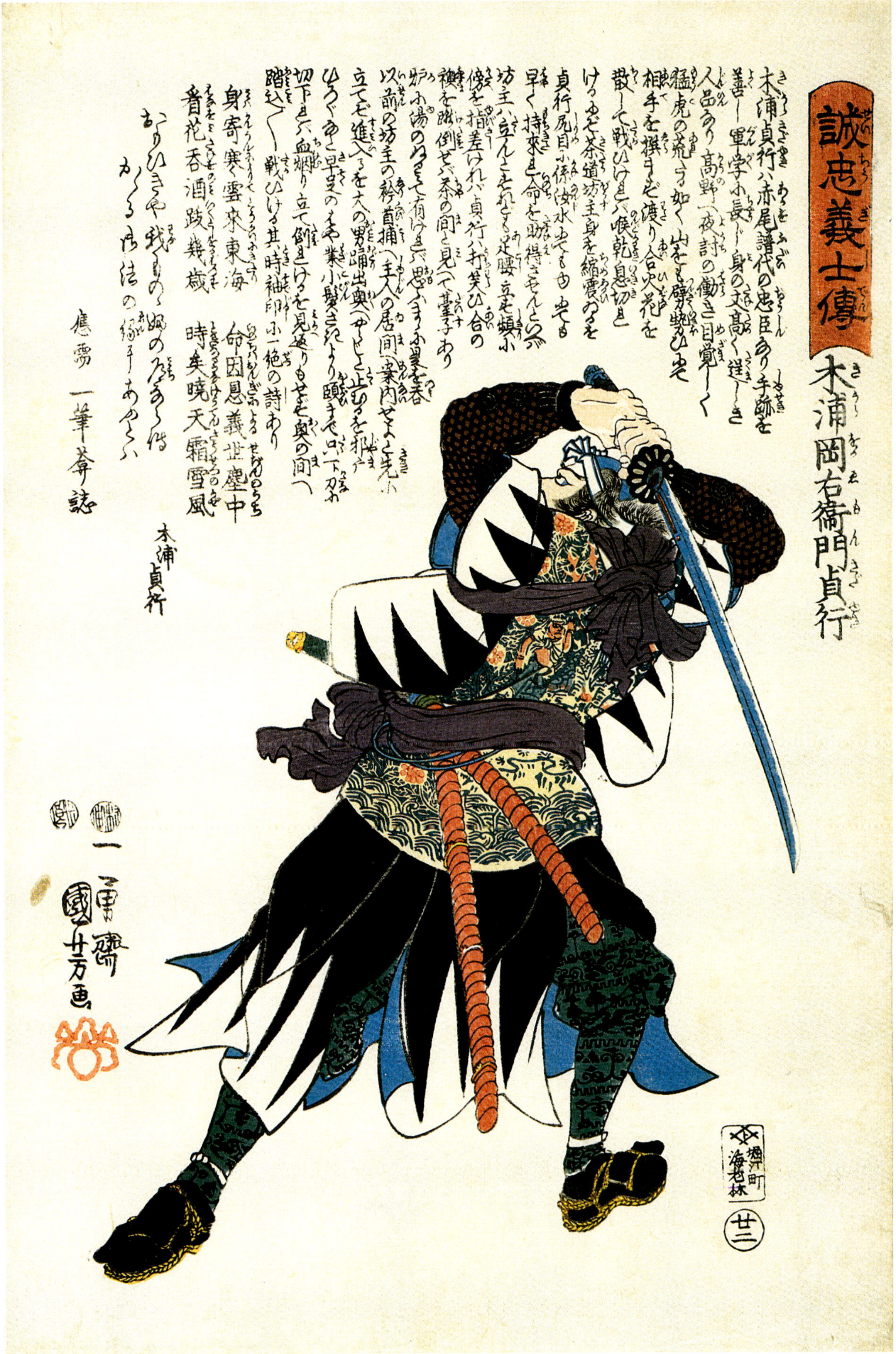

誠忠義士傳

木浦岡右衛門貞行

一勇齋國芳画

海老林

廿二

Katsuta Shinemon Taketaka

Taketaka was a strong man, and fearless.

He scrambled like a monkey up the ladder to the roof at the rear gate and looked down at the Kōno mansion, clear in the light of the full moon. It was as bright as midday, without a cloud in the sky. Under the fallen snow, the place shone like a mirror.

He didn't watch long. Saying, 'This is the time,' he jumped to the ground inside. The gate, he saw, was securely locked, so he took steps to get it opened. 'Sledge, sledge!' he called, and the attackers outside brought out their 150-pound battering ram and broke the gate open. Then they severed the bar with an axe and rushed in.

Alarmed by the noise, a gatekeeper ran out, half-dressed. Taketaka saw him and took appropriate action.

The shouts and crashes and noises of entrance at the back gate fell like thunder in the house, and panic-stricken occupants ran about in their underclothes. A child and its nurse screamed. Some crawled under the verandah.

The attackers saw none of this but struck against those who opposed them.[1] The air was filled with the sound of sword hilts striking. Thus Taketaka gained entrance to what seemed to be the room of Sahyōenosuke Moroyasu, Moronao's son, a room with an armour chest and other furnishing, and bed clothes that looked like someone had left in a hurry.

A brush and inkstone lay on the table there, and Shinemon took up the brush and wrote a scornful note on a sliding door pane: 'The Akao *rōnin* paid a visit to their esteemed adversaries and were disappointed that milord Sahyōe was not here.'

Then he entered Moronao's quarters.

1.23

Katsuta Shinemon Taketaka holding lantern aloft, discovers a dog at his heels

1. The scene in this print, however, depicting a beautifully combed and dressed dog, barking at a heavily armed warrior awkwardly lighting his way with a valuable but impractical lamp, is filled with humour.

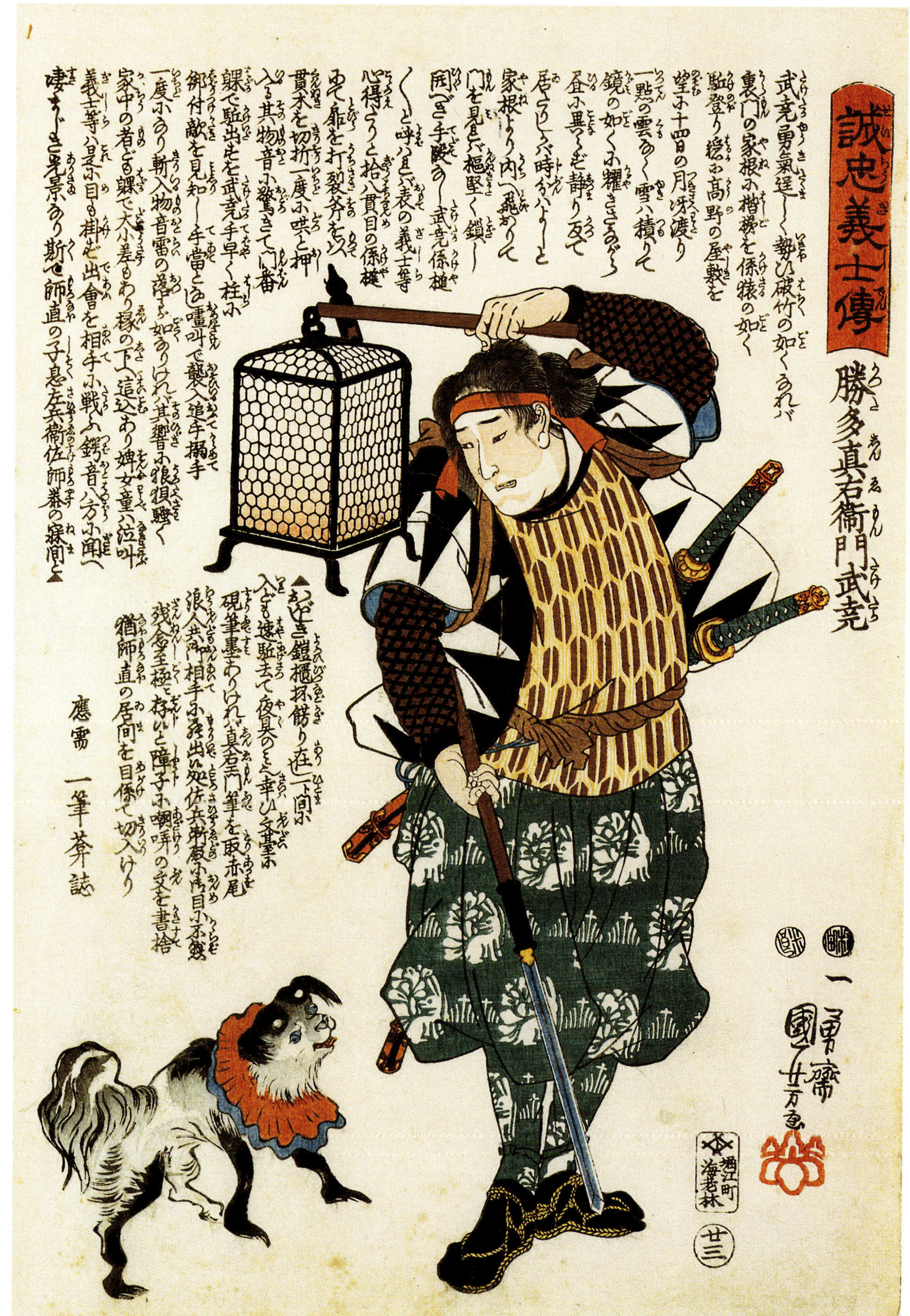
誠忠義士傳
勝多真右衛門武堯
應需 一筆菴誌
一勇齋國芳画
堀江町 海老林
廿三

Takebayashi Sadashichi Takashige

1.24

Takebayashi Sadashichi Takashige tying his waistband

Takebayashi Takashige was from a family of old retainers and was said to be a distant descendant of Bu Rin Ryū, who had been captured by Okuno Shōgen during the Korean invasion.[1] His mother had been a wet-nurse of Takasada, so he was a 'milk-brother' of the lord. He had lost his father, Sadaemon, to illness, and now he looked after his mother with unflagging devotion.

When the lord's house fell, he left Akao and took up temporary lodging in Kyoto and planned the vendetta with Ōboshi. When he informed his mother that he had signed the compact, she was overjoyed and set to work preparing for his journey and informed him about all the omens that must be observed if they were to succeed. Then, the night before they were to depart, she committed suicide.

At the end of the message she left behind, she had written this poem:

After I am gone,
remember me by looking at
the plum on my sleeve,
shining through a mist of tears
like the moon in clouded skies

This was March 15th. She was in her seventy-second year. Her death intensified the violent anger building up in her son, now driving a desire to destroy the enemy of not only his lord but also his mother. He informed Ōboshi of what had happened and, with blood in his eye, said he was leaving for the Kantō and hurried off.

I have dreamed for thirty-three years,
and dream still as I die for duty.
Both parents await me in the world of death.
Duty, vendetta, piety, dream: all meaningless.

How lucky it is
to see on death's mountain path
cherry trees in bloom

1. In the historical invasions of Korea of 1592 and 1597, the Japanese brought back a number of captives, primarily artisans and people with similar valuable skills. One was an ethnic Chinese named Meng Erh K'uan. A descendant of that Meng Erh K'uan, Takebayashi Tadashichi Takashige, took part in the historical night attack and died with the other condemned participants. Although his name was very much like the 'Takebayashi Sadashichi Takashi' of the Kuniyoshi prints, the Sino-Japanese pronunciation 'Bu Rin Ryū' given in the text of this print is surely a joke. The name would have been pronounced something like 'Mu Limnyung' at the time this fictional Korean would have lived.

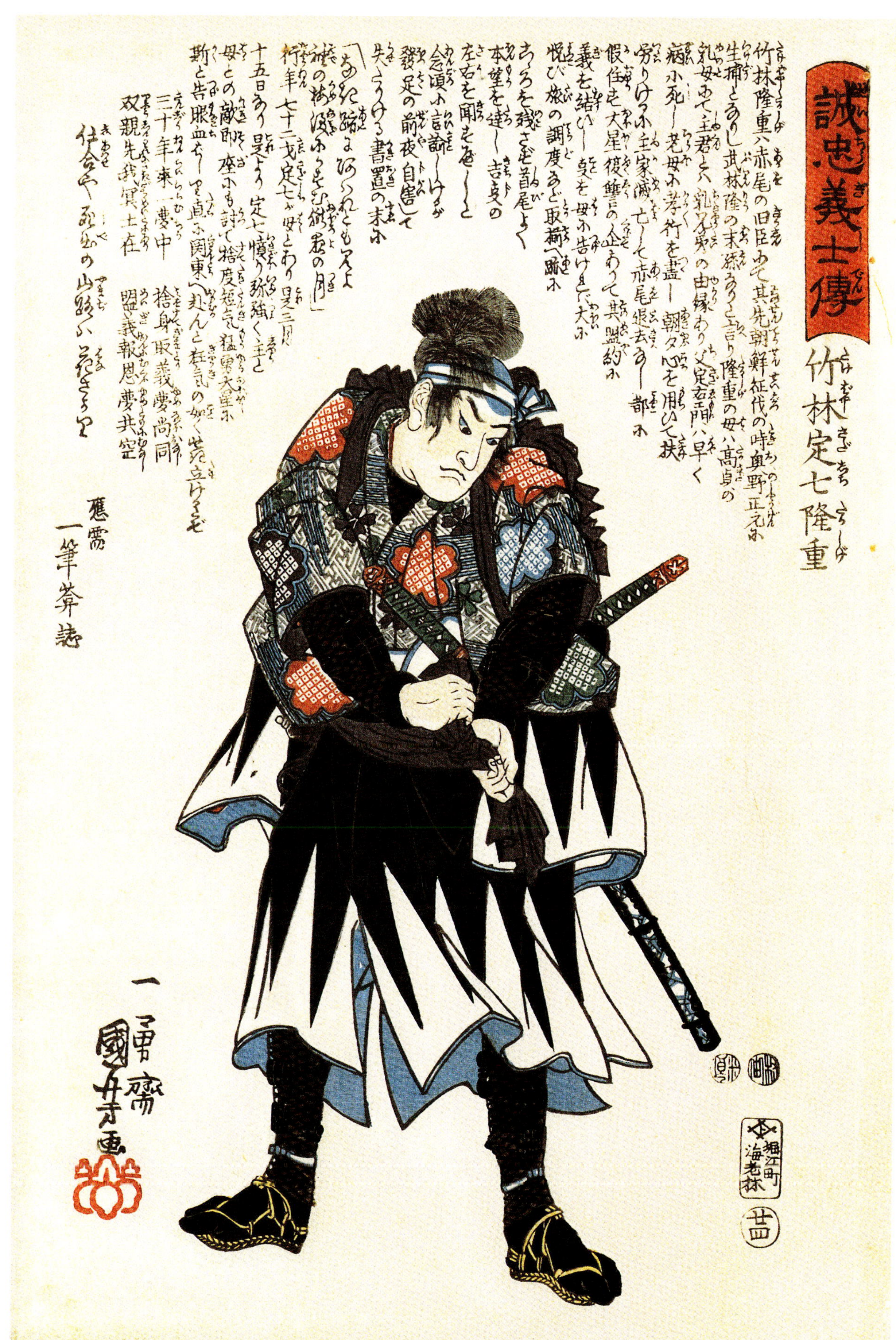
誠忠義士傳
竹林定七隆重
應需
一筆菴誌
一勇斎國芳画
堀江町
海老林

Kurahashi Zensuke Takeyuki

I.25

Kurahashi Zensuke Takeyuki, a wall scroll draped over his sword

Kurahashi Takeyuki was a fine hot-tempered swordsman and performed well in the attack on the Kōno mansion. He had studied the floor plan of the house, which the Yazama brothers had secured from Yasuemon, the chief carpenter. So he knew that there were certain hidden details in its construction.

He hacked his way into Moronao's bedroom just after Moronao had fled, leaving a rumpled bed. Takeyuki felt the bedclothes and found them still warm.

He knew Moronao could not have gone far, so he snagged the scroll out of the alcove and pushed on the wall it had been hanging on.[1] It was a secret door into the garden! He charged out through it and on seeing the storage shed for the garden apartments knew Moronao must be there.

Yazama, Senzaki, and Takebayashi circled the shed and poured arrows into it from their short bows. Two men ran out, and Takeyuki took them on.

1. The warrior in this print has the mock-heroic quality of Don Quixote as he uses his sword on the inoffensive picture scroll.

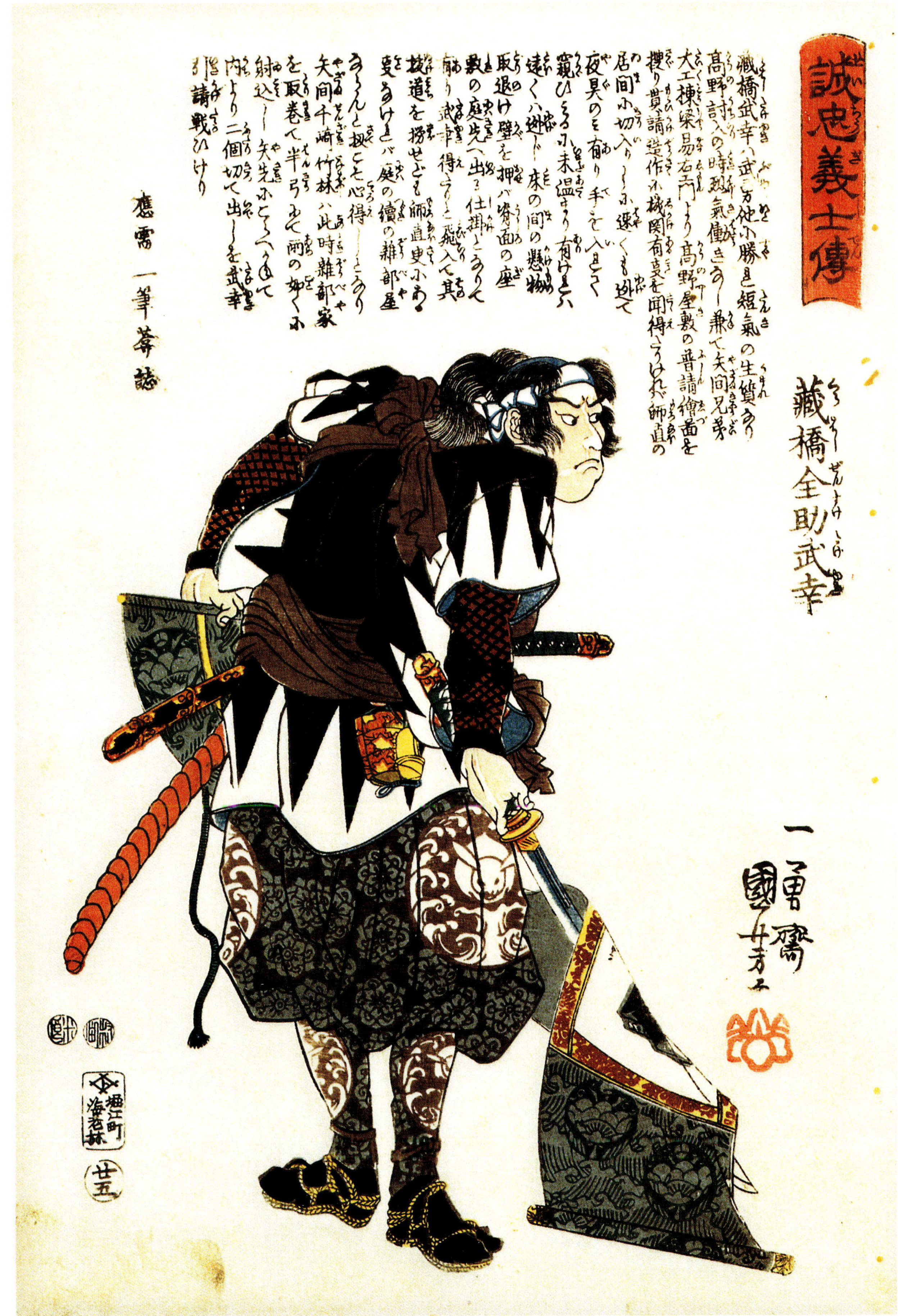
誠忠義士傳
藏橋全助武幸
應需一筆菴誌
一勇齋國芳画
廿五

Aihara Esuke Munefusa

I.26

Aihara Esuke Munefusa trampling over a screen

Munefusa was a straightforward and gentle man of few words. He was good at figures and worked in the business affairs office. Expert in martial arts, particularly archery, he was strongly loyal.

When the Akao was dissolved, he continued to follow Ōboshi's instructions and remained in the Yamashina area. Then he advanced to the Kantō region with Ōboshi.

He took up residence near the enemy mansion and peddled pipe tobacco, often discussing prices with the Kōno servants.

Before they carried out the attack, he wrote a farewell letter to his sister, who had married and lived in their home village of Ono, in Banshū:

Worlds that have not seen
or felt the depth to which
these snows have fallen
will find their spirits darken
with the ink laid by this brush.

Then he joined in the action and acquitted himself well, slaying many of the enemy.[1] The next day as he and his comrades were being interrogated, one-by-one, before their temple, he composed the poem:

As spring comes in,
with no one the wiser,
the years and the months
pass by with the aging hair
that makes human heads turn white.

He had a truly gentle spirit. He was not at all like Oyamada or Ono, who suffered lifelong embarrassment for failing to place their lives on the line in the face of danger.[2]
Comparing him with them is like comparing gems with gravel. He was truly a model of loyalty.

1. He seems to be running over a low screen behind which the women smoked from long pipes and wrote letters on sheets from the paper rolls he sends flying. His shoes, known as *waraji*, or 'straw sandals,' are conspicuously painted in most of the prints and emphasize further how incongruous these fully-armed warriors are amid the austere luxury of the mansion interiors. The Japanese have an inbred loathing of footwear, and it is never worn on the *tatami* mats the members of the band are treading on so brazenly. Shoes of this type, though of more durable material, were standard issue for Japanese soldiers even as late as World War II.

2. Ono Kudayū is a villain of the *Chūshingura*.

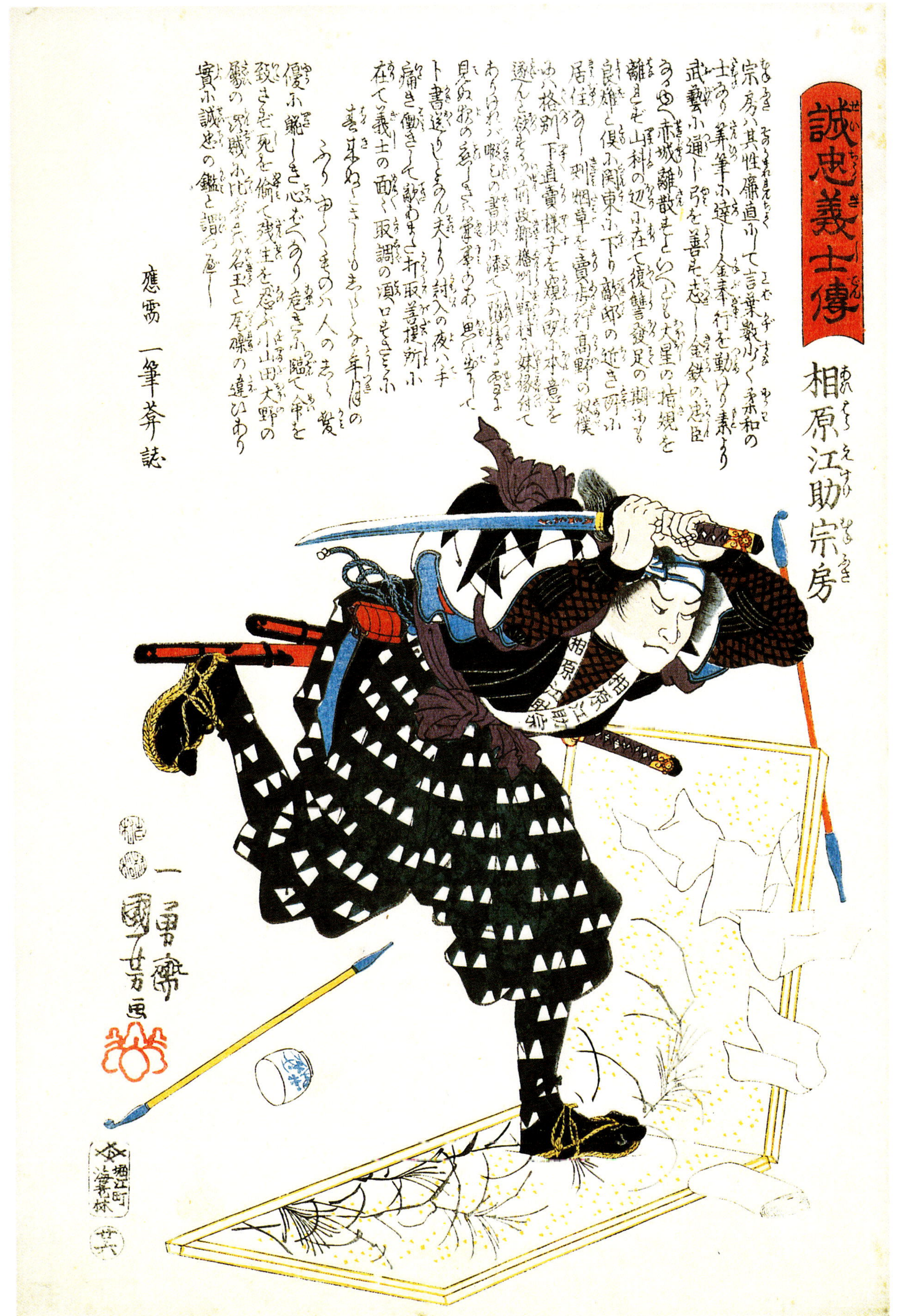
誠忠義士傳
相原江助宗房
應需 一筆斉誌
一勇斎國芳画

Tominomori Suke-emon Masakata

When Akao fell, Tominomori Masakata, his wife and their babe-in-arms, Chōsaburō, left for Osaka, with no way of supporting themselves. Ōboshi was living quietly in Yamashina, in Kyoto, and Tominomori got in touch with him and covertly went over plans for vengeance.

He was a dutiful son. His mother was absolutely devoted to their lord, and his father, Sukenoshin, served as intermediary between him and Ōboshi. His mother knew nothing about what was going on.

He felt that, if he wore a piece of his mother's clothing when they went into action, he would go happily to the land of the dead. So he contrived to get something of hers and wore it next to his skin in the assault.

They had had snow the night before, but when the time came for the attack, the fourteenth day moon was shining brightly, and the entrance stood out as clear as midday. When they broke down the cedar gate, he rushed in shouting: 'Get out of the way for the men of En'ya Hangan. We want the head of Moronao!' He had come, and now he engaged the enemy. Into the fray, with neither hesitation nor flinching, he plunged. His opponents didn't know whom they fought. When they used the password 'Mountain,' he said 'River.' His superb technique sparkled.

Then someone to the side of him threw an *hibachi* at him. Coals and ashes flew all about him. Dust got in his nose and mouth.[1]

The demoralized enemy were running around half-naked. But the Akao warriors were wearing protective gear, which made them that much more menacing. They killed all the defenders but two. Afterward they decided that the *hibachi* was thrown by the acolyte Suzuki Shōchiku.

1.27

Tominomori Suke-emon Masakata sustaining a blow from a charcoal brazier

1. This print has had metallic powder hand-applied after its printing to simulate the coal dust from the *hibachi* (see also note to plate 1.49). It is also one of many in which the artist seems to satirize the attack, showing that it was, after all, an armed incursion into a peaceful household, in which the attackers were opposed chiefly by home furnishings. The battle scenes in these sumptuous surroundings, however, gave Kuniyoshi marvellous props to set off his fighting men.

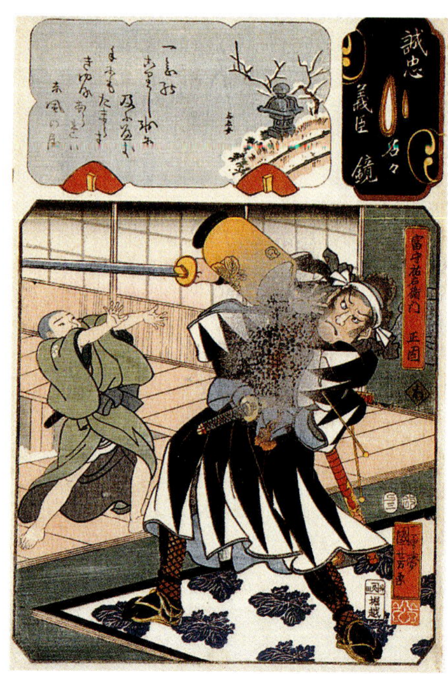

Fig. 8

Kuniyoshi: From the series Seichu gishin meimei kagami *or* Mirror of the true loyalty of the faithful retainers, individually. *Tominomori Suke-emon Masakata is struck by a jar of ashes thrown by an acolyte.*

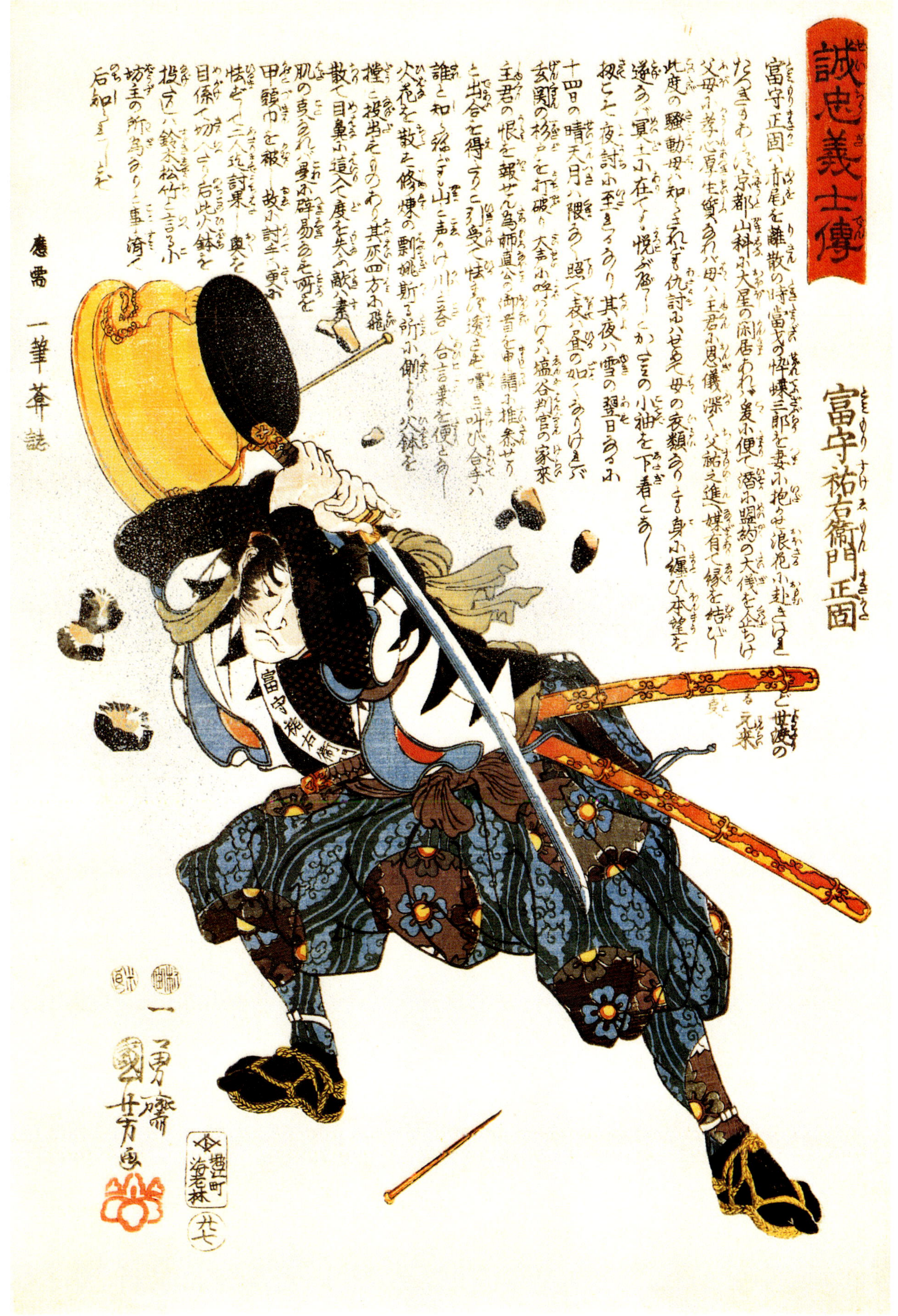
誠忠義士傳
富守祐右衛門正固
一勇齋國芳画

Ushioda Masanojō Takanori

1.28

Ushioda Masanojō Takanori fastening his wrist strap

Ushioda Takenori had been a retainer with the Yoshida family under the name of Ushioda Mondo. When that family went out of existence he became an Akao retainer and changed his given name to Takanori. He was talented with weapons, in particular the spear.

In the night attack he approached the back gate and threw the hooked rope, then launched himself like a bird over the wall and removed the bar. He was no laggard and once the gate was open, fought his way wondrously forward.

He moved into the garden in quest of Moronao's apartment, when a man with flashing sword leaped out and shouted, 'Shimizu Ikkaku here!' and swung it toward Takenori's throat.

Takenori reacted quickly and slid to the left, then swung his spear around and countered. His aim was true, but Shimizu was quick and twisted his body safely about. With sword parrying and thrusting, and spear skillfully stabbing, only to be kicked aside, they went on endlessly, gasping for breath, fighting like tiger and dragon. Both were so agile, and the outcome was in doubt, when Miura Jirōzaemon came running up, extended his lance, and stabbed Shimizu in the side.

Still active, even against so strong an enemy as Shimizu, Takanori thrust again, and this time caught his adversary in the throat, releasing a flood of blood. Shimizu died unable to utter a word.

The two men did not take a second look at the corpse as they hurried on into the centre of the house.

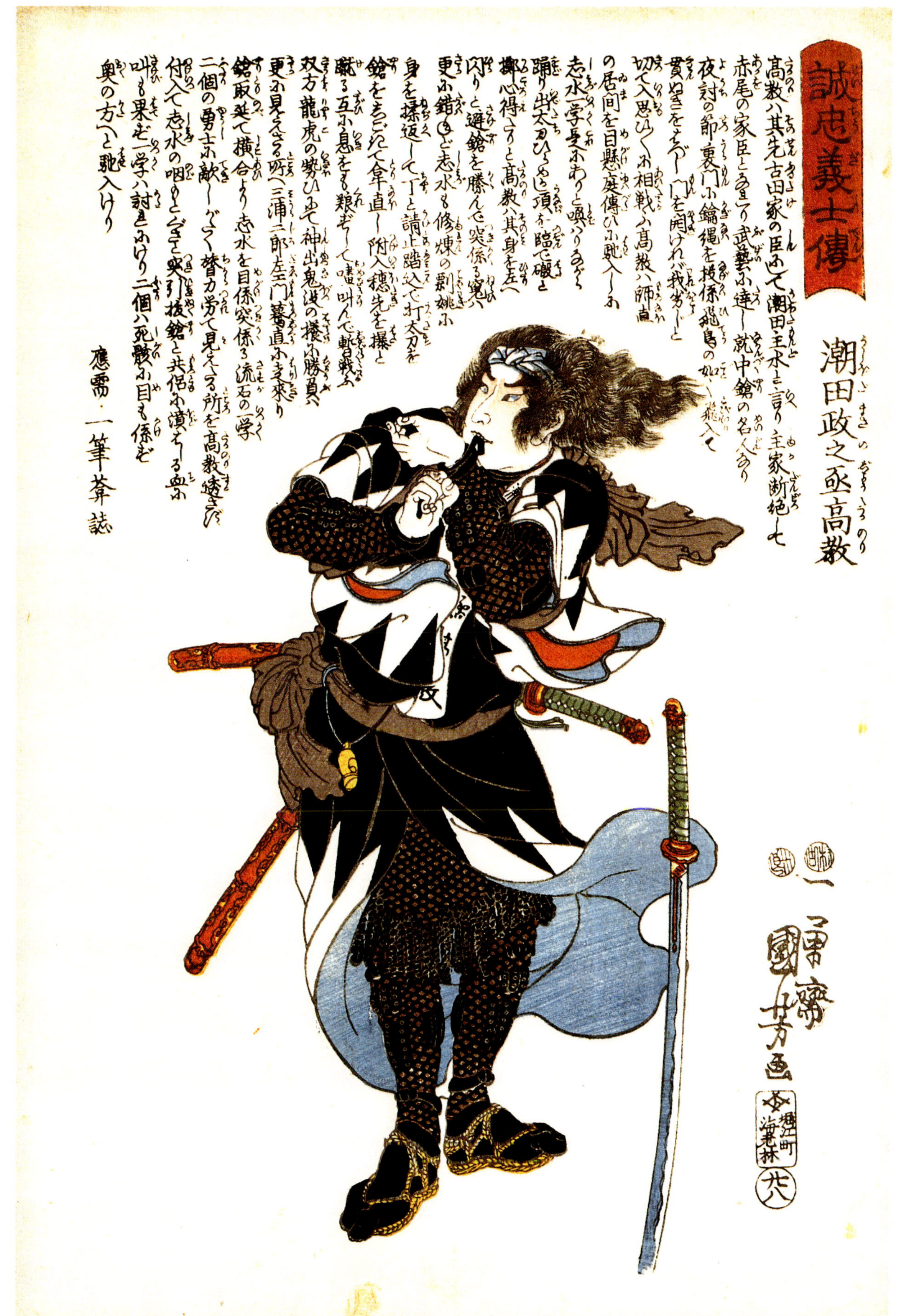
誠忠義士傳
潮田政之丞高教
應需一筆菴誌
一勇齋國芳画

Hayami Sōzaemon Mitsutaka

Hayami Mitsutaka was in service with the lord and retinue in Kamakura when the debacle occurred. He brought the news back to the home province and Akao, a distance of 170 *ri*, in 4 1/2 days, a journey like that of the 'Flying Prince' Tai Tsung, in *Water margin*, who went 800 *ri* astride four magic incantations.[1, 2]

Ōboshi praised him for what he had done when he made the formal announcement at Akao Castle, after which he went around to the various families and talked with them. Much was accomplished in that later trip, though there were craven people who failed to be counted among the faithful out of fear for their lives. Some of them, like Ono Kudayū, were unfaithful out of greed.

Thus, after a number of efforts, Yoshio was able to select a group of absolutely determined men and bind them in the compact through which they took the head of their master's enemy, Moronao, and offered it at Hangan's grave. Thus they achieved their goal, so that the names of these faithful warriors might shine before future generations.

On the night of the attack, Hayami Mitsutaka did distinguished work and prepared to fight to the death again later at Sengakuji, when word came that the Uesumi were preparing an assault.

At that time he went out the Mountain Gate and advised the priests to disperse the curiosity seekers. Then he raked up snow into a great pile and formed a barricade to ward off attackers. My, how Ōboshi praised his ingenuity!

Wind and water
and earth and flame and fire
have made this body.
In memory of this day,
it will return to the five rings.[3]

Mitsutaka

1.29

Hayami Sōzaemon Mitsutaka quenching his thirst from a water kettle

1. A distance of roughly 425 miles. One *ri* is approximately 2.5 miles. Thirsty after the battle or perhaps readying himself for his departure to Akao, the print shows Hayami Mitsutaka drinking from a metal vessel. The box behind him surely contains the head of Moronao.

2. See *Water margin*, translated by J.H. Jackson, I, 709, and passim and *All men are brothers*, translated by Pearl S. Buck, p. 946, and passim.

3. Literally 'the five wheels, or circles,' as of the five-layered pagoda.

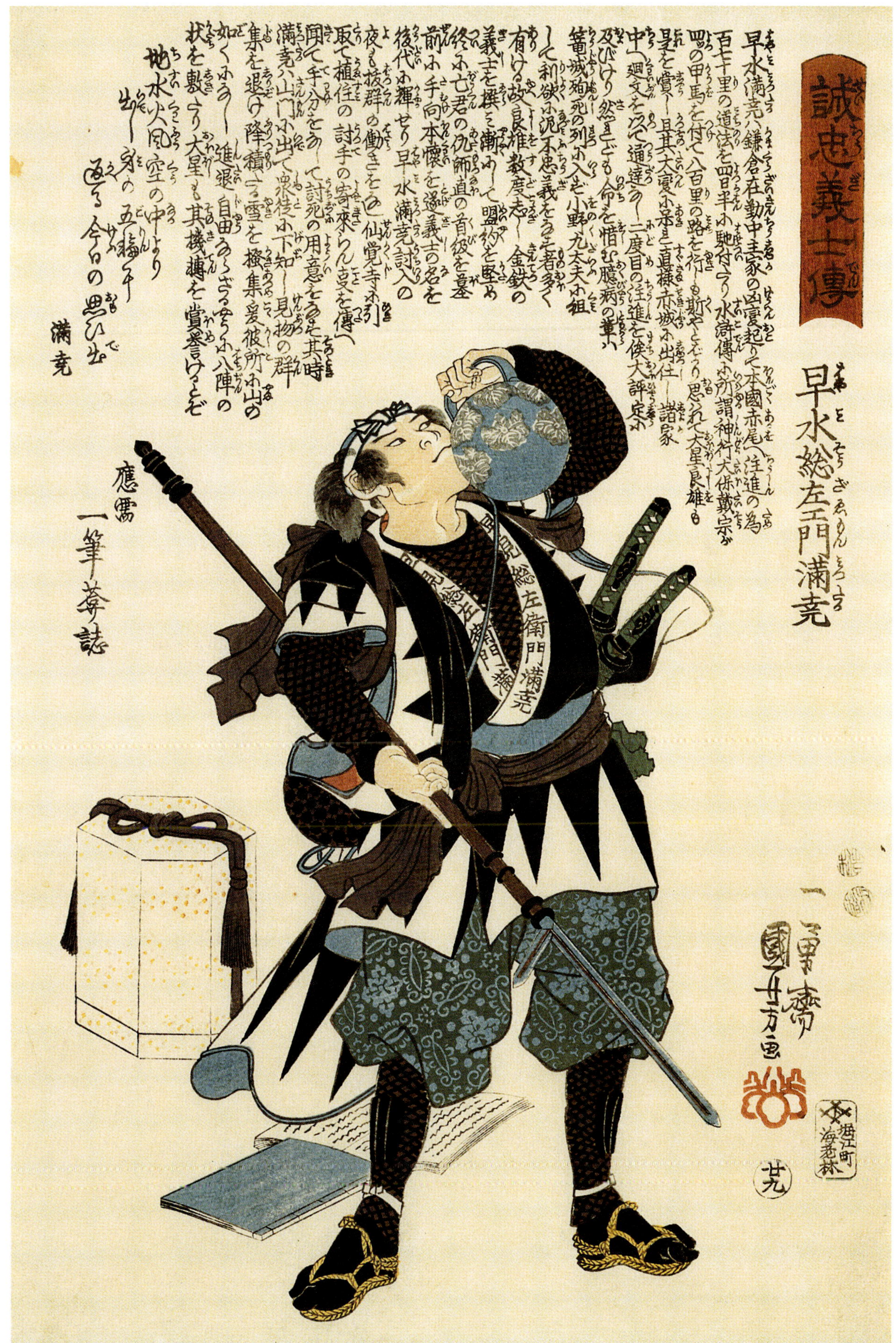
誠忠義士傳
早水総左衛門満尭
應需 一筆菴誌
一勇斎國芳画

Onodera Tōemon Hidetome

Hidetome was the foster son of Onodera Hidekazu, but since he had recently joined the Onodera family he received no stipend from Akao. He did receive the legacy of his foster father's declared purpose, however, and the two of them made their way to the Kantō to avenge their master's death, following Ōboshi's instructions.

Disguised as tradesmen, they gained access to the Kōno mansion and inspected it while no one was around. They worked valiantly to achieve their objective and left a heritage of fame for future generations.

On the 14th day of December in the 15th day of Kenroku, the *rōnin* gathered in three locations.[1] There they were told that the attack would take place at the hour of the rat. Then they had a parting fraternal draught of sake. With it they ate dried chestnuts, *konbu*, tiny dried sardines, and sweets, to symbolize how they would bring low the enemy's head. They also had duck, soup, and a feast of *soba* and went on toasting each other as much as they dared without falling asleep.

Then, when the time came, they donned their mail shirts and their spiked leggings and set out as if to fight a fire, a redoubtable group.[2]

If the lord is wise,
and his retainers good,
the people are happy.
The lord is like the head,
and the retainers the members.
If all is clear above,
all is good below.
If the lord is virtuous,
loyalty abides.
This is what we pray for.

This morning early
not even one word of mouth
passes among us,
as, for our lord's sake alone,
the dew begins to gather.

Hidetome

1.30

Onodera Tōemon Hidetome tying his sandal on a tipped go-board

1. The name of the reign - historically Genroku - has been changed slightly. Genroku 15 was 1702.

2. The redoubtable fighting man is here tying the cord of his thonged shoe, resting his foot on a massive overturned go-board. Go is a game the Japanese received from China, in which space on a board is ruled off in a grid of hundreds of squares, sections of which two players attempt to wall off from each other using black and white circles of stone. Only the black stones are visible in the print.

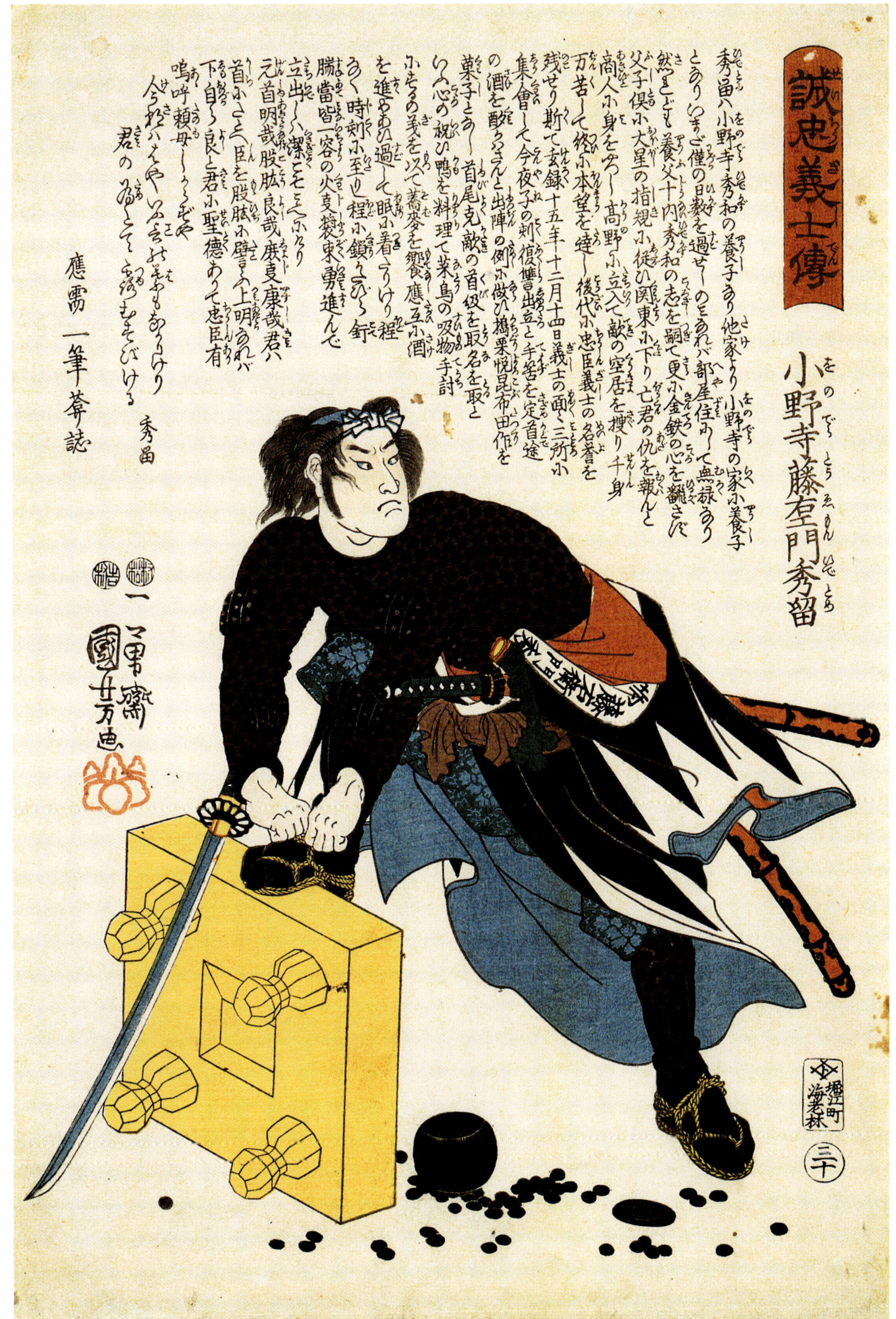
誠忠義士傳
一勇斎國芳画
堀江町
海老林
三十
應需一筆菴誌

Chiba Saburōhei Mitsutada

1.31

Chiba Saburōhei Mitsutada holding spear, helmet, and cape

Chiba Mitsutada was another hereditary Akao retainer, an ever-present confidant of the Lord Takasada, and at times even a critic. He was, however, undeviatingly loyal. When he questioned the conduct of Ono and the rest, he incurred the wrath of his lord and became a *rōnin*.

He sent his mother, wife, and children off to his home in Iyo, loaded his worldly goods on a boat, and was preparing to follow them when he heard of the calamity at Kamakura.

He returned to Akao, ready to join others in a fight to the death there, but then he had a serious discussion with Ōboshi. Yuranosuke praised him much but advised him that even though he was loyal, his *rōnin* status released him of any obligation. He therefore refrained from taking Mitsutada into the conspiracy.

Acting like he still bore a grudge, Mitsutada went to his home in the village of Iyo and quietly entrusted his mother, his wife, and his son, Fujinosuke, to an uncle. Then he went to the Kantō and took up lodging in Kōjimachi 4-chōme.

There he changed his name to Hara Misuke and, along with Yazama Kihei - who had changed his name to Somahara Kisai - opened a school of military arts in his home. He was an expert in the Heki school of archery.

In the night attack, he was in the third rank at the rear gate and inflicted many wounds on the enemy. He and Fuwa Masatane had both been *rōnin*, but in avenging the death of their former lord and sacrificing their lives in requital of care and devotion long past, they showed themselves to be men of truly unusual loyalty.[1]

1. The apology for *rōnin* status here shows that the word was normally pejorative, referring to a samurai who had been a bad soldier and was set adrift.

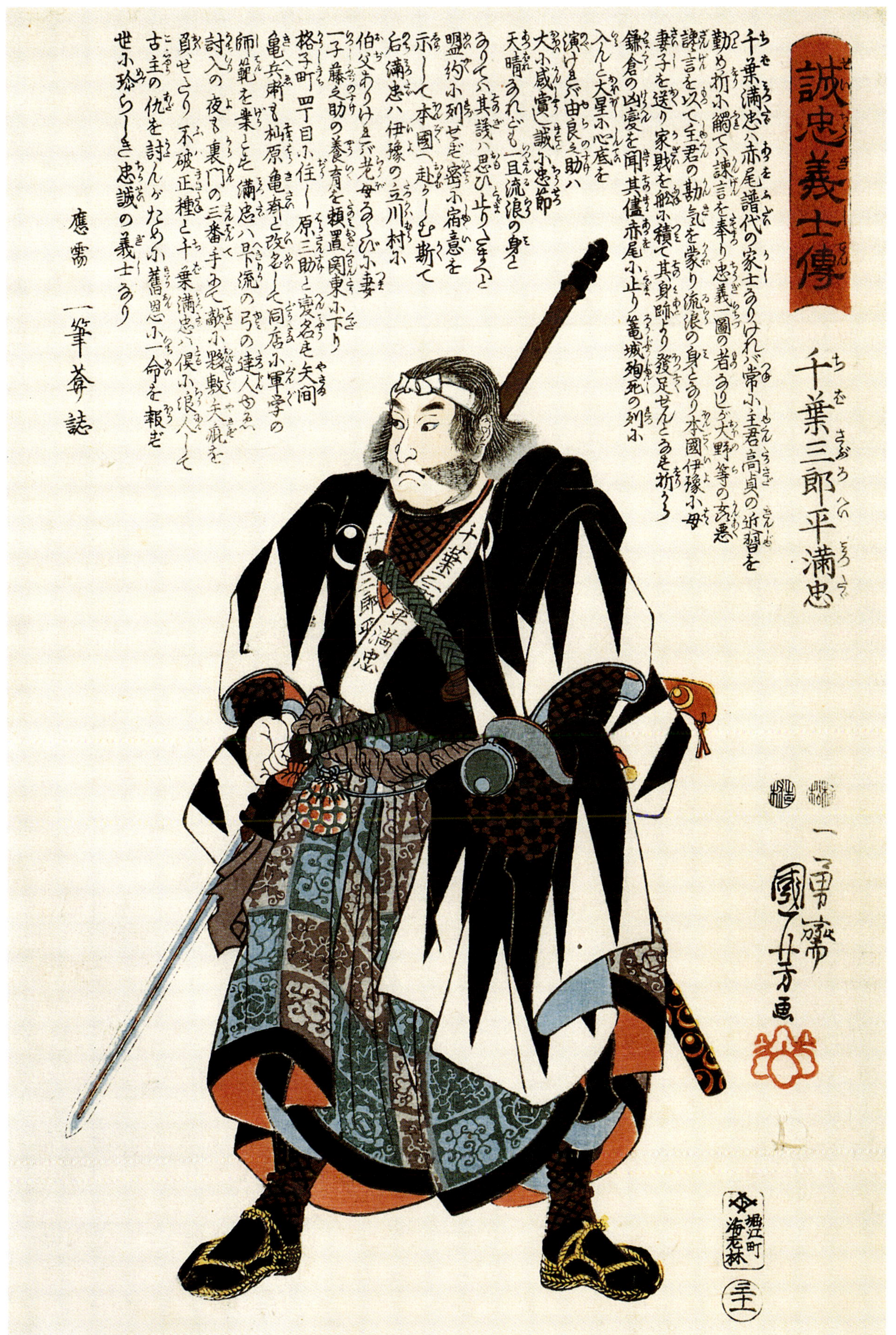
誠忠義士傳
千葉三郎平満忠
一勇齋國芳画
堀江町
海老林

Ōboshi Seizaemon Nobukiyo

I.32

Ōboshi Seizaemon Nobukiyo rushing on toward his next adversary

Ōboshi Nobukiyo was a cousin of Yuranosuke. He was employed by a collateral branch of the family as an armourer, at a salary of 200 *koku* of rice.[1] Ōboshi Magosaburō and Ōboshi Kondō Genshirō were also related and joined the conspiracy, but for some reason they remained in Kyoto on the fateful day and did not take part in the attack.[2]

Nobukiyo was deeply schooled in the martial arts and also an aggressive hot-blood who went to the Kantō early and waited impatiently for Yuranosuke to join him there. He, along with Hara and Yoshida, repeatedly petitioned for the attack to begin. Then, when the date was finally set, he rushed to the Oribe house in Honjō four or five days early, and fussed over the carefully prepared bows and arrows and spears and glaives.

He failed to sleep on the night of the 14th and charged into the rear gate with the fourth wave. Ready to cross swords with hordes of the enemy, he rushed ahead full tilt and, finding no one to attack at first, was finally accosted by Sudō Senemon, an aide of Kōno Uhyōe Moroyasu.

Nobukiyo rushed at his adversary with a scream, and their weapons crashed together. Sudō, too, was a skilled fighter, and he fought with a flourish. His was an astonishing display of agility and blade legerdemain, but the dazzling display of Nobukiyo's swordsmanship blinded and confused him, and the point finally slashed him from his shoulder to his ribs.[3] The blood cascaded down, and he died without a groan.

Nobukiyo never looked back as he made his way further into the interior.

1. The *koku*, which is equal to 4.9629 bushels, was the standard by which financial worth was measured. Thus the various *daimyō* were ranked by the number of *koku* they paid each year as tribute to the shogun's treasury. See appendix d.

2. See II.17, in which Ōboshi refuses to include another of the Ōboshi family in the attacking force on the grounds that it would involve the whole clan in the feud.

3. The blow which brought Sudō down is graphically depicted in this print, as the wounded man's headband is shown flying in one direction and his sword in the other.

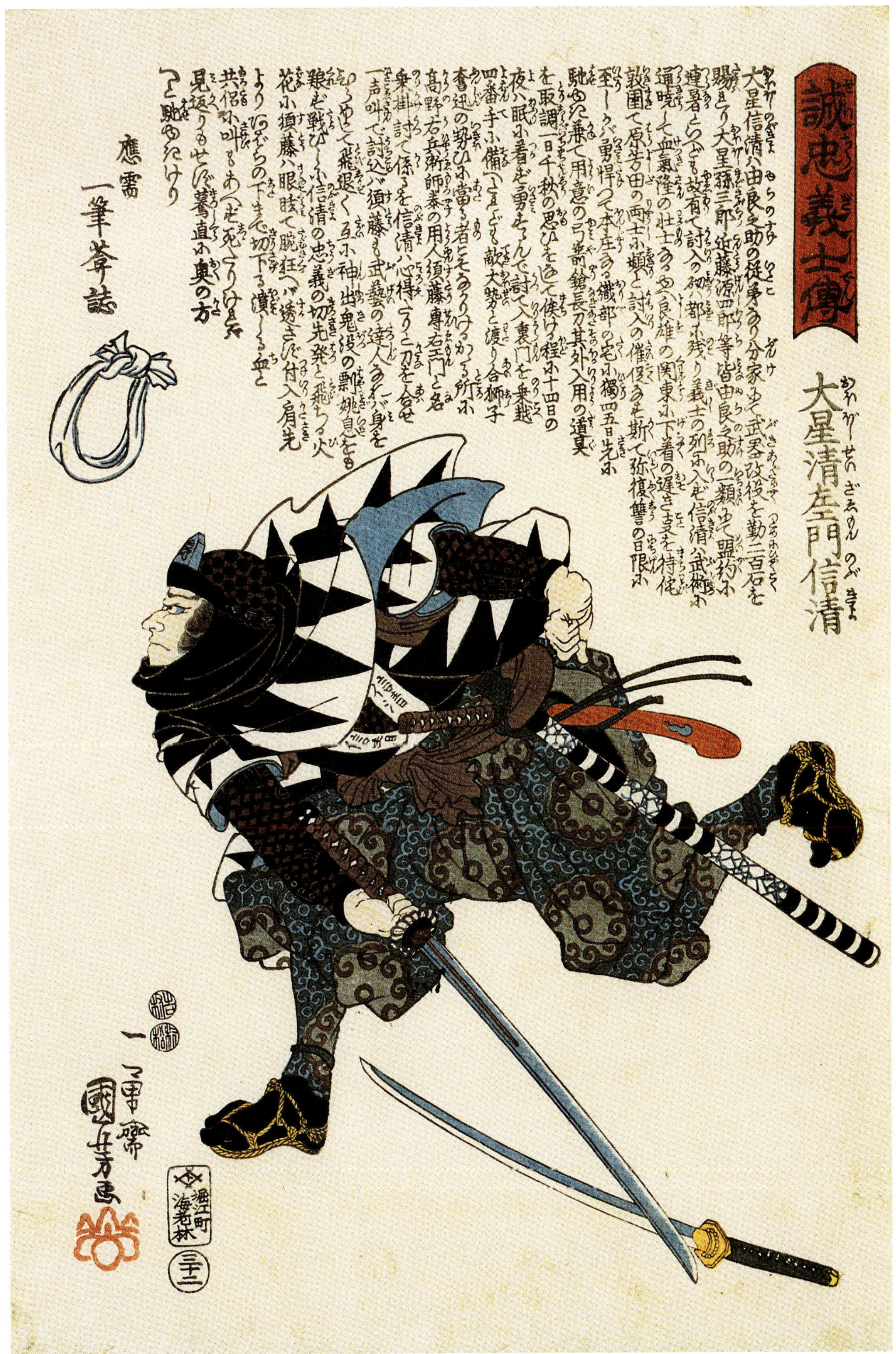
誠忠義士傳
大星清左門信清
應需 一筆菴誌
一勇齋國芳画

Sugenoya Sannojō Masatoshi

I.33

Sugenoya Sannojō Masatoshi entangled in the streamers of a *kusudama*[1]

Sugenoya Masatoshi was the adopted son and heir of Hanbei Masatatsu. A handsome young man, he served as page to Takasada.

His foster mother died young, and Hanbei married again, a girl as young as Masatoshi. She was not a virtuous person and lusted after Sannojō which upset him greatly. He loved and respected his foster parents, and he found an improper relationship with his foster mother to be more than he could abide.

As day after day went by with Sannojō's actions toward his foster mother being of absolutely correct deportment, Hanbei nevertheless began to suspect that Sannojō and his wife were having an affair. He then let his resentment be known.

The Lord Takasada got wind of the matter and, considering it a troublesome problem, quietly appropriated some funds on Masatoshi's behalf for a trip to the surrounding regions to visit shrines and temples. Then he ordered that the young man, upon completing the journey, should return to their home area, in Naniwa, to inspect the houses and storehouses.

After the confiscation, Sannojō hurried back from Naniwa to Akao and, mindful of his love for his lord, joined the conspiracy. His resolve was stronger than iron; for him waiting an hour and waiting a thousand autumns were the same thing. When the night of the attack came, he couldn't sleep for joy and, driven by valour, considered his life to be of no weight at all.

Thus he loved his lord with an incomparable love. One's lord is one's lord, and one's subject is one's subject. And that's the way it should be.

1. The great, highly ornamented and betasseled ball by the warrior's left cheek is a *kusudama* or 'scented ball,' used to deodorize garments and space.

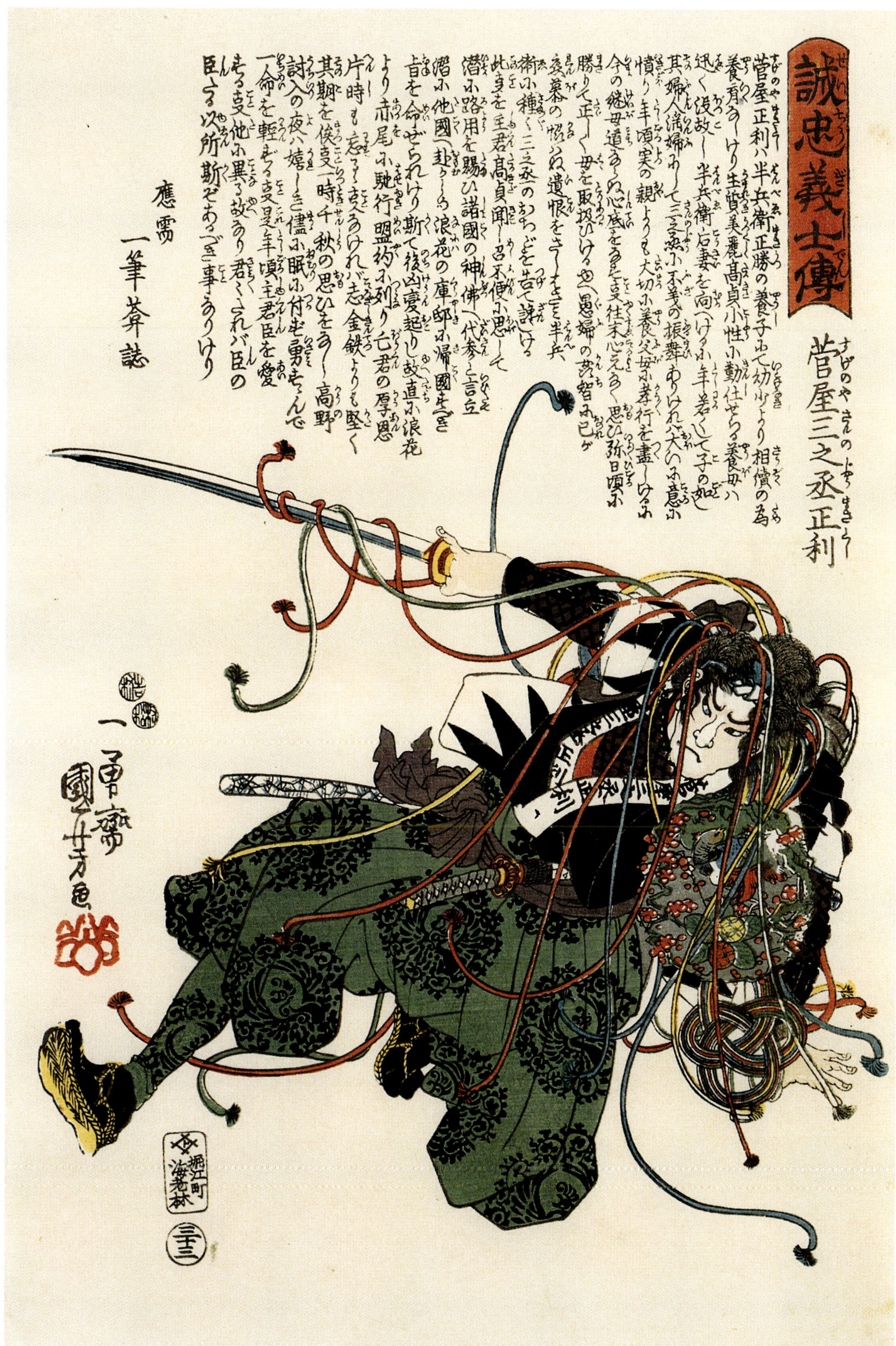
誠忠義士傳
菅屋三之丞正利
應需 一筆菴誌
一勇齋國芳画

Oribe Yasubei Taketsune

1.34

Oribe Yasubei Taketsune with Moronao's robe in hand

Yasubei was born Osawa Yasubei, the third son of Osawa Tadaemon, of the village of Osawa, in Echigo.[1] His childhood name was Tadanosuke. He was tall and powerful, well-schooled in weaponry, and had served with the Isoguchi family.

He became a *rōnin* and traveled through the various provinces perfecting his combat skills and then heard of Higuchi Jūrōzaemon, who lived in the village of Maniwa, in Jōshū, a great swordsman and founder of the Nenryū school. Yasubei became a disciple of his and mastered all the arts of the school. At that time he lived in Edo, in Utagawa Chō, in Shiba. He had an uncle named Osawa Sadashichi, who lived with two brothers named Takahashi Gumbei and Takahashi Sanya, who got in an argument with him and killed him. Yasubei then killed them.

After that, at Takata-no-Baba, he killed the enemies of Sugeno Rokubeizaemon, including Murakami Masazaemon and his brother Saburōzaemon, and thirteen students of the *kendō* school of Nakatsugawa Isamu - fifteen men all told. He did this amazing feat unassisted.

Oribe Yahei happened to be close to this when it occurred, and greatly admired the spirit of Yasubei. He therefore proposed that the young man marry his daughter and take his name. Thus Yasubei became a part of the En'ya clan.

Immediately thereafter, however, the En'ya house was dissolved, whereupon Yasubei joined his foster father in the vendetta against Moronao, along with all the other brave men whose fame has gone beyond anything ever accomplished.

Celebration of their exploits is going on even now on Kaneyasu Yuemon's stage in Utagawa Chō.[2]

There is not enough room on the page to recount the exploits of Yasubei in the night attack.[3] Even though they are not told here, they are known to all.

1. Echigo is the traditional name for Niigata.

2. Surely the artist was rewarded somehow for this advertisement of a play currently on the stage. It seems likely, too, that the prints were conspicuously hung in restaurants and teahouses to advertise the play.

3. The raging frustration of Yasubei as he stands here holding the enemy's sleeping garment is terrible to behold.

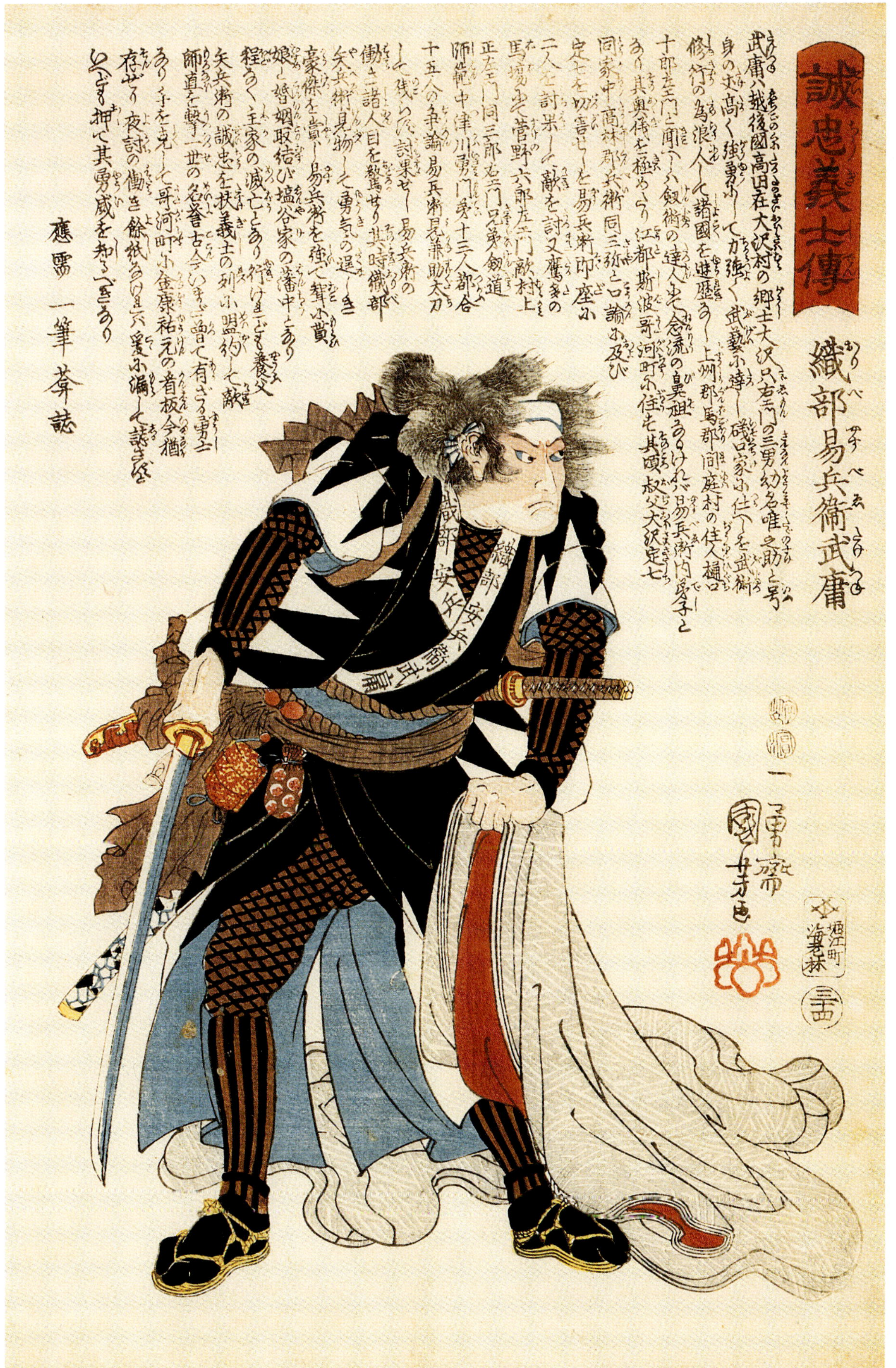
誠忠義士傳
織部易兵衛武庸
一勇斎國芳画

Hayano Wasuke Tsunenari

Hayano Tsunenari was an excellent bowman. He could hit 100 bull's-eyes with 100 arrows. On the night of retribution, Ōboshi had him carry on his spear a pennant that read 'Hayano Kampei, killed in battle,' in memory of his brother, who died for the cause. That night he went in the back gate, and he transfixed a guard with his spear - a blow for Kampei!

Then he jumped to the roof of the barracks and sent such a volley of arrows down on the doorway that they thought at first a fire had broken out. They ran out only to be wounded and then ran back inside and stayed there.

After that he ran deeper and deeper into the house in search of Moronao and fought with whomever he met, a frightful man to face.[1] Then he heard the whistle and ran to the utility shed, where everyone gathered and took the enemy's head.

Tsunenari enjoyed *haikai* and was a student of Sentoku. He wrote about their victory using the name Jōryū.

A show of spirit:
a kite in the distant sky
carried by the wind.

Jōryū

On his quiver he carried a poem card bearing a poem:

My catalpa bow:
I have not so much as set foot
on Yamato's road,
but on the field I aim at
snow may now be coming down

Jōryū

1.35

Hayano Wasuke Tsunenari piercing a cord-bound chest

1. The only explanation of the action taking place in the print is that he suspects Moronao might be hidden in the chest he is puncturing. Hiding a hunted lord is a favourite ploy in Kabuki.

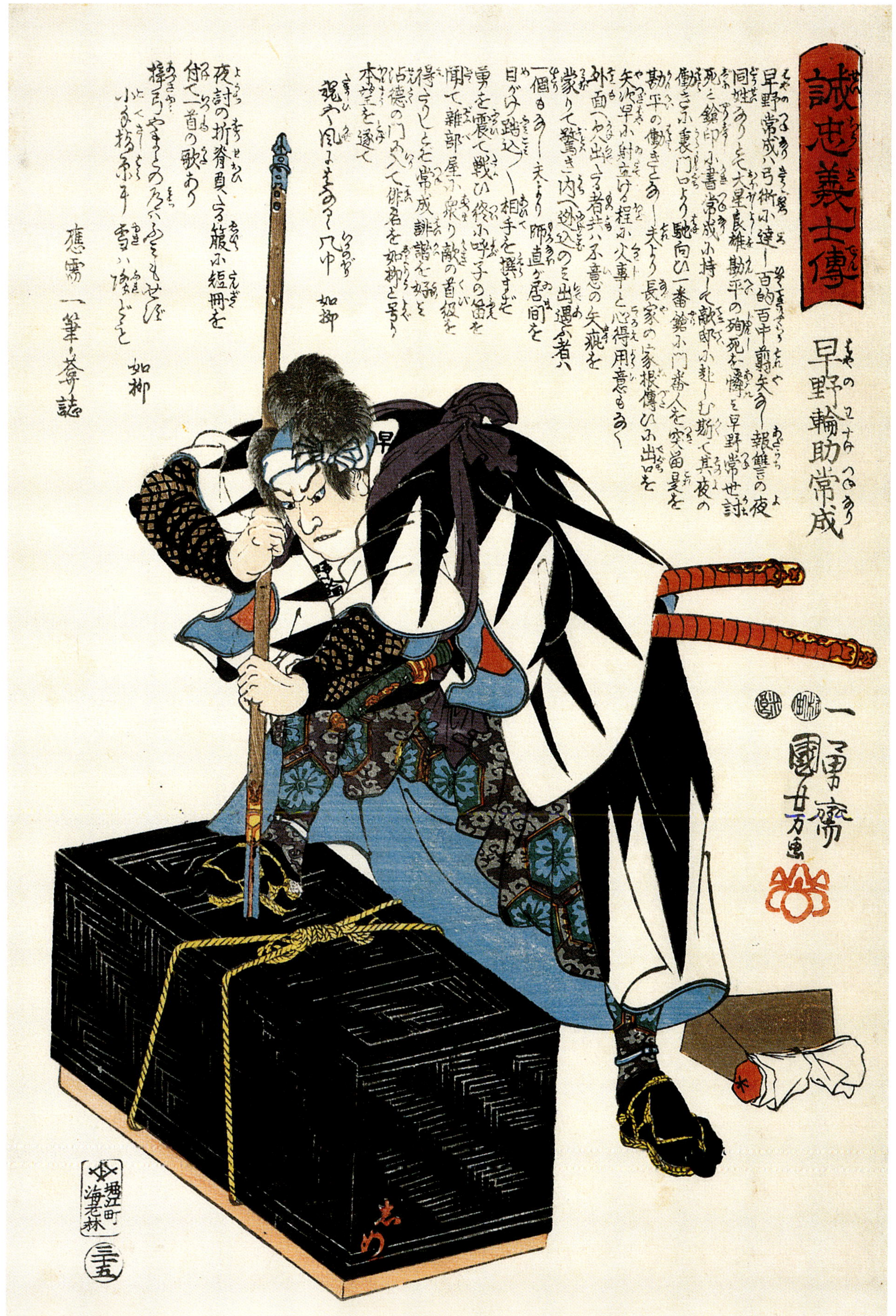
誠忠義士傳
早野輪助常成
一勇齋國芳画
三十五

Yata Gorōemon Suketake

1.36

Yata Gorōemon Suketake amidst flowers and pieces of *shoji*

After Suketake left Banshū, accompanied by his wife and seven year old son Sakujūrō, he moved to the village of Totsukawa, where he had relatives. Before long, he received word from Ōboshi that they were moving to the Kantō. He proceeded first to Kyoto, then, along with his wife and child, followed Yoshida Chūzaemon to Azuma, where he settled in Shiba Kawarakemachi. There he assumed the name of Hanawa Busuke and taught ju-jitsu.

On the night of the attack, a lamp, a flower vase, a tea bowl, and an earthen pot were thrown at him from the secretary's room. This infuriated Suketake, who shouted: 'Cut the foolishness, and fight as you should!' Then Tsuzuki Jitsuemon stepped out swinging his sword and announced his name. They exchanged thrusts, high and low. Tsuzuki, too, was a skilled swordsman, an Uesumi assistant, and fought with might and main. Suketake was amazed at his ability. Finally Suketake's sword point cut Tsuzuki from the right shoulder to the ribs on the left side and killed him.

Suketake's sword bore the characters of Kunitoshi. His technique was brilliant. The inspectors who came a day later marvelled at his swordsmanship.[1]

1. The inspectors might have marvelled at his skill with a sword, but all we are shown in this print is a samurai running amuck, smashing *shoji* and scattering flowers.

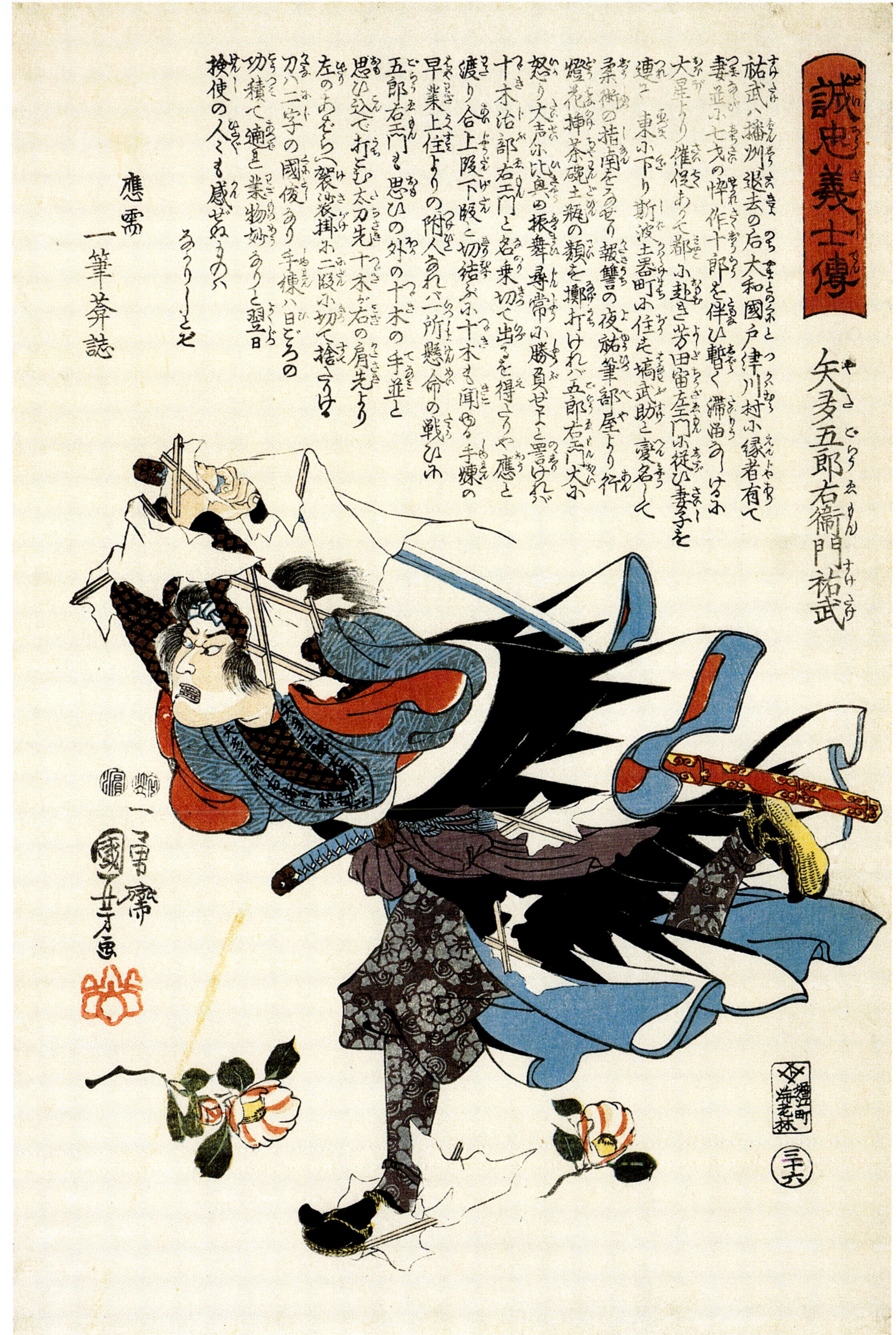
誠忠義士傳
矢多五郎右衛門祐武
應需 一筆菴誌
一勇齋國芳画
三十六

Tokuda Magodayū Shigemori

Shigemori was an excellent swordsman of the Shintō school.[1] He and his son Tadaemon joined the band sworn to take vengeance on Moronao for the death of their lord. Thus it was that they entered the enemy mansion behind Ōboshi.

Shigemori was fifty years old but in no way inferior to the younger men. His hands were supple and free of pain. He mistook Moronao's son Uhyōe Moroyasu for his father and almost killed him, but held off when he heard the signal whistle. Then he rushed to where Yazama Takebayashi and the rest were finishing off Moronao.

The faithful warriors were overjoyed and raised a shout of triumph. Yabei and Magodayū quietly withdrew from the mansion as the last to depart.

1.37

Tokuda Magodayū Shigemori beside a tall painted screen

1. Tokuda Shigemori with both hands on his uplifted sword, wary and coiled behind a tall decorated screen, illustrates once again Kuniyoshi's genius for representing battle tension.

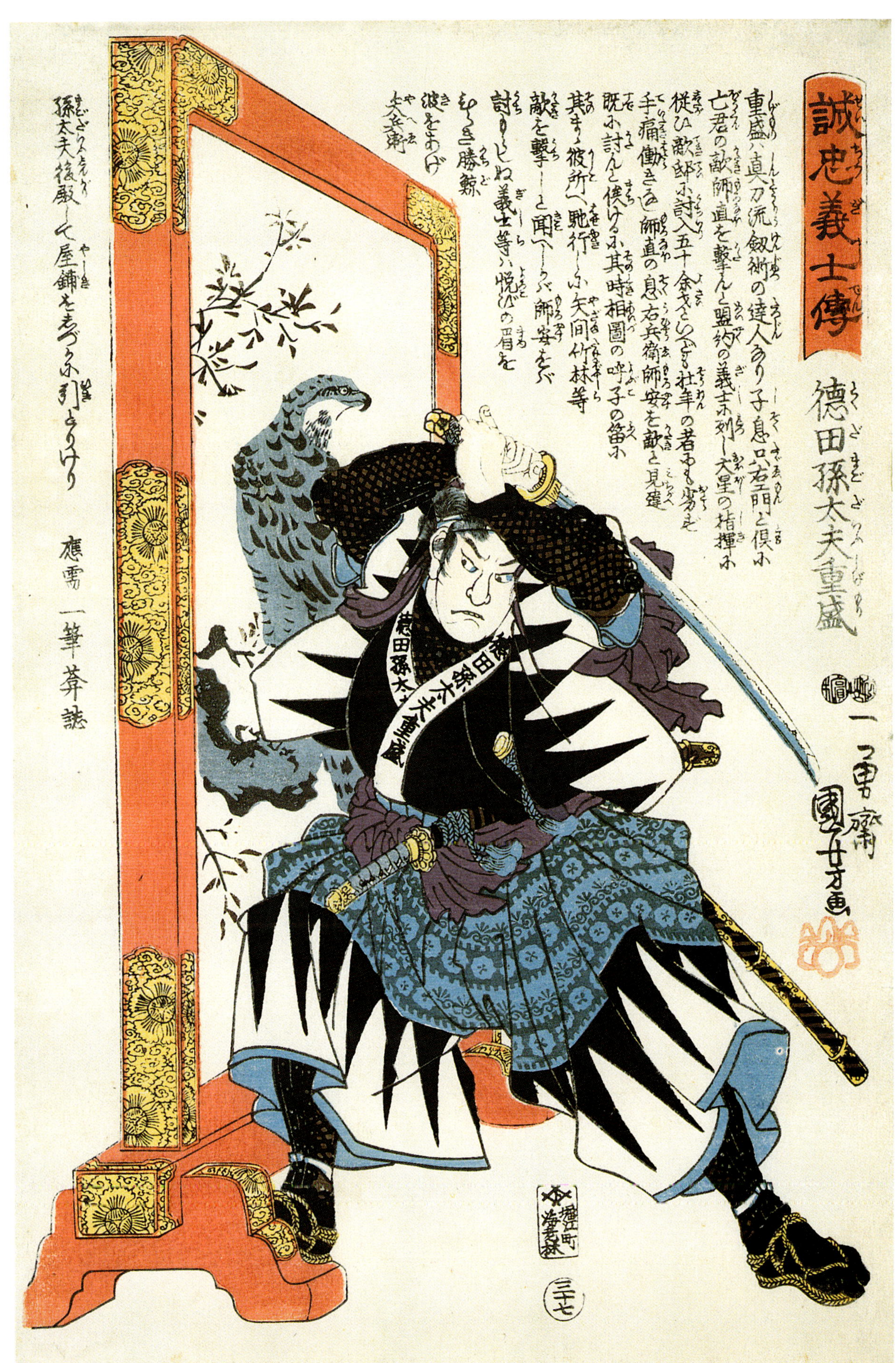
誠忠義士傳
徳田孫太夫重盛
一勇斎國芳画
應需 一筆菴誌
徳田孫太夫重盛
三十七

Kōno Musashi no Kami Moronao

1.38

Kōno Musashi no Kami Moronao cowering in fear

Ill-gotten wealth is like a floating cloud. Kōno Moronao was one whose covetousness threw a nation into disorder. His was inordinate greed and a lust for power. He pursued profit and coveted earthly goods, and in the end lost his house and his life, and befouled his name for a thousand years thereafter. How pitiful! All of this because he did not accept his lot, but instead used position in defiance of his peers and plundered when he should have served.

Let us start at the beginning. The function of serving as Imperial Messenger to the Tsurugaoka Shrine was carried out annually, and this particular year En'ya and Momonoi, based on their rank, had been ordered to take charge of the banquet. Kōno Moronao, who had great experience, had the duty of instructing them in protocol and procedure.

The two lords had departed from the scene, but Momonoi Wakanosuke had informed his retainer Kakogawa Honzō sometime earlier of Moronao's acquisitiveness, and Kakogawa exercised all care to advance bribes as he received instruction. En'ya Takasada's retainer, Kasui Fujie, however, was close-fisted and unwilling to respond as the occasion demanded.

Because of this, Moronao was upset with En'ya over what he considered to be gross neglect and insulted him twice before the entire gathering, accusing him of being tardy and generally derelict in the discharge of his duties.

Takasada was thunderstruck and infuriated by Moronao's twisted wiles and, even though he was in the Kamakura palace, found the vilification more than he could abide and wounded Moronao. How regrettable!

Moronao's family had held this post through many reigns, and he was the senior elder in the palace.[1] No position was so honoured by the lords of the nation. His overweening pride, however, was the cause of the Akao calamity. Heart of a brute and face of a man - wickedness and lawlessness should respect and fear the manifest judgment of the heavens.

1. The official post of Kira Kōsuke-no-suke, the historical model for Moronao, was *Kōke*, or 'Master of Court Ceremony.' Moronao's ceremonial dress in this print is 'The *daimon*, worn for very formal occasions, consist[ing] of a wide-sleeved top garment with prominent crests [thus, *dai*, meaning 'large,' and *mon*, meaning 'crest'] and a pair of *naga-bakama*, long trailing trousers in which the feet are hidden. The costume combines regal dignity and grace.' Shaver, p. 120.

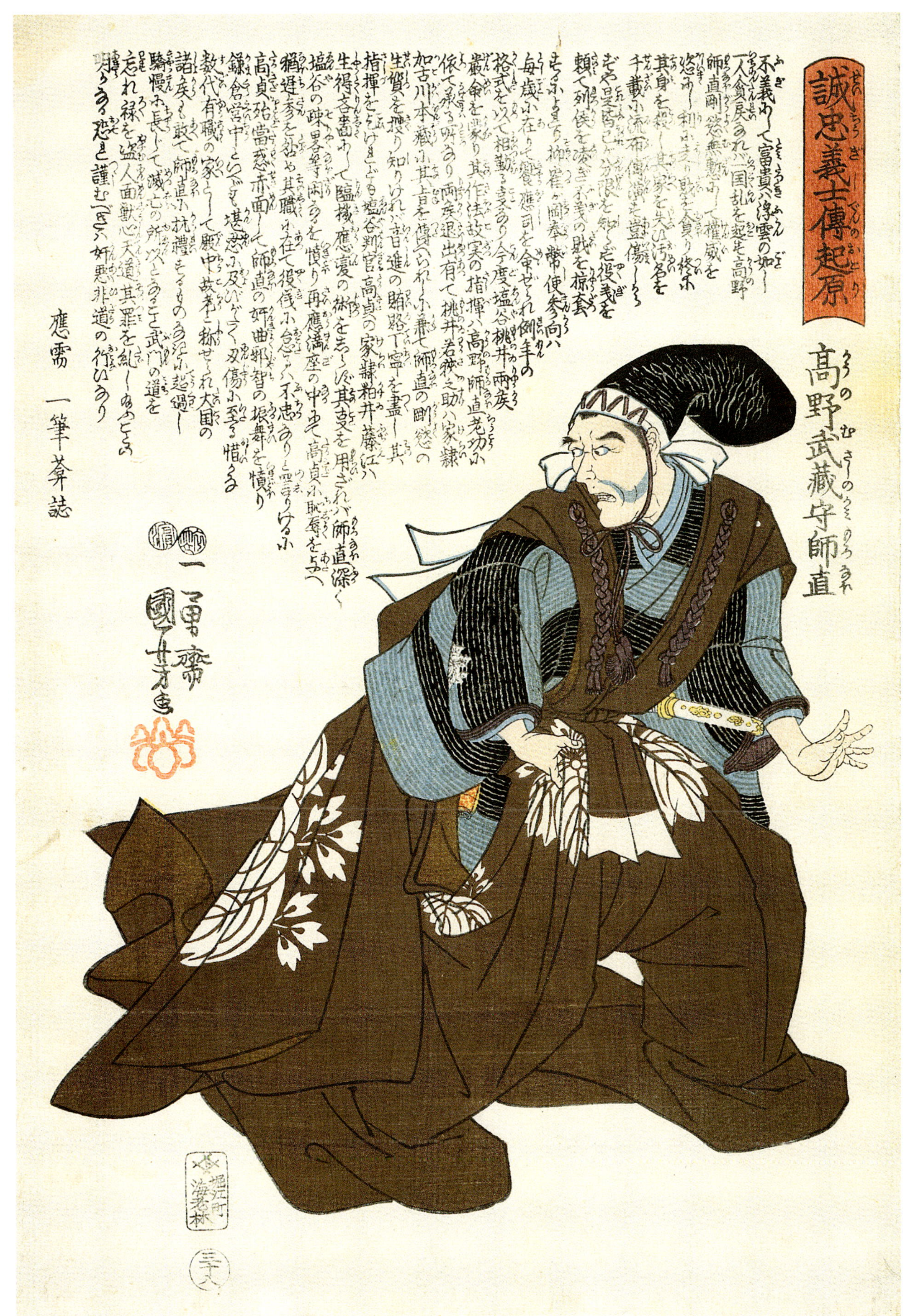
誠忠義士傳起原
高野武蔵守師直
應需 一筆菴誌
一勇斎國芳画

En'ya Hangan Takasada

I.39

En'ya Hangan Takasada in a threatening stance

En'ya Takasada was talented in both literature and the military arts. His family had been known for generations in the surrounding regions for its benevolence. He was by nature respectful and warm-hearted. He always treated his retainers with gracious affection and deported himself properly, never violently. Who but those who had served in that gracious warmth would be able to become part of that dedicated band, laying down their lives for their beloved lord? With his upright and generous nature, Takasada found an unkindness shown him impossible to bear and, place and time notwithstanding, went so far as to shed blood. We must not say that this lord was wrong.

These were times when one had to restrain oneself, even in the face of direct attack. The period of the warring states had come to an end fairly recently. Although the way of governing was not greatly different, customs were much simpler. One took care to treat underlings with courtesy, and if it came to combat, warriors were in demand and literature was scorned. It was not a time for short tempers.

Moronao had slighted Takasada a number of times. On the day of the ambassadorial banquet, even though he had been given the wrong instructions and been insulted, En'ya remained composed. But then anger clutched at his vitals in a way he could not control, and in the Maki corridor he drew and cut Moronao.[1] He was restrained by Katsukawa, but he shook loose and was finally separated from Moronao only with great force. Moronao was not dead, but when the furore quieted down, Takasada had to die.

Moronao lived, but En'ya's lands were confiscated and his clan dissolved. In these dire straits, his beloved retainers, tormented constantly by grief in an upside-down world, organized themselves into a loyal confederacy of forty-some men under Ōboshi. In accordance with their master's last instructions, they presented his enemy's head at his grave.

Their prayers had been answered. They had fulfilled their purpose in life, and their fame now sounded to the four seas, a model for warriors, of undying praise.

1. Takasada's ceremonial dress in this print is the *naga-gamishimo*, a broad-shouldered garment worn with *naga-bakama*. It is not as formal as the *daimon*. (See note to I.38.) 'It is interesting [ironic] to note, historically, that the wearing of *naga-bakama* at court is said to have had the advantage of hindering a man's movements, thereby preventing him from getting involved in swordplay.' Shaver, p. 120.

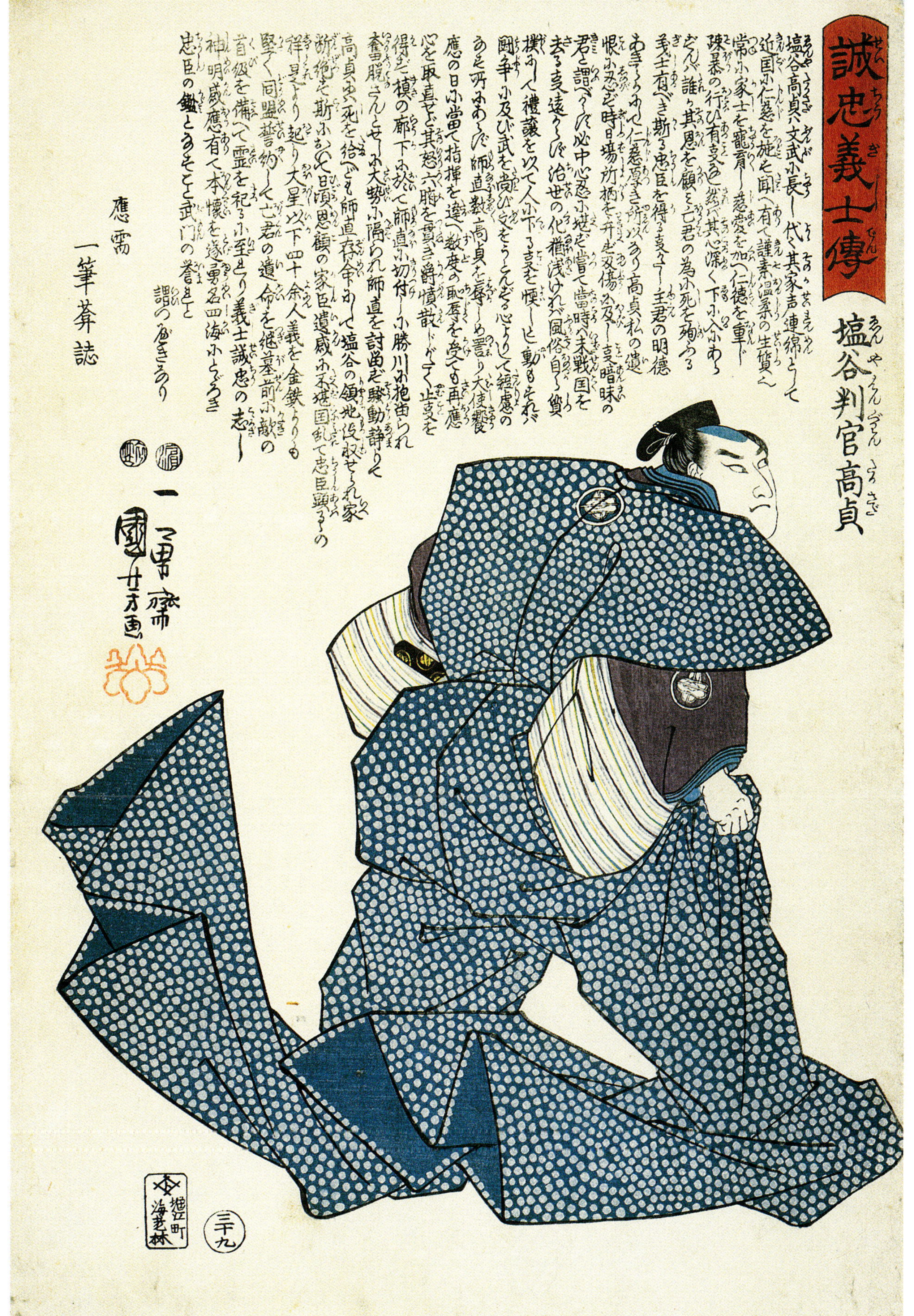
誠忠義士傳
塩谷判官高貞
應需 一筆菴誌
一勇斎國芳画
堀江町 海老林
三十九

Yazama Shinroku Mitsukaze

Shinroku was the third son of Yazama Kihei, a courageous and skilled fighter, another determined and absolutely prepared loyal man.

When the band moved to the Kantō area, he took up residence in Kojimachi, in Edo. There he, his father, and his brother Jūtarō were able to observe the enemy mansion and to move about along the route between the Uesumi and Kōno houses and inspect Moronao's premises when he was not at home. Impatient about the delay in Ōboshi's arrival, they demanded of Hara Gōemon that the raid take place.

Then, suddenly, they learned that a master builder was in possession of the plans for the Kōno mansion. Delighted, Shinroku set about securing them.

A member of the group named Nakada Riheita, who was living with the Yazamas, heard about this and quietly arranged for the carpenter to sell the plans to Shinroku for ten *ryō*.[1] Fearing that Riheita might defect and leak word of the action to Moronao's spies, Shinroku set up a meeting with him at a bathhouse in Kanda, where they argued and Shinroku killed him.

In flight from a warrant for murder, Shinroku hid in an empty house Ōboshi had rented earlier from a man named Seo Magozaemon. There, in the village of Hirama, in Kawasaki, he bided his time.

He received word from Senzaki Yagorō about the impending attack, went to Honjō with great joy, and performed brilliantly in the battle.[2]

I.40

Yazama Shinroku Mitsukaze with flag on his back bearing death name

1. See appendix d.

2. On the flag is written 'Shakuso Teishinshi', which is Shinroku's chosen death name.

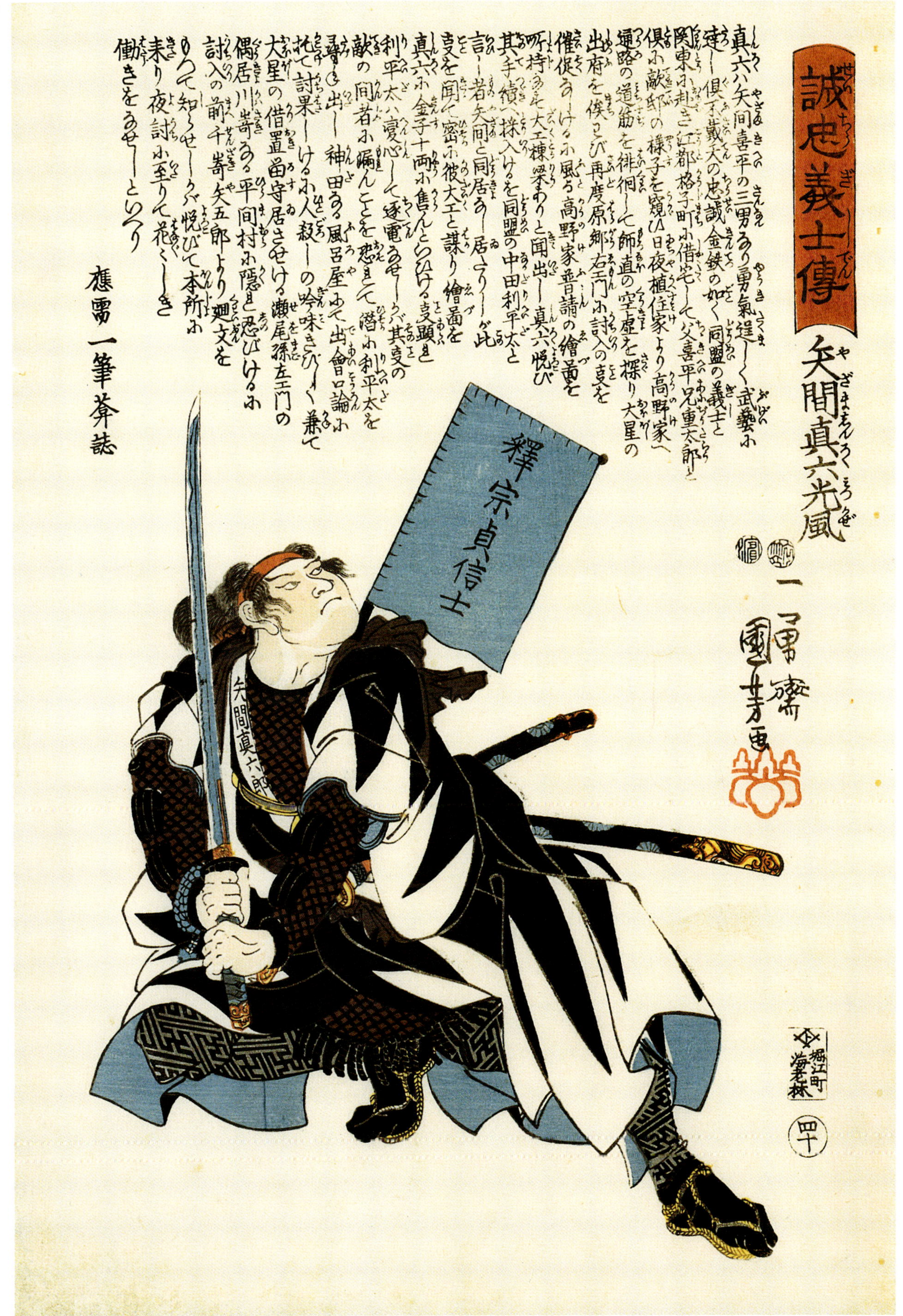
誠忠義士傳
矢間真六光風
釋宗貞信士
一勇斎國芳画
應需一筆斎誌
堀江町 海老林
四十

Mase Magoshirō Masatatsu

Magoshirō was the son of Kyūdaiyu Masa-aki and an able swordsman, but he had been suffering from blisters on his hands.[1] Wrapping his sword-hilt with cotton strips improved his grip somewhat, but did not make him confident that he could defend himself properly with the sword. Therefore, he entered the attack using a bow, and after he had shot all his arrows at the enemy, took up a spear.

In the garden of the mansion, he met Torii Riemon. He gave the password *'yama?'* and received the reply *'yama.'* There in the dark it was impossible to discriminate one man from another, but the reply from a friend should have been *'kawa.'*[2] This was clearly an enemy. Masatatsu then pulled back his spear and thrust it.

He faced off against Masatatsu with high and low strokes, using all the tricks he knew. Masatatsu took a wrong step, slipped on a snowy spot and fell into a pond. Torii brought up his sword to finish him off, but then, at the very moment he was to strike, Ōboshi Rikiya, some distance away, saw what was happening, drew his bow and shot. The arrow pierced Torii in the chest. At the same time, Magoshirō cut him from below, from the ribs to the nipple. Torii fell to his back and died without a sound.

Magoshirō jumped up, wrung the water from his clothes, and penetrated further into the house.

1.41

Mase Magoshirō Masatatsu smashing an earthen vessel with a mallet

1. In the print, Masatatsu, his hands too sore to grip a sword, is using a great mallet to smash a large earthen vessel, perhaps a brazier. He would have had to use the mallet before he took up a spear.

2. The complete password was *yamakawa*, or 'mountain-river.' The challenge was the first half of the phrase and the proper reply, indicating a friend, was the second half. Of course, reply with a repetition of the challenge indicated an enemy.

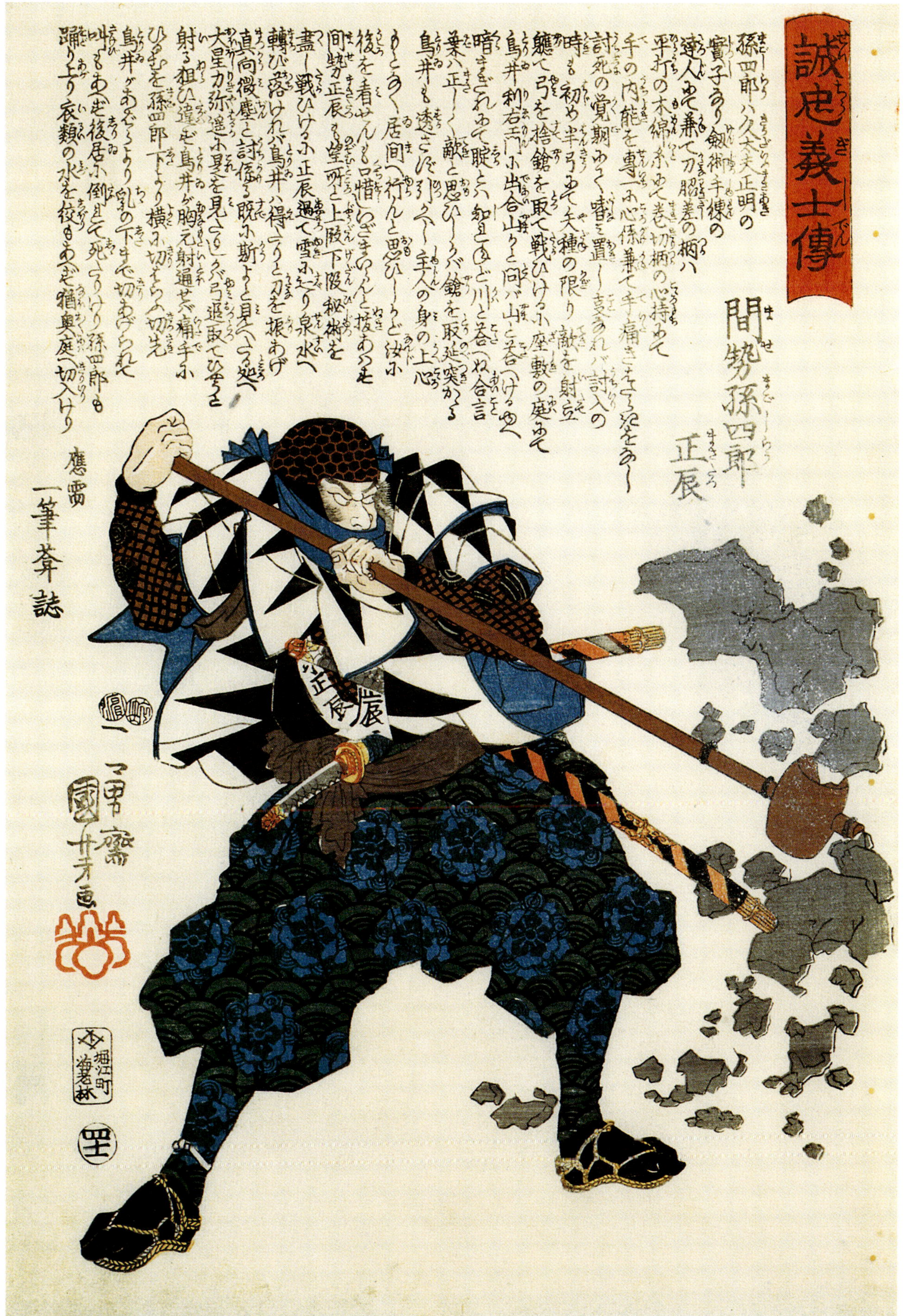
誠忠義士傳
間勢孫四郎
正辰
應需
一筆菴誌
一勇齋國芳画

The lay priest Ryūen, Uramatsu Kihei Hidenao

1.42

The lay priest Ryūen, Uramatsu Kihei Hidenao, behind a rack of kimonos

Hidenao was living in Kantō when Lord En'ya met his end, and he immediately began preparations to go to Banshū. At that time he was sixty-two years old. His son, Handayū, tried to dissuade him but finally gave in, and they set out for Akao together.

They had great respect for Ōboshi, who advised them to put off dying for the cause at this time. The castle was then surrendered, and they signed a compact agreeing to head for the Kantō and plan vengeance.

Hidenao returned and took up residence in Kōjimachi. On the night of the attack, when their hopes were realized, he carried his last words sewn into his skull cap:

Giving up this life
for the sake of his dear lord,
to the samurai
means the fulfillment of all
he has wished his life would bring.

And that is not all.
You may try to get away a hundred or a thousand times,
but do not forget these words:
In the light of duty, life is light.

Life doesn't tell you
that you are never able
to lose even one.
You may try to run and hide,
but life, you cannot escape.

Uramatsu Kihei Hidenao,
lay priest[1]
62 years old

1. Priests are frequently the butt of humour in Japanese art and literature. Ryūen, seeking cover behind a rack of gorgeous kimonos, his sword engaged against one, is far from a warlike figure.

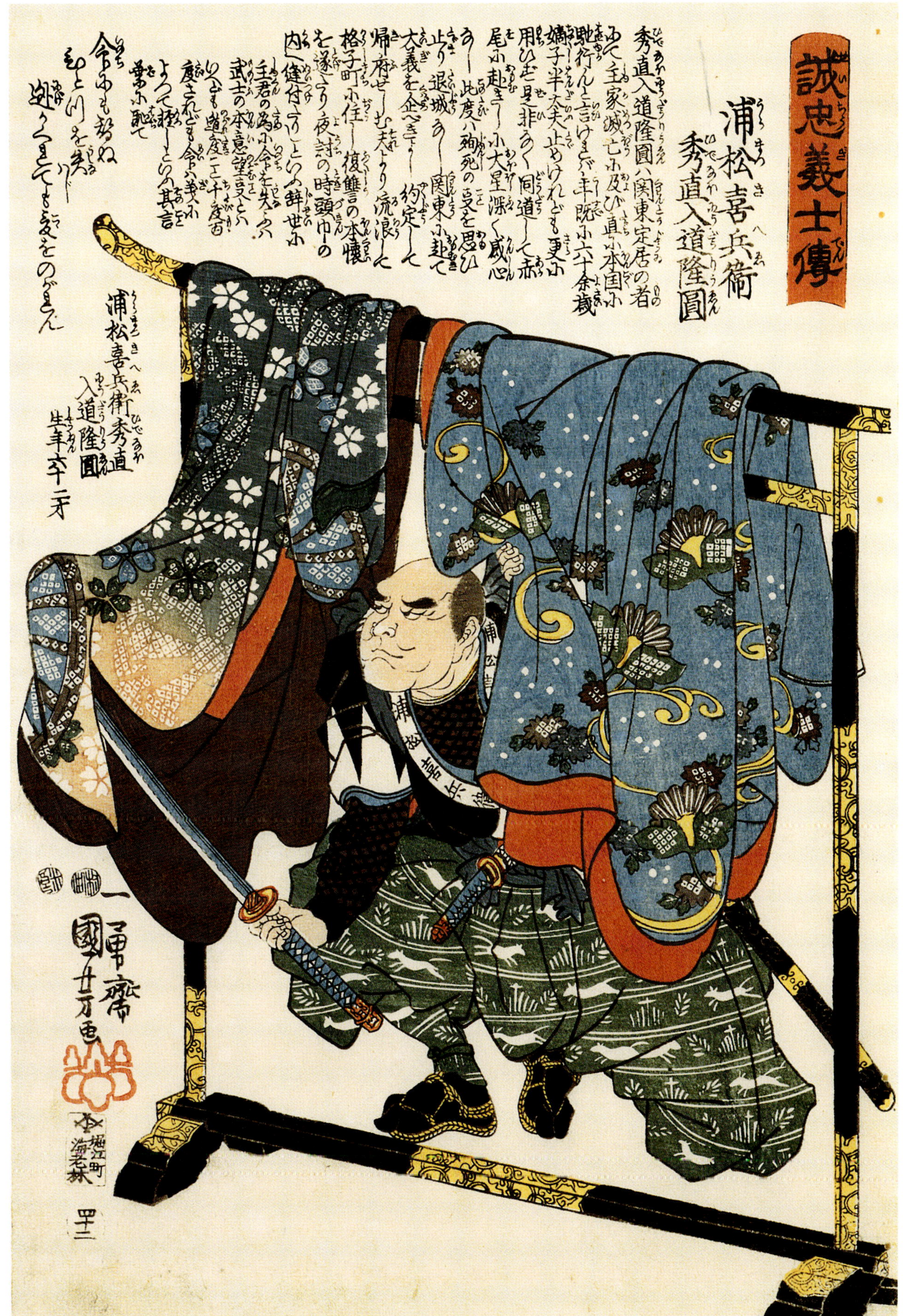

誠忠義士傳
浦松喜兵衛
秀直入道隆圓
一勇齋國芳畫
堀江町 海老林

Yazama Kihei Mitsunobu

I.43

Yazama Kihei Mitsunobu with helmet and cape on blunt end of *naginata*

Yazama Kihei Mitsunobu was a loyal hereditary retainer of the En'ya clan. He had two sons, Jūtarō and Shinroku, and all were strongly determined men. When Akao fell, they immediately made their way to the Kantō and, unaware of the dedicated group around Ōboshi, set to work to kill Moronao.

They frequented the roads Moronao took near the Kōno mansion and did all they could to waylay and kill him, but Moronao's karma was strong, and they were never able to confront him.

Then, one day, Kihei happened to meet Senzaki Yagorō, who told them the whole story of the loyal band and how they were in the process of moving into the area. They were overjoyed and went to where Hara and Yoshida were staying and signed on with the conspiracy.

Kihei changed his name to Somahara and rented a house in Kōjimachi and then, it is said, moved to Honjō just before the attack.

He had many years of acquaintance with all the secrets of the spear and was in no way inferior to men much younger. He was particularly deft with the short bow and could shoot a fantastic number of arrows in quick succession. When he had emptied his quiver he could fight with the spear.

He left his spear with this poem on it at the gate of a samurai house:

Put the question to
the wise oystercatcher bird[1]
of the capital,
whether this world can know shame
or whether it knows it not.

Kōshū Gamau School
Yazama Kihei Fujiwara Mitsunobu
69 years old

1. The *miyakodori (Hoematopus ostralegus)*, literally 'capital bird.' It is referred to in the ninth century classic *Tales of Ise* when the poet Arihira no Narihira asks the bird for news of the capital. It is also referred to in many Kabuki plays.

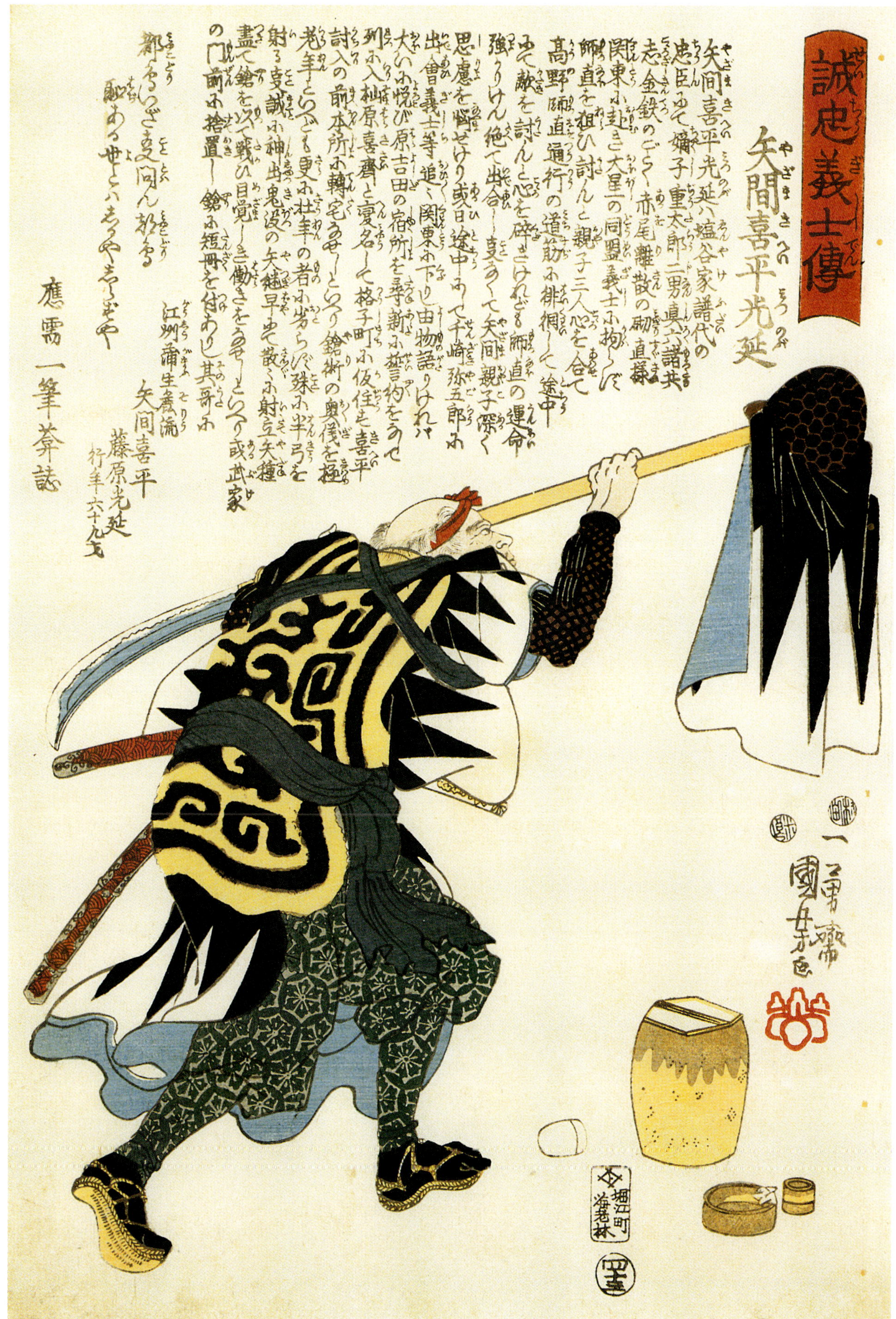

Mase Chūdayū Masa-aki

Masa-aki changed his name to Mitsuhashi Jūtei, rented a house in Kōshimachi and set up practice as a physician. His son, Magokurō, changed his name to Koichirō. Three or four confederates, who pretended that they were busy petitioning the ruling powers to allow them to collect money to construct a shrine to a local deity, lived with them.

On December 14th, the day of the attack, Chūdayū was in his sixty-second year. He was nevertheless a strong man, not at all inferior to those younger. He entered the gate with the second wave, shouting with each arrow from his bow.[1] He came upon Mori Banzaemon as men fought to the death all around him. Hara Mimura saw this and, aware that Mori was a crack swordsman, tried to divert him in order to spare the old man.[2] Mase, however, dauntlessly pressed forward without let-up, shouting, sparks flying from his sword hilt, and with one leap, sent his unerring blade forward and sliced Mori through the headband and down between the eyes. His sword, a Kunitoshi, cut this practiced swordsman right in two. The mortally wounded Mori died without a sound, his wounds smoking.

Off to a good start, Mase pressed forward again, with his bloody sword. As he did so, Komori Genji, his sword drawn and ready, blocked the doorway. They exchanged blows, downward slashing, upward thrusting. Komori was an excellent swordsman, but he was overmatched and tried to escape. He could not back away, however, and was unable to ward off a horizontal blow that severed his ribs and killed him.

The truly admirable old man's work received the plaudits of all.

1.44

Mase Chūdayū Masa-aki aiming with deadly precision

1. This print is a *trompe l'oeil* - from whatever angle it is viewed, the arrow will point directly at the viewer.

2. Hara Mimura - a name difficult to identify. Perhaps Hara Gōemon Mototoki's assumed name.

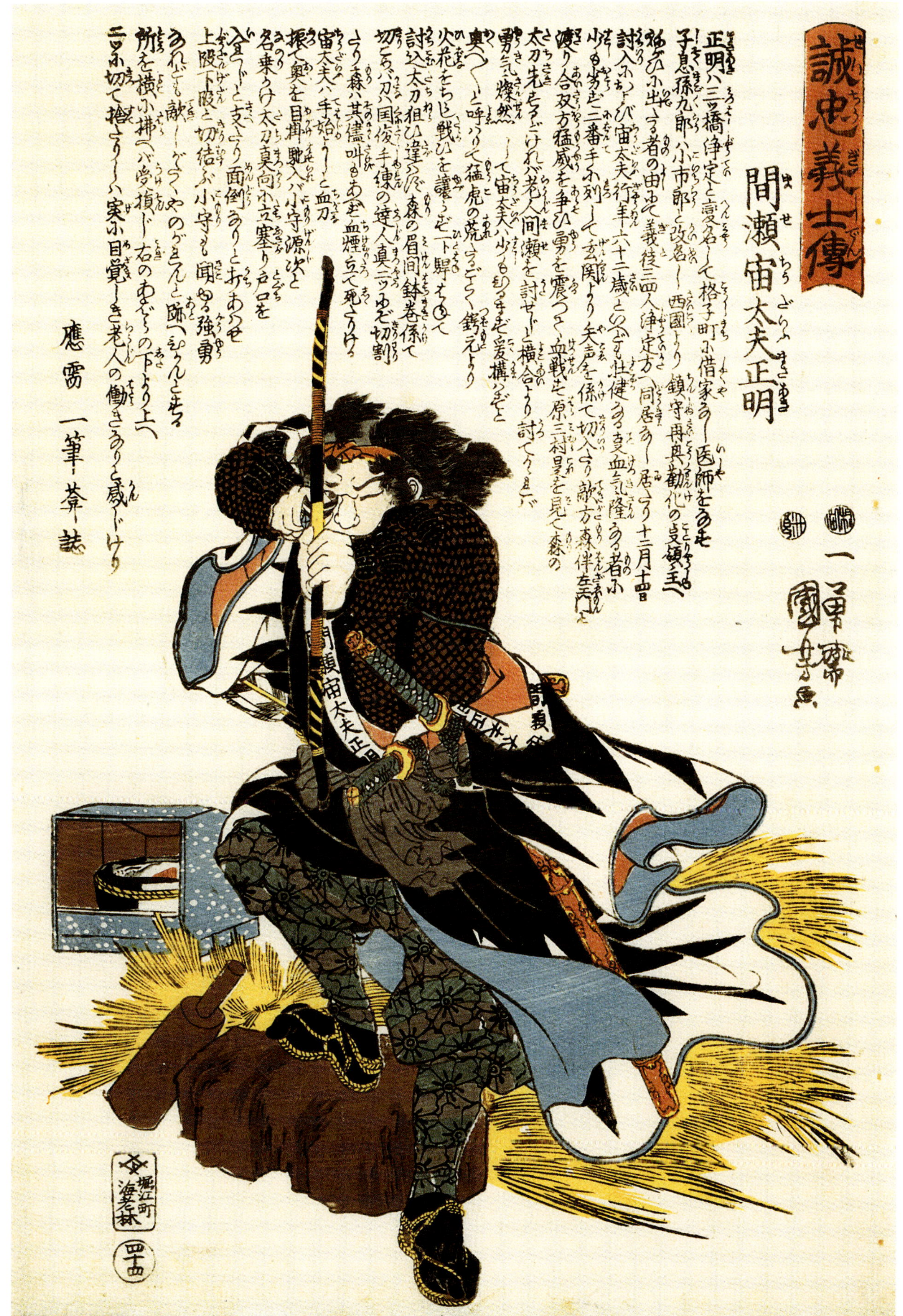
誠忠義士傳
間瀬宙太夫正明
一勇斎國芳画

Sumino Jūheiji Tsugufusa

1.45

Sumino Jūheiji Tsugufusa with his arm under Moronao's quilt

After the dissolution of Akao, Sumino Tsugufusa wandered aimlessly about Kyoto, and not until the conspirators were about to move out did he inform his old mother of the obligation he was under. Then, at the last minute, he said to her: 'Ōboshi and some other men are going to the Kantō to visit our lord's grave, and very soon I would like to go with them. I shall be back to Kyoto soon. So you be so good as to stay here, and don't worry.'

Then he took out ten *ryō*, which he had received from Ōboshi, and gave it to her. The old mother was sincerely pleased and counselled him, saying: 'I assume that a party of men is ready to attack and, if so, I pray that your plans coincide with those that are fated in the heavens. Fight to the death mindful that the name you leave will be eternally compromised if you show cowardice. Please don't expect to see me again. There are all kinds of things you will need on your journey, so take that with you,' she said, and returned the money.

She went on chatting happily that day and retired even more cheerfully than usual. The next morning the son found that she had written a note and committed suicide.

Jūheiji was shocked. He informed Ōboshi of what had happened, and they laid her to rest, mourning this parting of son and mother. Then Jūheiji set out with his heart at peace.

His departed master's enemy had now become his mother's enemy. On the night of the attack, he towered above the throng. With murder in his heart, he charged into Moronao's bedroom ahead of Uramatsu Kihei and Ōboshi Seizaemon but found only the bed from which Moranao had departed. He gnashed his teeth when he ran his hand under the quilts and found the bed still warm.[1] Moronao couldn't have gone far!

Tsugufusa ran from corner to corner of the mansion searching.

1. Kuniyoshi catches the moment Jūheiji discovers that Moronao's bed is 'still warm.'

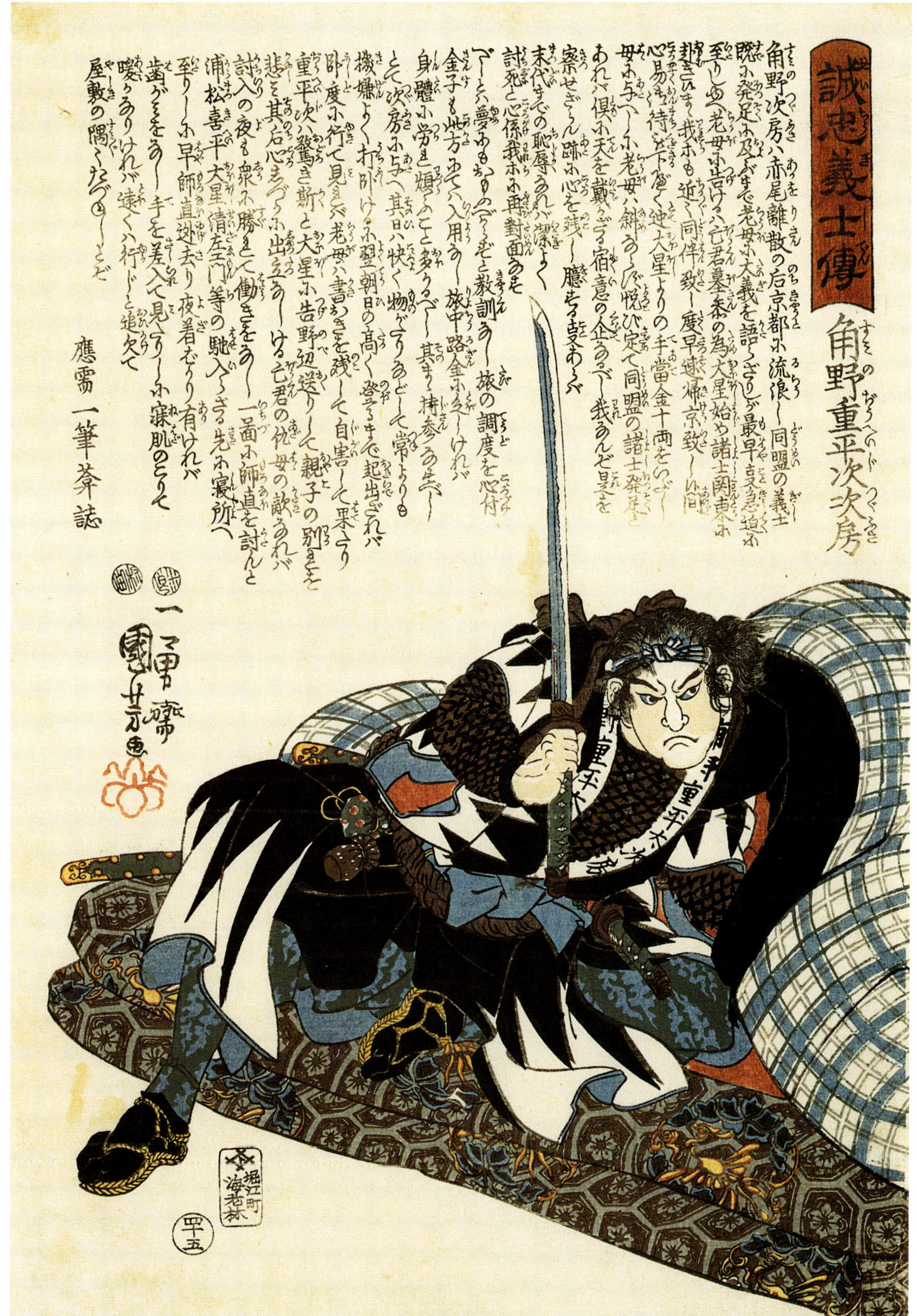

誠忠義士傳
角野重平次次房
應需 一筆菴誌
一勇斎國芳画
堀江町 海老林

Hara Gōemon Mototoki

I.46

Hara Gōemon Mototoki with sword in one hand, spear in the other

Hara Mototoki was a grandson of Hara Heida Masatoki and commander of the En'ya samurai detachment in the Kantō area. He was a celebrated student of Yamaga Jingozaemon and was well-versed in the secrets of military lore and the arts of combat, in particular the uses of the sword and the spear.[1]

He first served the Matsuda family, in Banshū, but then moved to the En'ya clan. When that fief fell and the time for dispersal came, he took charge of the movement of effects, complete with flags, with a minimum of disturbance. He was skilled at taking responsibility and issuing commands, and for these reasons Ōboshi placed him in charge of strictly controlling the transfer of the hot-blooded young samurai to the Kantō.

He was a strong, heroic man and during the interim period lived in Kōjimachi, where he was known as Wada Genshin, physician. He made a trip back to Kyoto to confer with Ōboshi and returned to the Kantō with many of the men who were ready to take part in the action. A story has gone around that, when he left for Kyoto, his old mother committed suicide, but that is not true. He had lived in Tokyo from the beginning, with his parents, his wife, and his children, and anything conflicting with that is a falsehood.

Hara's adopted son, Heidayū, joined with the vendetta when Akao fell, but he disappeared before the attack, no one knows where.

A rich full moon in a wide sky
after thunder and unceasing rain
after piercing cold, a refreshing breeze
a rich full moon in a wide sky.

Last poem:

How unexpected:
to survive into the dawn
of this New Year's Day
and now to go on waiting
the inevitable end.

1. Kuniyoshi illustrates Hara Mototoki's abilities with 'sword and spear' in this print, where we can also clearly see the sole of the *waraji* straw sandal mentioned in the first note to I.26.

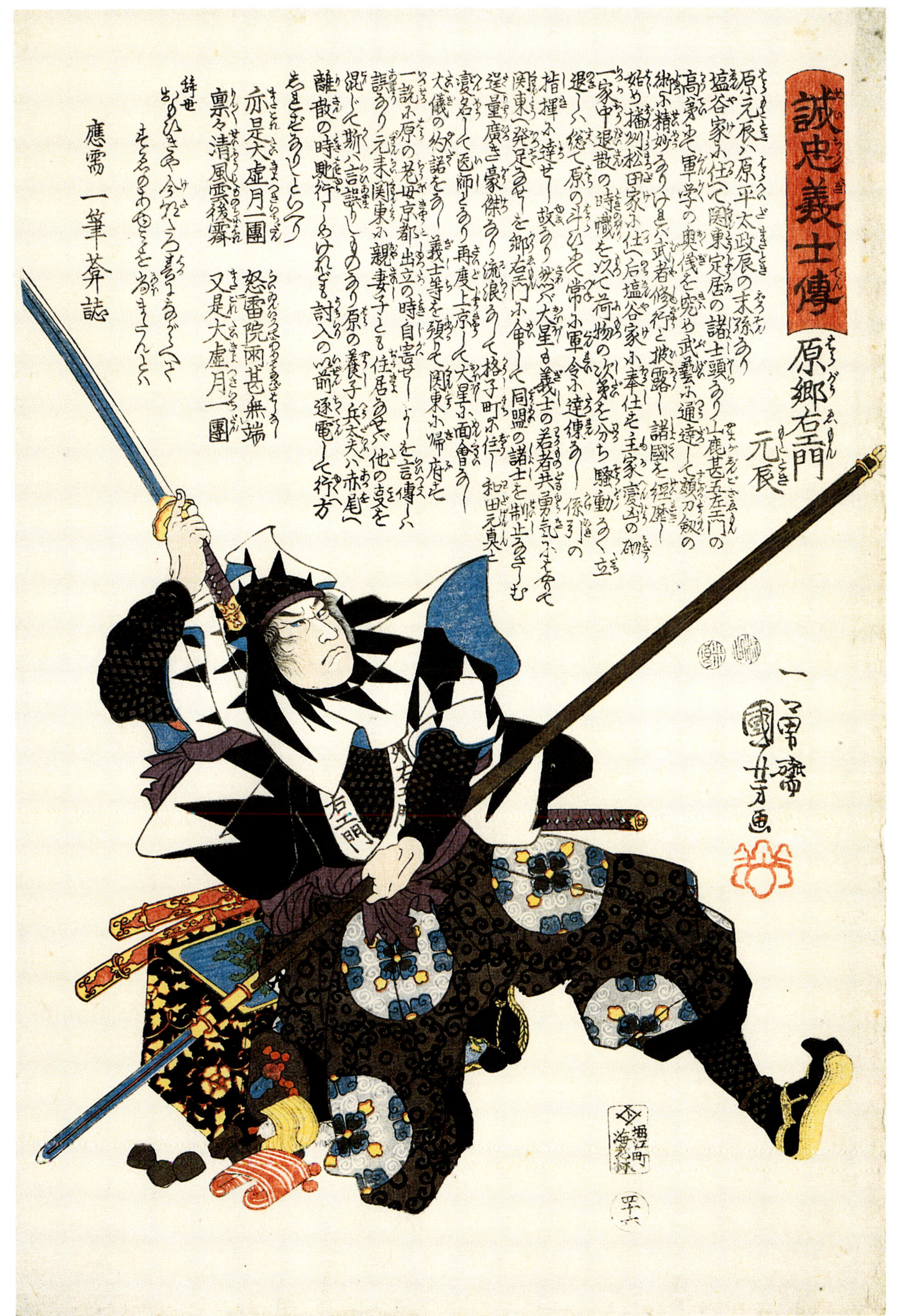
誠忠義士傳
原郷右エ門
元辰
應需 一筆菴誌
一勇斎國芳画

Hayano Kampei Tsuneyo

1.47

Hayano Kampei Tsuneyo as a ghost-like figure

When Akao was dissolved, Hayano Kampei and his brother lived in various places, but then, when the time came for the band to move on the Kantō area, they went to their home village, Kayano, in Seishū, to take leave of their parents. They arrived to find a funeral in progress - their mother's. Absolutely shocked, they took their places in the procession.

Then Tsuneyo sent his younger brother, Wasuke Tsunenari, to Yamashina with a message for Ōboshi, informing him that their mother had died unexpectedly and that he would have to remain in their home village for thirty-seven days, until the observance of a mass for the dead.

He took care of his father, as a good son should, and as the time to depart drew near, told his father about the group of men he had sworn himself to become part of, that they were on their way to the Kantō region, and that he would have to leave soon.

His father told him that he was old and had lost his wife and that he was at his wit's end, and that Kampei's having become a *rōnin* was bad enough, but now he had sent his brother, Wasuke, off to the Kantō area. And even though he had made commitments to a body of men, was he not abandoning his father? He then asked his son not to go.

Hayano agreed with his father completely. He knew that if he disobeyed his father, even covertly, he would stray from the path of filial piety. And yet if he turned his back on his sworn comrades he would be deficient in loyalty and would fail to render love and fealty to his lord in accordance with the warrior code. He then wrote to Ōboshi that in this conflict between the two paths - loyalty and filial piety - he had no choice but to sacrifice his life.

So, on the 14th day of January, in the year of the horse, he cut his stomach and died. Unable to do anything about it, his determined comrades mourned, overcome with sadness. In the attack, however, Ōboshi had Wasuke carry on his spear a pennant carrying the inscription 'Hayano Kampei, killed in battle.'[1] If Wasuke killed so much as one of the enemy with it, Tsuneyo's spirit would become part of the battle.

1. Kampei in this print is a ghost-like figure. Except for the *rōnin* uniform, his flesh and clothes are without colour.

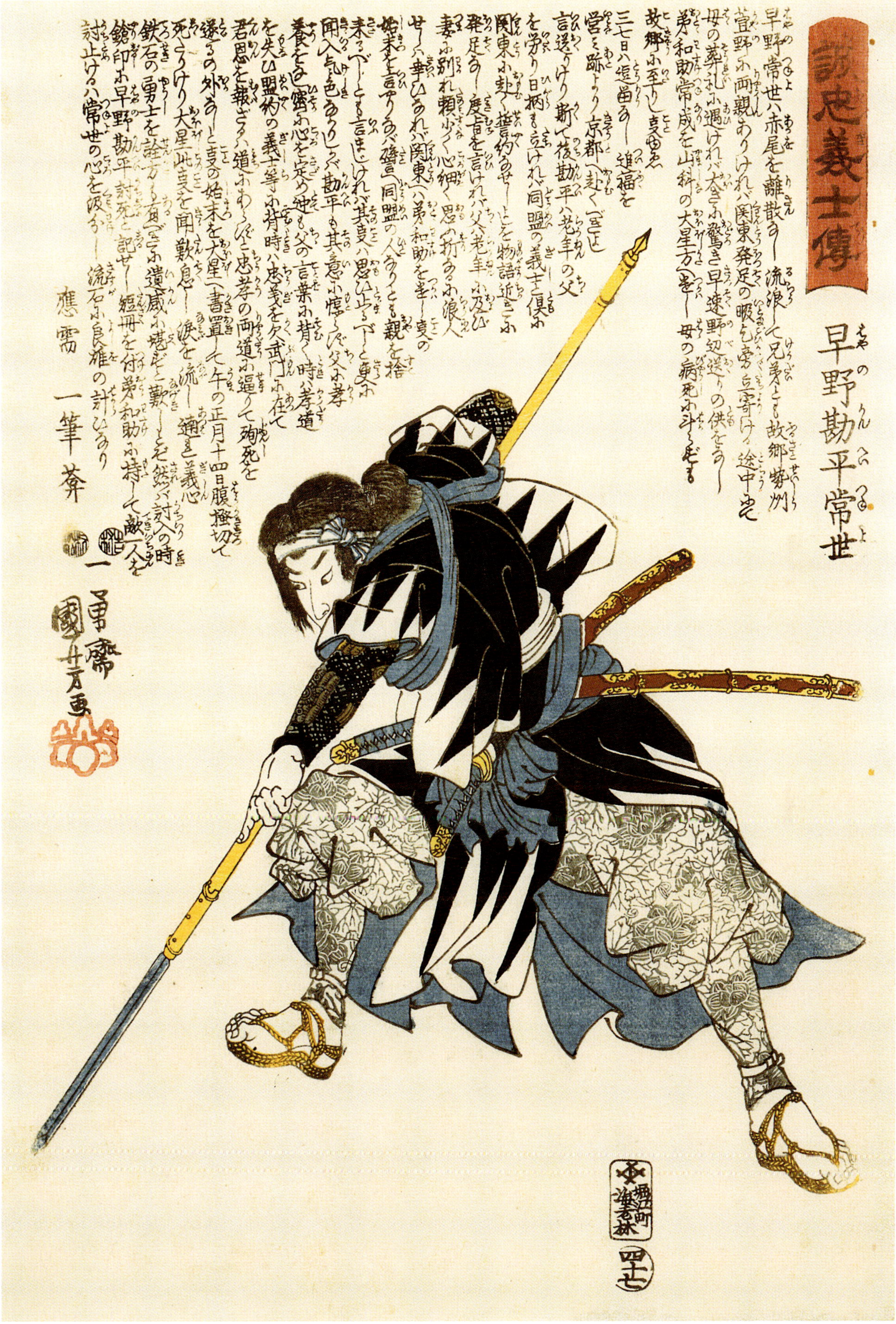

誠忠義士傳

早野勘平常世

四十七

Kaida Yadaemon Tomonobu

Kaida Yadaemon served in the accounting department, a man of rectitude. He was also expert with the sword and the spear.[1] After Akao fell, he lived in the Yamashina area of Kyoto and circulated in the amusement districts in various disguises, ferreting out Moronao's spies and reporting back to Ōboshi.

Ōboshi, too, played a part: that of a roistering frequenter of brothels. At the same time he gave Yadaemon fifty-eight letters from loyal men, swearing that they would take part in the conspiracy. Yadaemon was asked to inform them that plans for the vendetta had been postponed.

Some had their doubts; some were turned off. None knew what Ōboshi had in mind. A number of them changed their plans and left for other provinces. The iron-minded ones moved on the Kantō area.

Moronao's spies gradually diminished in number. Ōboshi's dissolute behavior gradually intensified. Everyone spoke ill of him, saying that he had backed down out of cowardice. This was a brilliant use of disinformation: intelligence designed to throw the enemy off the track.

I.48

Kaida Yadaemon Tomonobu using a *koto* as a shield

1. In this print, Kaida Yadaemon is warding off enemy arrows from behind a *koto* in its cover.

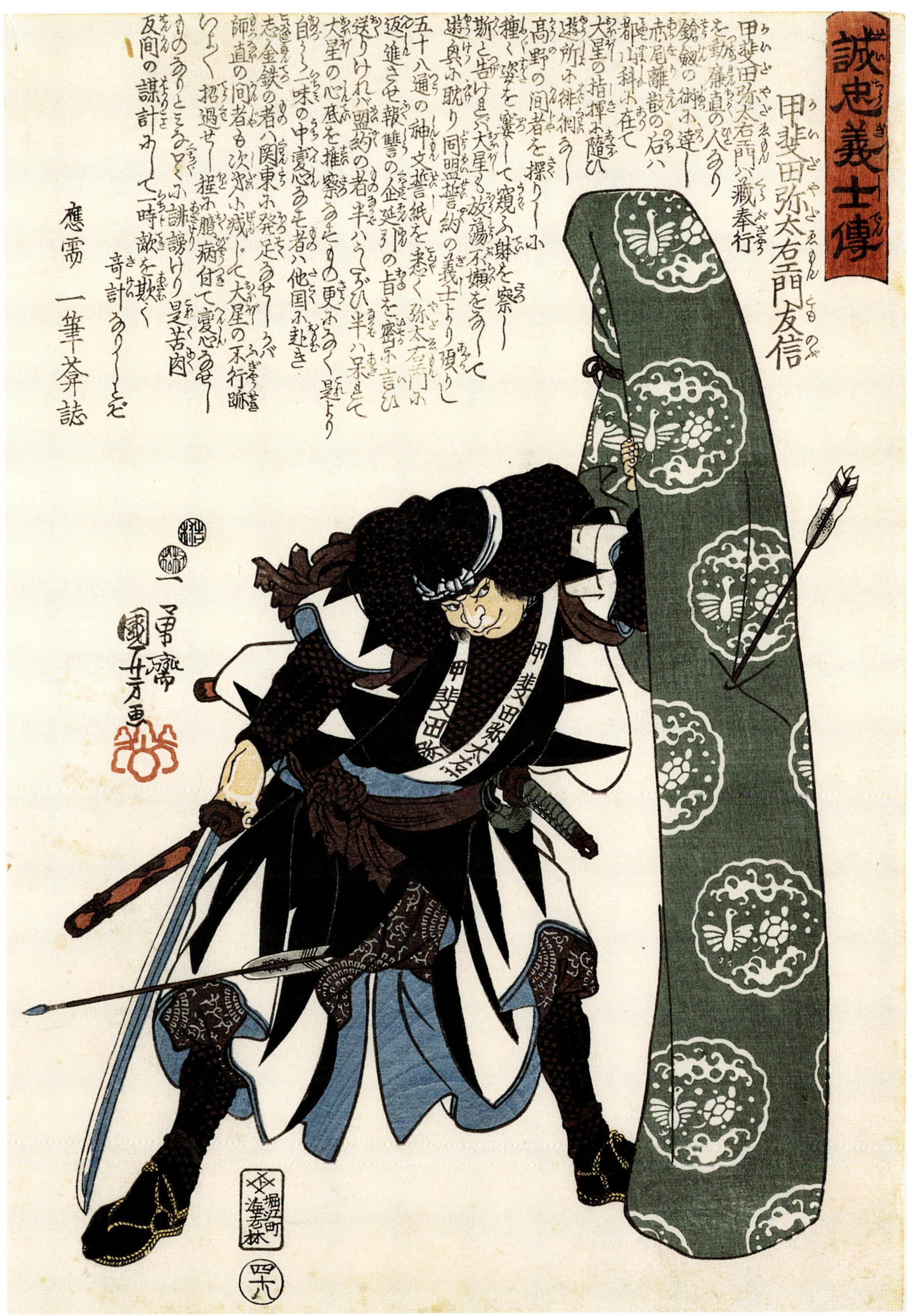
誠忠義士傳
甲斐田弥太右衛門友信
應需 一筆菴誌
一勇斎國芳画
四十九

Miura Jirōemon Kanetsune

1.49

Miura Jirōemon Kanetsune falling backward into a hearth

Kanetsune was a chef, in charge of food service, and though he was of low rank as a samurai, he was honest, sincere and dutiful. He looked after the lord's alimentary needs day and night in incomparable fashion. If the food had been around too long, whether fish, fowl or vegetable, he would not use it. He would say: 'Human life depends on food. Long life depends above all on food preservation.' Even something the lord enjoyed, he wouldn't serve if he couldn't get it fresh, at the risk of getting scolded. Hangan appreciated his integrity and treated him with love and affection.

Then, when the Akao fell, Kanetsune took the oath drawn up by Ōboshi with his whole heart. Thereupon he scouted around the enemy mansion in the Kantō and reported his findings to the retainers in Kyoto, urging Ōboshi to move.

Then he worked as an aide to Ōboshi in the house they rented in Kokuchō and took part in the glorious attack.[1] He was a truly loyal man.

1. Kanetsuke, like the priest Ryūen (plate I.42), is not the complete fighting man and thus provides the artist with another comic figure as he slides into a hearth imbedded in the floor and overturns a basket of charcoal. Metallic powder has been hand-applied to this print to simulate the coal dust from the hearth (see also note to plate I.27). Collectors should be aware that these prints are sometimes offered for sale without the metallic powder.

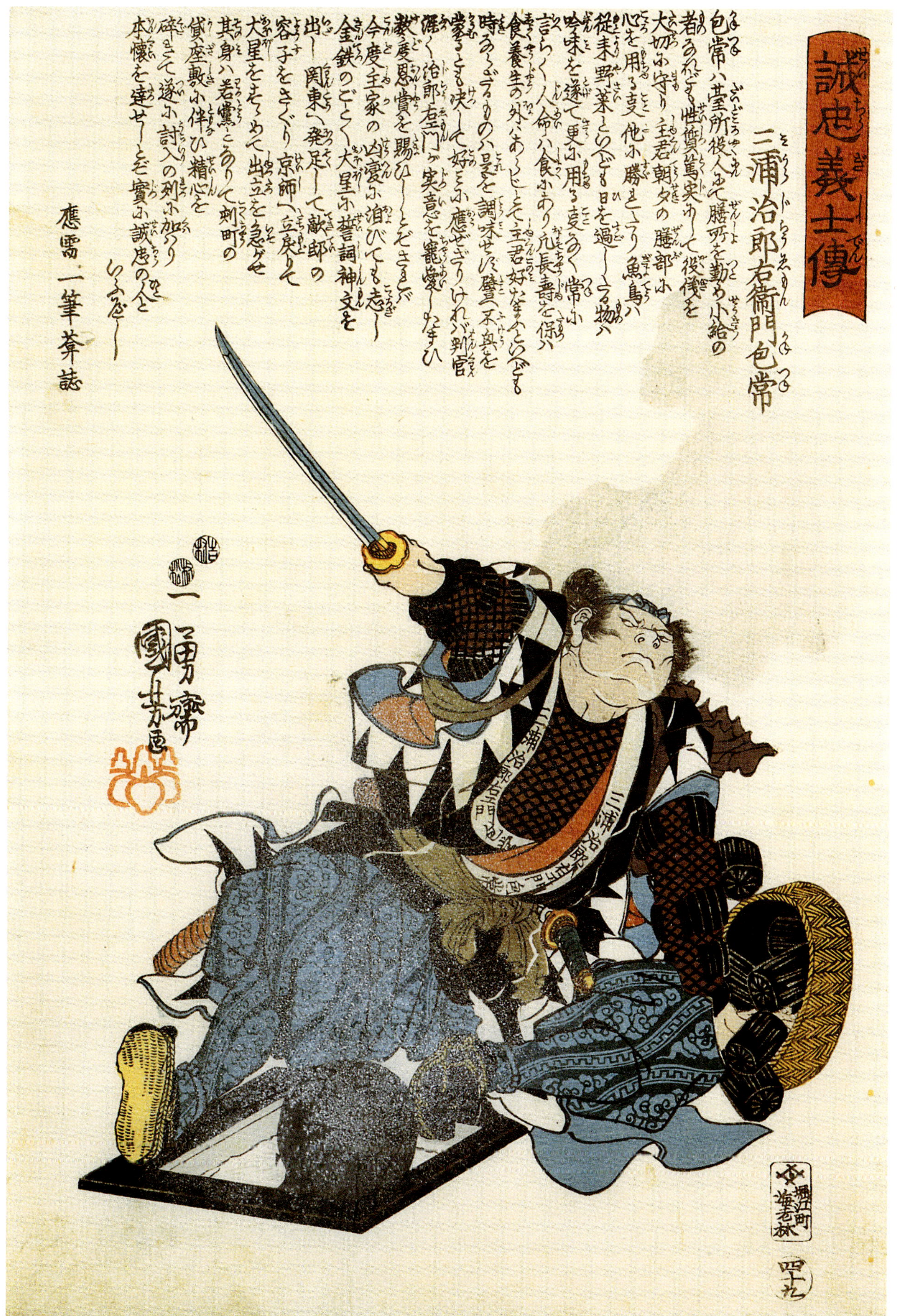
誠忠義士傳
三浦治郎右衛門包常
應需一筆菴誌
一勇齋國芳画
四十九

Yoshida Chūzaemon Kanesuke

1.50

Yoshida Chūzaemon Kanesuke pointing with a battle fan

Yoshida Kanesuke was part of an old retainer family. He was expert in all the elements of warfare, a master of the Yamaga school, and trained his men well. He also enjoyed poetry, in particular *waka*.

Thus, when Ōboshi set the conspiracy in motion he appointed Kanesuke as commander of the troops. Then, on New Year's Day of the year of the horse he let Kanesuke know that he wanted him to be his representative in the Kantō area.[1]

On receiving Kanesuke's consent, Ōboshi said: 'Please inform the young men who have signed this oath with such unwavering determination that I hereby place them under your command. Take that important message to their homes in the various provinces and at the same time inform them that we shall be holding a worship service to dedicate a tablet to be placed on our deceased master's grave on February 19th, at the Zuikō-In Temple, in Danshō Machi, Murasaki-no, Kyoto.'

Hara Gōemon, Kaida Yadaemon, and Onodera Jūnai were with them as they met the group. They had a big meal; then Ōboshi spoke to them, saying: 'I do not plan to arrive in the Kantō until late. In the meantime Yoshida Kanesuke will be here and take charge as my representative.' Happy that plans were moving ahead and pleased that they could now do their duty, the men celebrated with high morale. On the 21st, Kanesuke left Kyoto, accompanied by Shikamatsu Kanroku and Teraoka Hei-emon. As they came to the Ausaka checkpoint, he recited:

A mist of nine folds[2]
clears away before our eyes
and reveals the sun
shining on a cloudless reign
over the Ausaka gate.[3]

Then they visited various scenic spots and historic monuments on their way to Kamakura. Kanesuke took lodgings in Kōjimachi under the name Taguchi Isshin. During the attack he was in command at the rear gate. He was truly a hero in both literature and war.[4]

The loyal samurai, begun early in July, completed on December 14.[5,6]

The publisher humbly announces that the *Record of the loyal samurai*, received with such acclaim when it came out in July, will be ready again on December 14th, with all the 47. We pray that the sequel to that *Record* will receive the same favourable reception.

1. Meaning 1702.

2. The word translated as 'ninefold' is *kokonoe*, associated with complex structures and even clothing and thus with the imperial court.

3. 'Ausaka,' or 'Osaka,' gate was often referred to in traditional poetry as a place where lovers or others coming to or leaving the capital meet or part. This poem shows Yoshida acting like a courtier observing the time-honoured tradition as he leaves the capital and writes a *tanka*, a thirty-one syllable poem, about the experience.

4. In the print, Yoshida is holding a *jin-sen*, or battle fan, used in Kabuki by theatrical warriors. The banner on his sleeve reads: 'Yoshida Chūzaemon Kanesuke, Akao retainer.'

5. Literally 'seventh month' under the lunar calendar, really August of 1847.

6 Still the Goat year, under the lunar calendar, but also January 20, 1848.

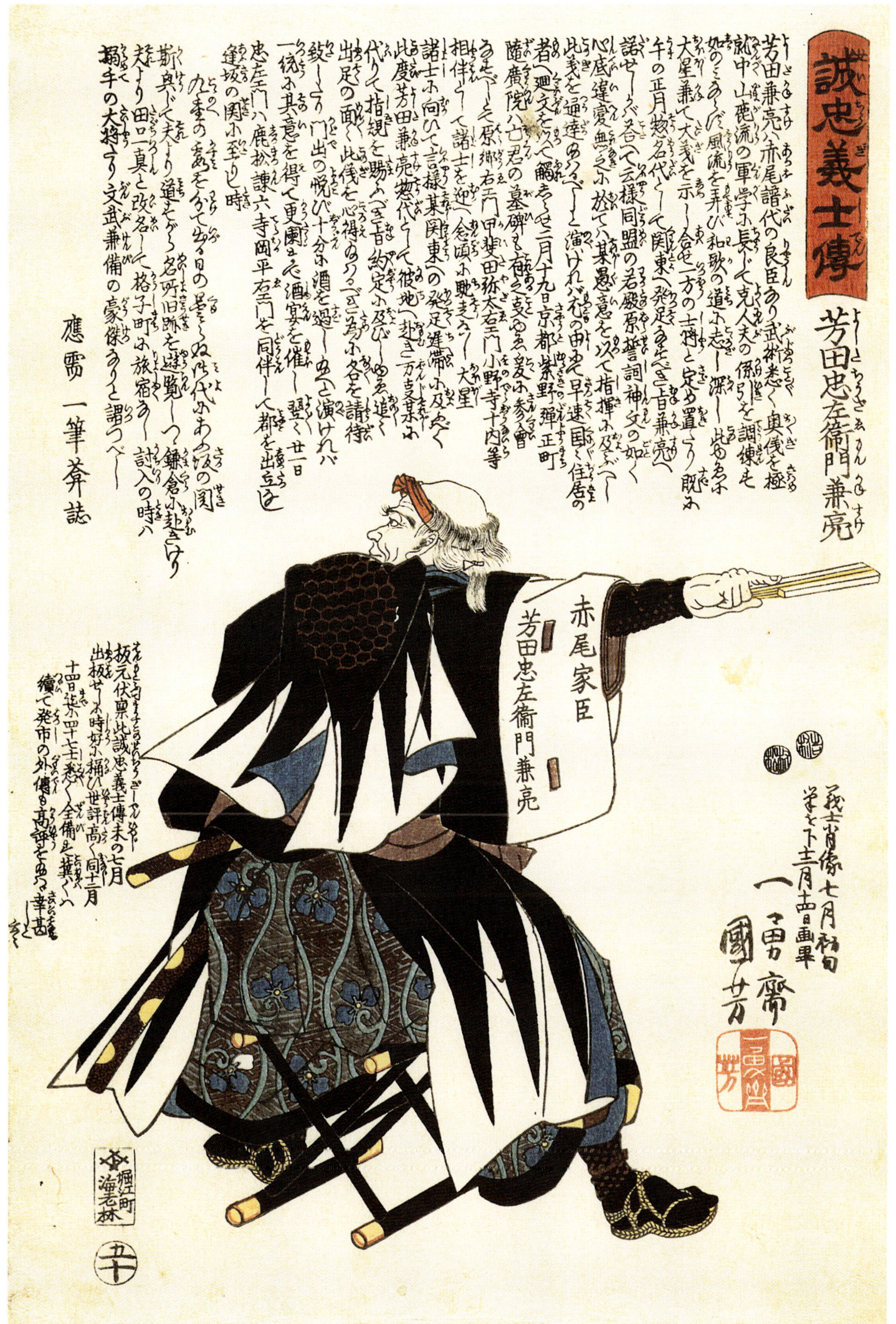
誠忠義士傳
芳田忠左衛門兼亮
赤尾家臣
芳田忠左衛門兼亮
應需 一筆斎誌
一勇齋國芳
五十

Jinzaburō, retainer of Shikamatsu Kanroku

1.51

Jinzaburō, retainer of Shikamatsu Kanroku, offering refreshments

Jinzaburō had served the Shikamatsu family faithfully for years and followed his master, Kanroku, when he became a *rōnin*. In the Kantō in their bare lodging, he endured privation while caring for his master's every need.

When the time for the attack approached, the various members of the band started giving their landlords notice and selling their household goods. Kanroku then approached Jinzaburō and told him that he was about to take a trip to the eastern provinces with some other *rōnin* and would be gone for a long time and now wished to reward him for his long and faithful service. Then he suggested that Jinzaburō take up employment elsewhere and handed him five *ryō* in coins.

Jinzaburō, however, was severely put out and tearfully rejected the money. 'I am a simple person, and you have never confided in me, but I have, after all, been at your side day and night and have drawn certain conclusions about great plans you may have. I know that when those plans are realized they will be magnificent and will establish your fame throughout the nation. So being let go by you is a terrible blow to me. Isn't there any other way?'

Kanroku said: 'I have never had any doubts about your loyalty, but my oath prevents me from taking along a retainer's retainer. You must understand the reasons for that.'

Jinzaburō took those words to heart, but during the attack he carried a ladder and a basket of provisions, and as the faithful ones left the scene he passed out water, rice crackers and tangerines so that nobody went hungry.

Afterward, he shaved his head and tended the graves at Sengakuji. At that time, a humorous poem went around having fun with what might have happened if he had made a mistake packing his basket.[1] It went:

In the confusion
Jinzō carted everything
including the cat

1. Jinzō's mammoth basket is visible in the print, along with the pole that went through the two loops and over his shoulder. The print is numbered *taibi*, meaning 'the end.'

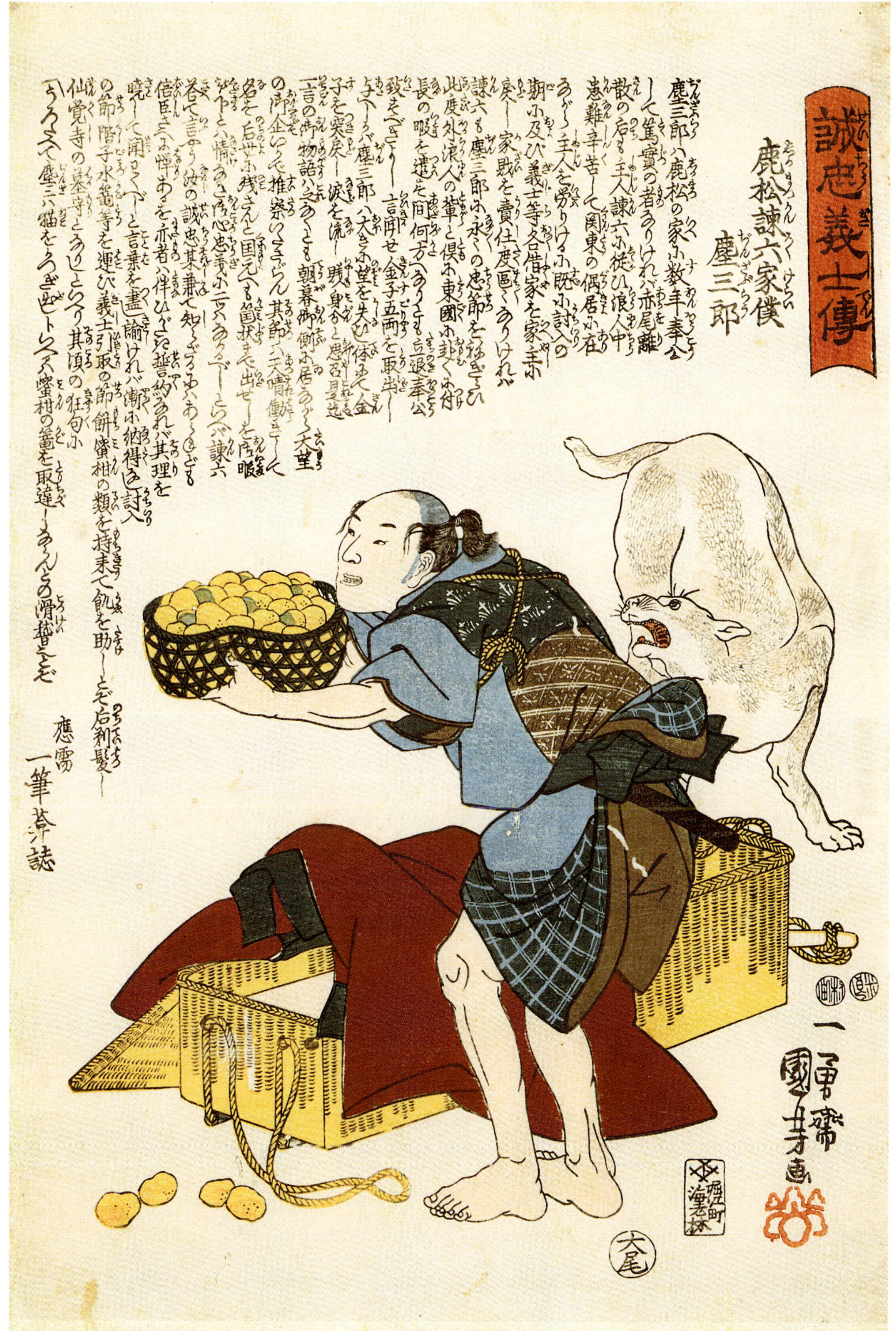
誠忠義士傳
鹿松謙六家僕
塵三郎
應需
一筆菴誌
一勇斎國芳画

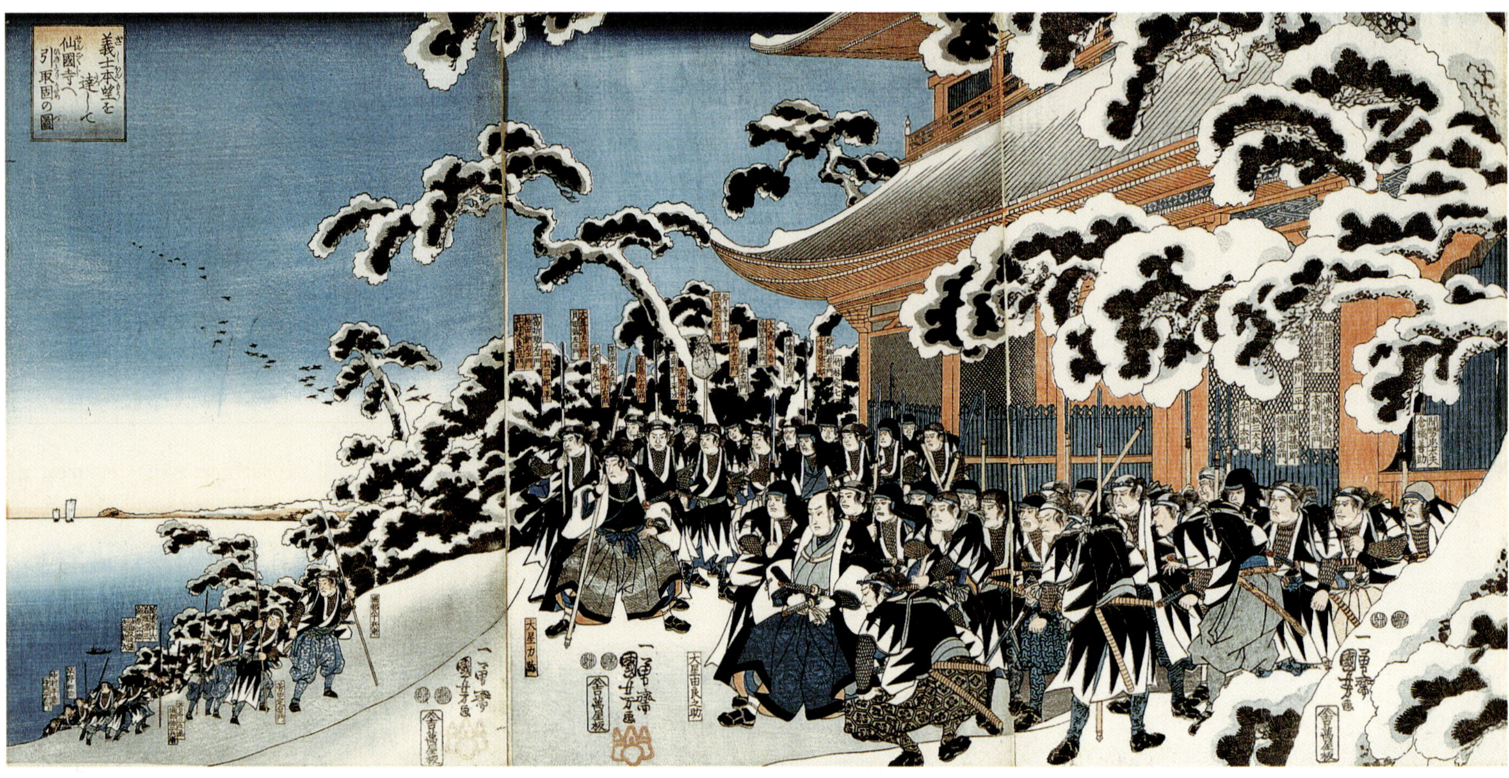

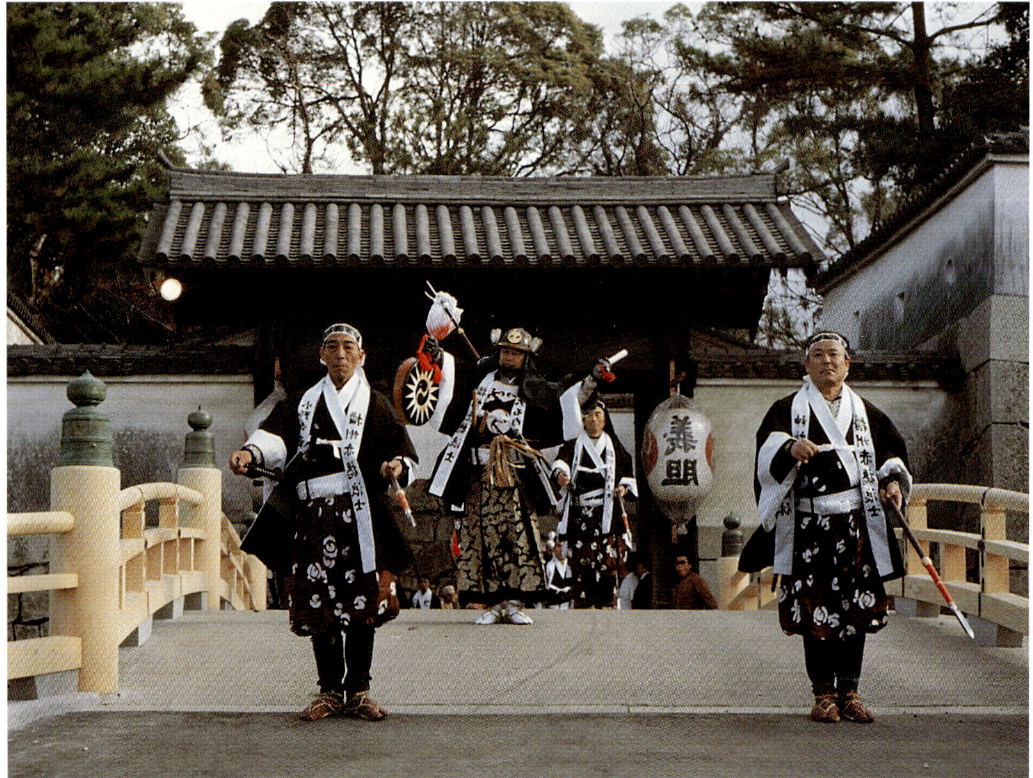

Fig. 9. Kuniyoshi. Triptych of the forty-seven rōnin gathering at Sengakuji Temple with the head of Moronao in a sack.

Annual 'Ako Gishi Festival' commemorating the night attack of the forty-seven rōnin.
Photo courtesy Ōishi Shinto Shrine, Akō.

Stories of the faithful hearts
Seichū gishin den

Series II

The subjects of the *Seichū gishin den* are the silent heroes and heroines drawn into the vortex of the Akō disaster. The series depicts family members of the forty-seven *rōnin:* mothers, widows, wives, sons, daughters, sisters and brothers, as well as courtesans and servants. It is further evidence of Kuniyoshi's fascination with this event and story, for here are the peripheral players in the drama, not just the legendary heroes.

The charm of the *Seichū gishin den* lies in the fullness of its social representation. We are shown Lord En'ya's widow, Yōshinin-ni (plate II.8), elegantly dressed in a long and flowing, floral black kimono, the flowers vined in gold tassel, standing beside a screen decorated with a colourful bird in the snow. We are also shown Amagawa-ya Gihei, the *rōnin* armaments dealer (plate II.6), playing with his small child on the floor. A blue and white robe is loosely draped over his semi-nude body.

Though most of these prints at first appear to be the traditional *ukiyo-e bijin-e* or 'pictures of beautiful women' highly dependent for their effect on kimonos with brilliant patterns and designs, it is the delineation of character and situation to which we really respond. Indeed, Kuniyoshi's sensitivity to the predicaments and tragedy of these people is as poignant and subtle in its expression as is the boldness and combativeness of the warriors. For example, Ishi-jo, wife of Ōboshi Yoshio (plate II.1), exudes the strength and determination of a leader's wife. In her face and stance we see 'a model samurai wife.' With Onodera Jūnai's wife (plate II.4), we read in her eyes her sad resignation to suicide. In Toda no Tsubone (plate II.5), seated before the burning incense by the head of her late lord's enemy, we sense her 'feminine gentility' and her 'dignity and correctness.' In the wife of Uramatsu Handayū (plate II.13), despite the humour of the print, we witness the trials and tribulations of the woman in a household bereft of men. Perhaps the most moving print of all is that which concentrates its visual effect in the expression on the face of the old servant, Katsusuke (plate II.18), holding up his token of friendship from Ōboshi Yuranosuke.

Our aesthetic appreciation is further enhanced by the translations which are perhaps even more critical to an understanding of these prints than in the *rōnin* series. We learn from the texts that of the seventeen individuals depicted, four committed suicide and three renounced their former lives to become nuns or priests to tend the graves. All the rest lived out their ordinary lives with the burdens and memories of lost loved ones.

The *Seichū gishin den* at present consists of seventeen prints. B.W. Robinson lists number sixteen as 'not seen.' Indeed, there is no record of it in any museum or private collection. Perhaps the *hanshita* was lost before it was cut into a block. On the other hand, it may surface one day as did number eighteen after the publication of *Kuniyoshi: The warrior-prints*.

The eighteenth print, which is listed in Robinson's unpublished 'Supplement to Kuniyoshi: The warrior prints,' is included in this book (plate II.18).

Series II

Stories of the faithful hearts
Seichū gishin den

The plates

Ōboshi Yoshio Naishitsu Ishi-jo
Ishi-jo, wife of Ōboshi Yoshio

II.1

Ōboshi Yoshio Naishitsu Ishi-jo in a heroic stance

The proverb goes: 'The samurai is to men what the cherry tree is to trees.'

When it comes to higher office, one cannot govern unless one has the ability to treat one's people benevolently. Governing a nation is like governing a household, but governing a household is the task of a woman.

Ōboshi Yoshio's wife governed her womanly virtues with all the intelligence of a warrior. When the messenger came from Kamakura with the tragic news, and Yoshio and his son went to the castle planning to sacrifice their lives as easily as removing teeth from a comb, she was outwardly unmoved.

She said to her son Rikiya: 'You are now fifteen years old and an adult. You must do as well as your father. Show your worth as a samurai, and leave a name that will last to the end of time.'

She took care of all the household details and gave the younger children all the advice and encouragement a loving mother can impart. Then, after the father and the son had departed, taking their underlings with them, O-ishi went into the living room, took out all the private and business documents and put them in a chest and sealed it. Next, while it was still dark out, she had the maid wash everything from outside the gate to the threshold, missing nothing.

Thus she and the maid worked every day, without flagging, even though there was no man in the house, with even more care than when Ōboshi was home, without complaint. When people were told later what they had done to prevent robbery, they were all amazed.

Thus, when the estate had been dissolved and Ōboshi was in house arrest in Yamashina, and it was said that he was frequenting brothels, she registered no complaint. And when the Kantō move began, she continued to take care of her home and saw to it that Kishi Chiyo and Daisaburō were cared for and educated.

When Teraoka Heisaburō informed her that the deed was done, she was overjoyed. Then she gathered the family relatives together, placed the two sons in their care, and committed suicide.

She sacrificed herself for her husband. She was a model samurai wife, a heroic and virtuous woman for all ages.[1]

'Women in Kabuki are not without their means of protection, for they quite often have to defend their husbands', their lords', or their own honour.'
Shaver, p. 298.

1. Kuniyoshi has chosen to depict Ōboshi Yoshio's wife, O-ishi, in a heroic stance of 'a model samurai wife.'

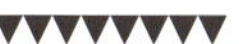

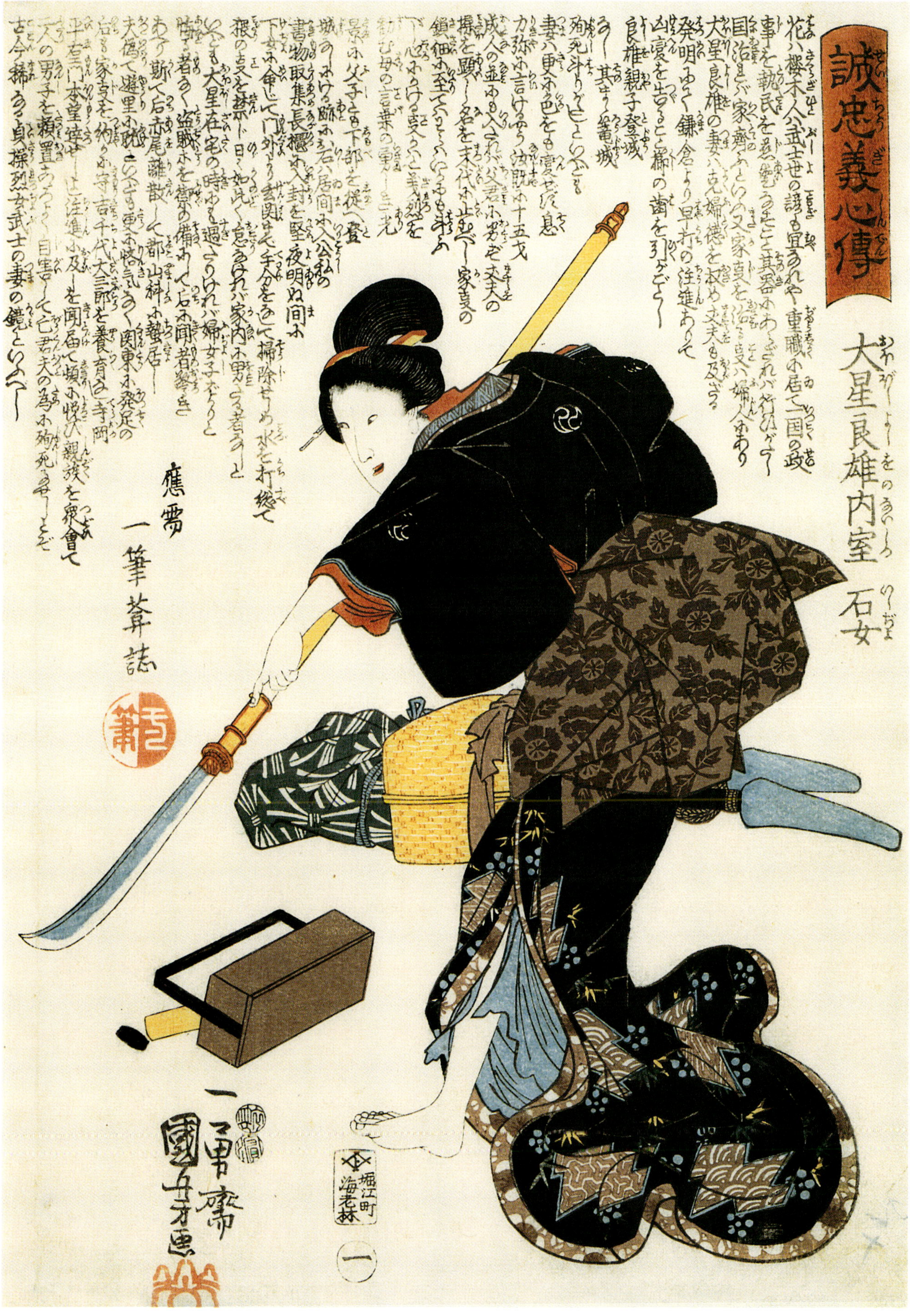

誠忠義心傳

大星良雄内室 石女

應需 一筆菴誌

一勇斎國芳画

堀江町 海老林

一

Take-jo, wife of Yamaoka Kakutei

II.2

Take-jo, wife of Yamaoka Kakutei, weeping next to her child

Tokiwa Gozen, in sacrificing her chastity, showed herself to be a virtuous woman.[1] After the fall of Akao, Yamaoka Kakutei Morisata, with his wife, O-Take, and their three-year-old son, Matsukichi, went to the village of Kuretake no Fushimi and stayed with friends. Then he joined Ōboshi and his comrades in the conspiracy. He was making plans to leave for Kamakura when he suddenly died.

O-Take, grief-stricken, picked up her child and went to visit Ōboshi. She informed him that Kakutei had died the night before and that he was by nature a quiet man who kept things to himself, but that he had worn a charm with his dead lord's name on it close to his body. Also written on it were the words: 'Will the heavens not accept ...' That was all there was.

'Perhaps he was planning to visit his master's grave sometime in the distant future, but life can be unpredictable,' she said.

Then Ōboshi asked her how she would feel if other men like him should be planning to take vengeance on Moronao. He waited silently for an answer.

O-Take adjusted the fold of her kimono.[2] 'I am a daughter of the Kasaokas, hereditary retainers of En'ya. We are all upset about what has happened. Although I am only a weak woman, I will tell you that when the time comes for your men to go to the Kantō area to assassinate Moronao, I will kill my son, Matsukichi.'

'Then I want you to add the name Matsukichi, son of Yamaoka Kakubei, to your rolls as a remembrance of his father's part in this action.'

She went to wiping away her tears with her sleeve, unable to say more, thus demonstrating her commitment before Ōboshi's admiring eyes.

O-Take was able to use her charms to get into Moronao's home and then to lead in the avenging forces. Thus she sacrificed her chastity but brought about the fulfillment of Kakubei's desires. Through her loyalty she made herself a great heroine in the eyes of the world.

1. Mother of Yoshitsune, one of the greatest heroes of Japanese history and literature. She became a concubine to save her mother and children. See Will. H. Edmunds, *Pointers and clues to the subjects of Chinese and Japanese art*, p. 631.

2. Literally, 'correcting her knee,' describing a woman's gesture of arranging the skirt of her kimono as she sits on the *tatami*. It is a gesture indicating that she is very serious.

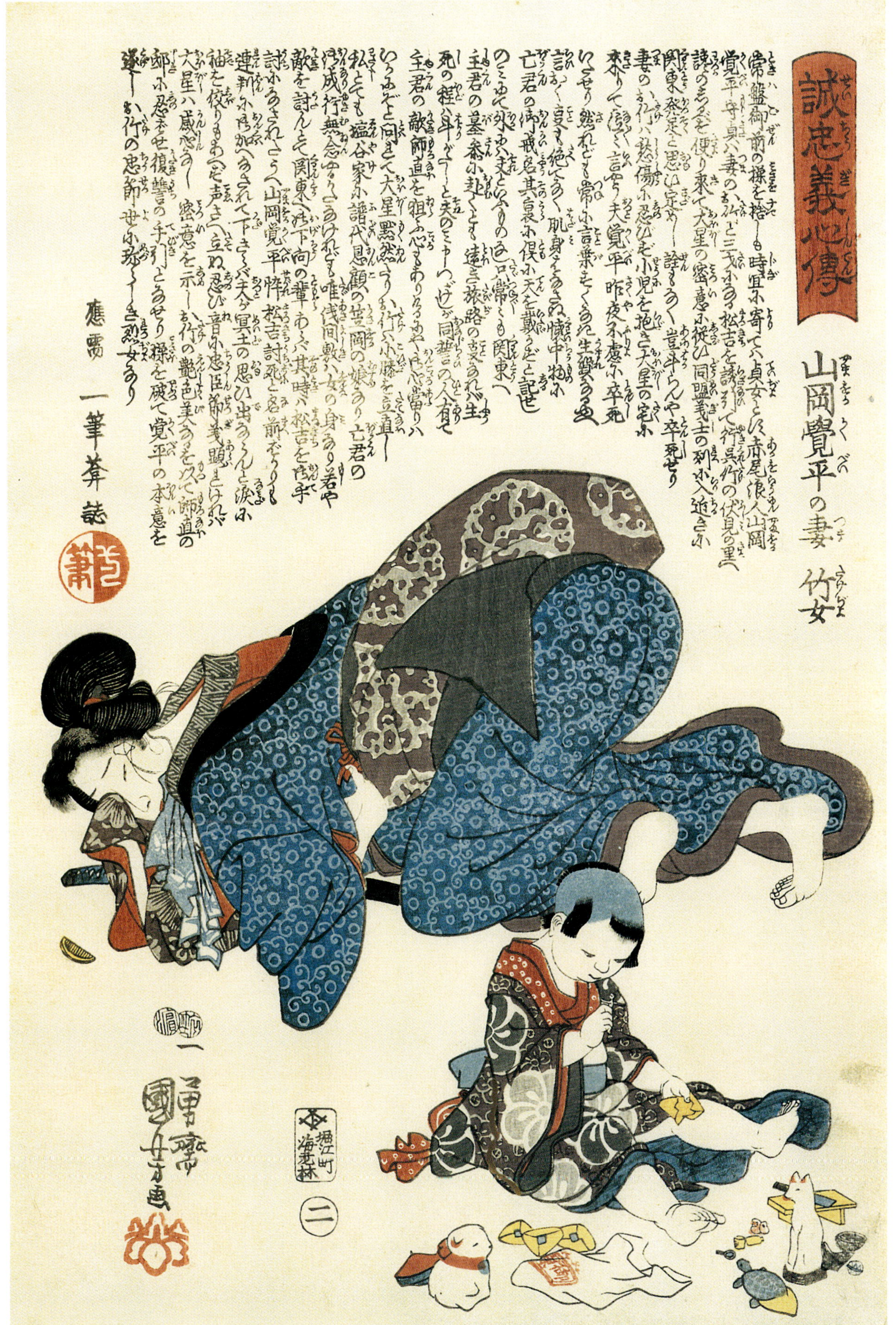
誠忠義心傳
山岡覺平の妻 竹女
一勇齋國芳画
二

Hana-jo, daughter of Oribe Kanamaru

The *Honchō bonsui* speaks of: 'A hundred-year-old inn, at which he was the most honoured guest.[1] Man is mortal, but fame lasts forever.'

Oribe Yahei was a man who abided by the laws of the sword.[2] His wife and children also loved the martial arts. They admired the deeds of Nakayama Yasubei, whose name was synonymous with martial fame and who had wrought vengeance at Takata-no-Baba. So they took him into the family as the husband of O-Hana.[3] They rejoiced in the association with this great name in warfare.

Not long after that, however, the central family was brought low, and Yasubei became a *rōnin*. He was, however, a man of iron will, determined to clear the shadow from his master's name. He and his parents made covert plans to realize this.

In this very year, incidentally, in Kameyama, in Seishū, the Ishii brothers carried out a vendetta against Akabori Mizuemon, something the Oribe family heard about, though it did little to assuage their torment.

Yasubei was informed of Ōboshi's plot and joined with him. He and his comrades worked with every fibre of their beings and eventually carried out their plan, but then they had to die for having defied the law.

At that time Yasubei's wife, O-Hana, was eighteen years old. Her mother was over fifty. Both of their husbands had committed suicide, but, concealing their sorrow and with altered hairstyles, they appeared before the magistrates with perfect deportment. Then they carried out a mass for the salvation of the loyal retainers and donned the charcoal-coloured robes of the sisterhood, wearing the faint smile of enlightenment.[4]

The mother took the name Myōshin, and the daughter the name Myōkai. At eighteen, she had left the floating world. She then spent three years living in a grass hut that she had built for herself at Sengakuji, near Amida of Kamedo.[5]

She lived to be eighty years old, leaving behind an admirable life, an unclouded mirror, that of a woman of singular virtue.

II.3

Hana-jo, daughter of Oribe Kanamaru, holding both ends of her sash

1. Obscure allusion to the *Honchō monsui* (same characters, different pronunciation), the *Choice literature of the realm*, published in the early part of the 11th century.

2. See I.21 and I.34.

3. And thus Nakayama Yasubei became Oribe Yasubei, and his wife's parents became his parents.

4. Allusion to an incident during a sermon by Buddha, when only one disciple registered the faint smile of complete comprehension.

5. One of six temples of Amida Buddha in Tokyo, favorite destinations of pilgrims during spring and fall equinox observances.

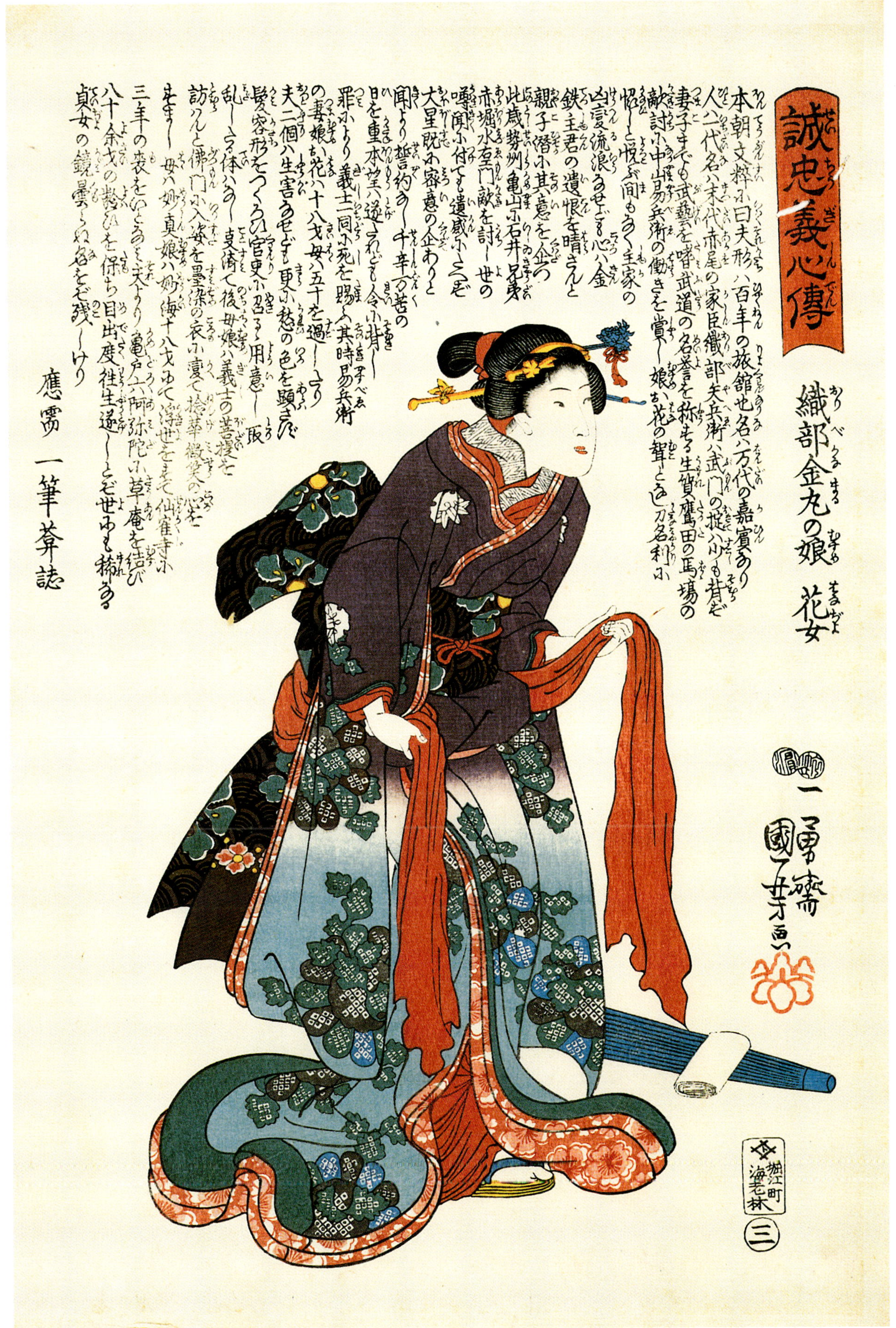
誠忠義心傳
織部金丸の娘 花女
一勇斎國芳画
應需 一筆菴誌
堀江町 海老林

Wife of Onodera Jūnai

Onodera Jūnai Hidekazu was not only a famous swordsman, but he was also a devotee of *waka* poetry.[1] He also took pleasure in refined pursuits and wrote a number of excellent poems, which established his reputation. His wife was a very beautiful girl from Kyoto who also wrote poetry. People envied the way the two of them enjoyed themselves with words and poems. At first they lived in the mansion in Kyoto and, after the dissolution of Akao, went on living in that city. When the time came for the movement to the Kantō to visit the grave of their departed lord, he travelled with Rikiya and sent this poem back to his wife from Seta, in Kōshū:

As I look about
at the colours of the fall
on Otowa mountain,
I recall our parting words
and the dampness of your sleeve.

Then, when he was in the Kantō, someone brought this to him:

To my husband, I send not a letter but this poem:
When I read the words
your pen left upon the page
a shower of tears fell
And now all the leaves are gone
that I might use to answer.

He replied thus:

Limits there may be
on whether I shall return
but as I travel
my love goes along with me
like a garment of nine folds.

After she received word that her husband, Hidekazu, and their son, Hidetomo, had completed their mission and committed *seppuku* after the New Year, she went to Honkokuji, had a Buddhist mass said for them and erected a stone in their memory. Then, her earthly duties behind her, she went to their graves, placed this poem as remembrance and ended her life:

Real though they appear
the dreams of life melt away
before you realize
an undying principle
that even the flowers obey.

Her death name was: Sekishin-In Myōkun Nissei Shinjo, and her stone still stands in Kyoto's Honkokuji. She was all that a samurai's wife should be.

II.4

Wife of Onodera Jūnai, legs bound in preparation for suicide

1. Identified as Onodera Jūnai Hidetomo in I.9. The lady in the print is dressed in preparation to commit suicide. Since women perform the act by cutting the vein under the arm, she is technically not committing *seppuku*, or *hara-kiri*, both of which mean 'cutting the stomach.' Her legs are tied to keep her from falling in an unladylike manner.

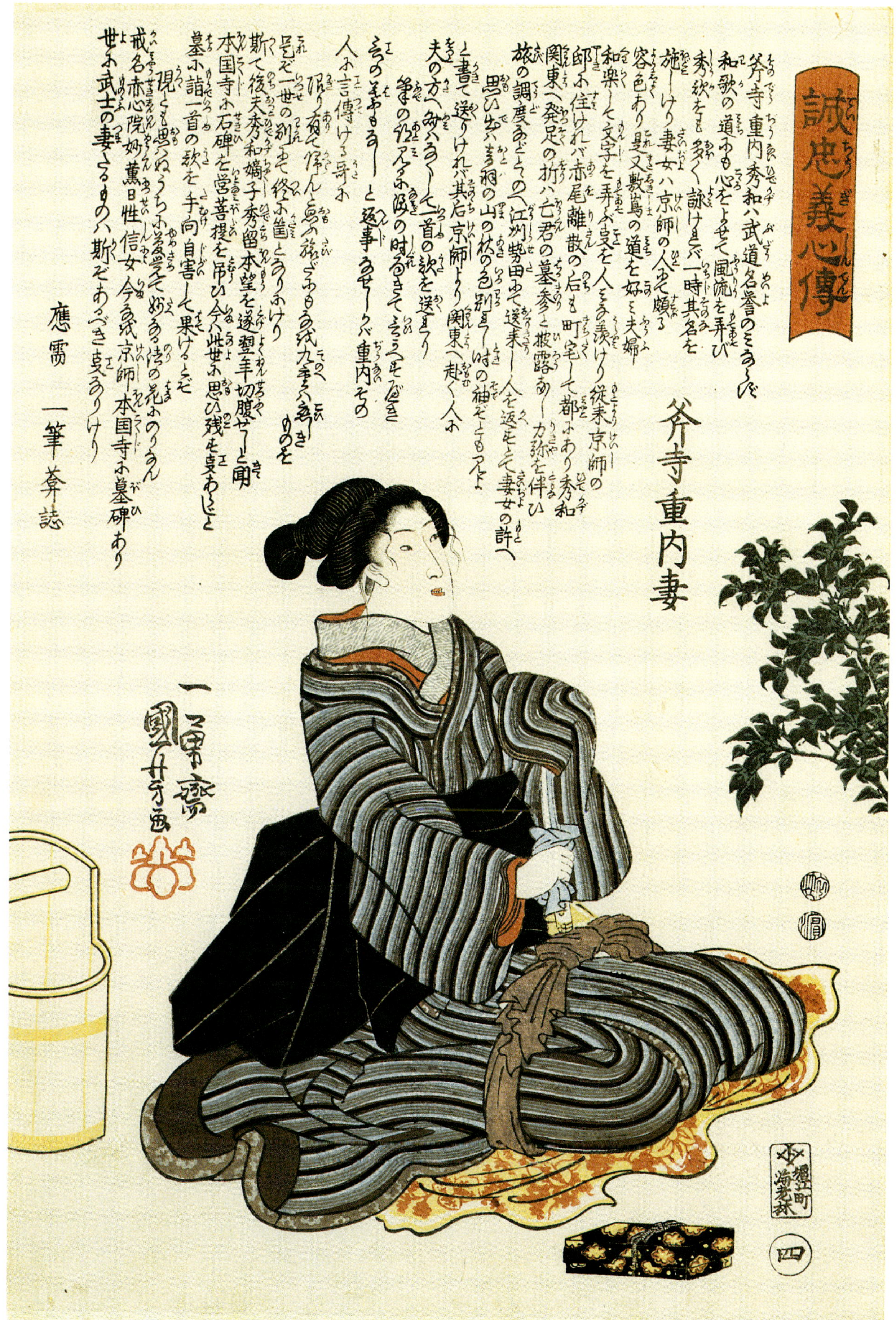
誠忠義心傳
斧寺重内妻
一勇齋國芳画

Toda no Tsubone

II.5

Toda no Tsubone seated before a box and burning incense

Hangan Takasada's widow was living quietly in the Aoyama mansion when, on the morning of December 15, Teraoka Hei-emon arrived and called: 'I have a message for you, ma'am.'[1] She rushed out and took the letter which was from Ōboshi, saying that on the day before, the 14th, a loyal group of forty-seven men had attacked the Kōno mansion, taken the head of Moronao, and achieved the heavenly-ordained vengeance. They had carried out their mission and were now at the place of the Bodhisattva, Sengakuji. He was writing at the first opportunity. Having delivered his message, Teraoka Hei-emon stood there in the great room as the noble lady asked him for all the details of the attack. She was obviously pleased, and in order to show appreciation for this courageous action, soon ordered Toda no Tsubone to express her gratitude and called for a palanquin to take that lady to the temple.

Toda greeted Ōboshi and all the warriors and gave them the message of the lord's widow:

You loyal men have expended incalculable effort on behalf of your late lord to carry out this difficult attack against a powerful enemy force. My joy is great, and your lord must be feeling admiration in his grave. The clouds of delusion have been dispelled, and the other lords must be feeling overwhelming gratitude. Because of public concern, I have sent this messenger to express the warmth of my appreciation.

With that, Toda bowed and said no more.

The loyal band wept in unending emotion. Ōboshi then politely replied:

We retainers know that we cannot repay so much as one ten-thousandth of the debt we owe our departed lord. Under his governance we have been treated warmly and graciously, and we receive the words we have just heard as a divine blessing.

With that, they took Toda into the sanctuary and showed her Moronao's head.[2] She inspected it with all feminine gentility and deep feeling. Then, after a time, she gracefully thanked the men, entered her palanquin, and departed. The men marvelled at the dignity and correctness of Toda. Not one of them felt that a man could act as she had.

1. See II.8.

2. The round box in front of the lady Toda seems to be the container in which Moronao's head was transported. The incense reminds us that she is in a temple.

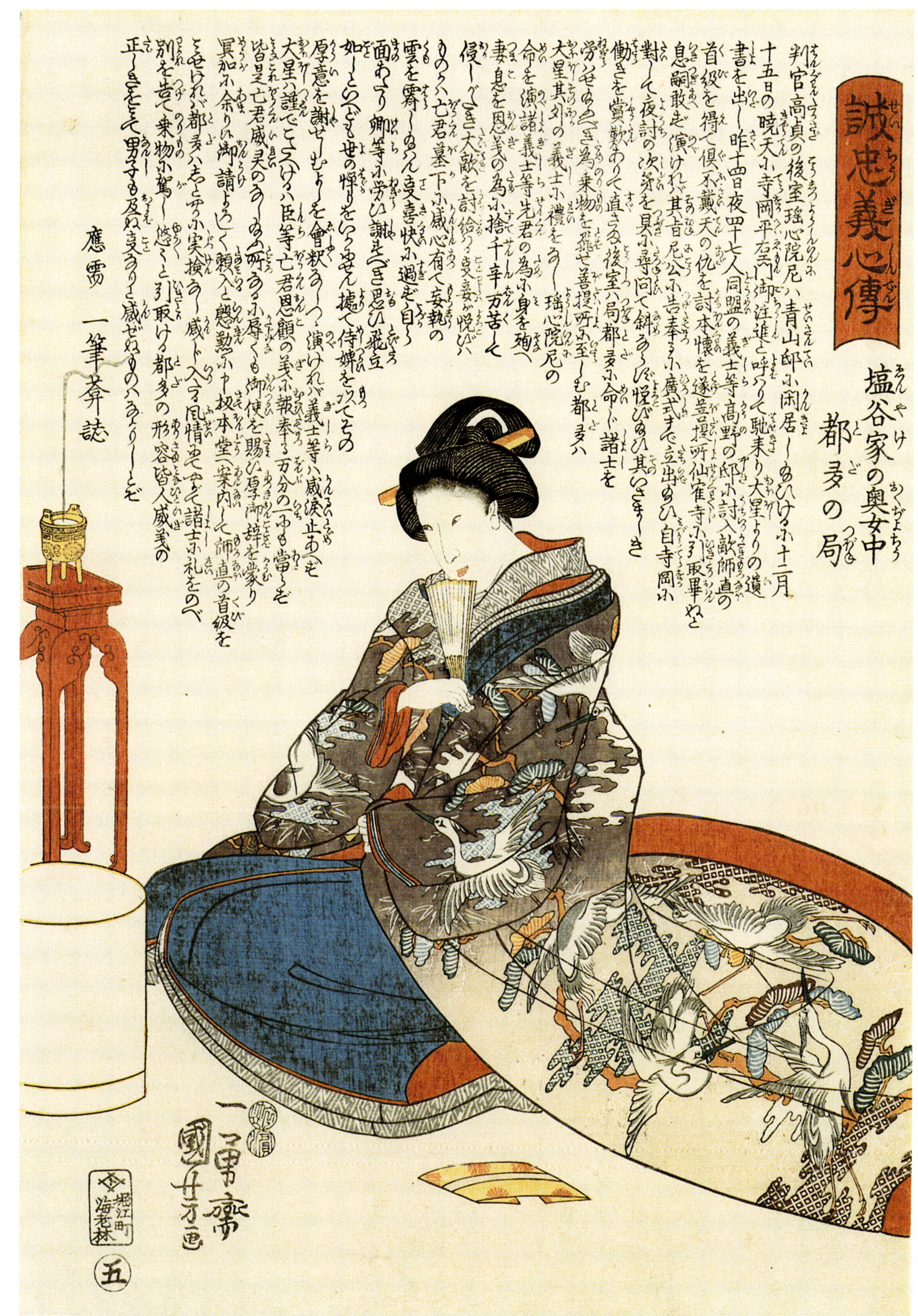
誠忠義心傳
塩谷家の奥女中
都夛の局
一勇斎國芳画
五

Amagawa-ya Gihei

II.6

Amagawa-ya Gihei cupping the chin of his child

Although he owed fealty to the En'ya family, Amagawa-ya Gihei lived in Tsu, in Senshū Sakai. When he heard about the confiscation of the Akao estates, he hurried to see Ōboshi, offering his services in whatever way needed. Ōboshi was deeply touched by this, but told him they were leaving the castle and dispersing to their home provinces and that he would be in touch later. With that Gihei returned home.

Even though he was of merchant stock, Gihei was a man of broadly human qualities, deeply honest, of a masculinity beyond even that of the samurai, and Ōboshi had been aware of this for some time.[1] The secret he would not lay bare even to the oldest hereditary retainers to test their devotion, his plans for the vendetta, he discussed with Gihei.

Gihei was careful not to excite suspicion, but he stored weapons for the attack: a spear, chains, keys, and various ropes, in a cottage he owned in Kitano Kasasagi, in Sesshū. He also went to the swordsmith Shinryoku-maru and ordered a new sword. The swordsmith, however, informed on him, and Gihei was thrown into jail. He was tortured at length but did not confess.

Time went on, and he forgot his travail, but then news came of Ōboshi's successful raid, and Gihei turned himself in with the request that he be punished. The authorities, however, rather admired this show of knightly derringdo on the part of a merchant. His punishment was reduced, but he was expelled from Tsu, Sakai.

He took orders, changed his name to Dosai, and retired to Higashiyama. There he took up tea ceremony and poetic pursuits and prayed for the salvation of the forty-seven loyal men. He lived till he was past eighty years old, when he went to his heavenly reward.

1. The print shows Gihei in a *yukata*. He seems to be clutching a wash-towel. It is a very sentimental pose, showing a man in the bosom of the family.

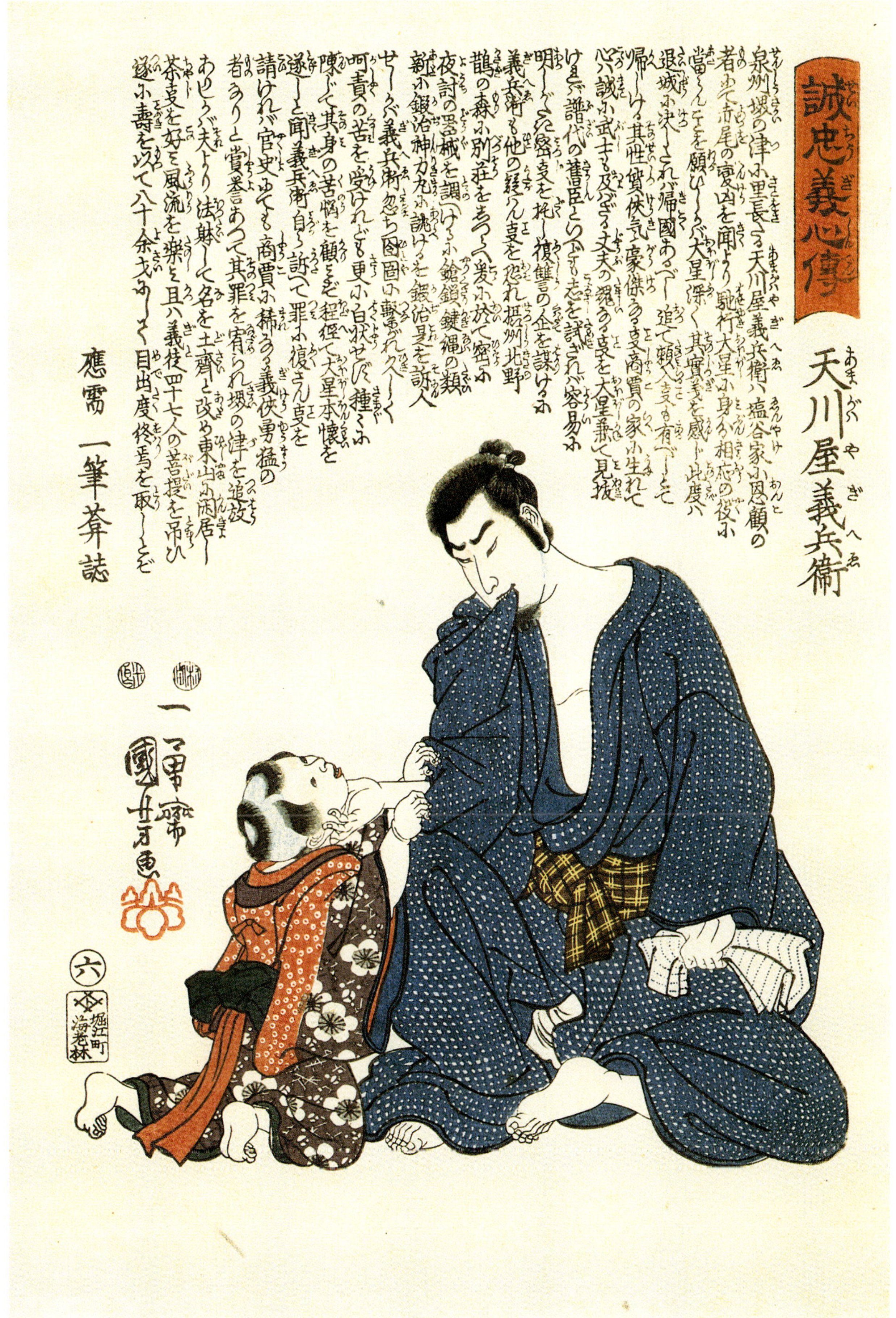

誠忠義心傳
天川屋義兵衛
應需 一筆菴誌
六
堀江町 海老林

Ueshima Monya

II.7

Ueshima Monya raising sleeve to chin, wearing one sword

Ueshima Monya was the son of an Akao retainer named Ueshima Yasuke. He was fourteen years old and served in the retinue of Takasada, who showered him with affection. When the lord's estate was confiscated and the clan dissolved, he went to live with his parents in Kishi no Wada, in Sesshū.

His father, Yasuke, followed Ōboshi first, and took the oath of martyrdom at the castle and became a part of the loyal band in iron resolution. When the time came to go to the Kantō, however, he changed his mind for some reason and turned down Ōboshi's invitation. When all the other members of the group set out, he went to the Arima hot springs.

Though he was quite young, Monya was aware of the plans for revenge and, fired by grateful devotion to his lord, wanted to make the journey to the east. But his father went on dallying in the warm water, and his mother was ill and infirm. Then, two months later, when Yasuke returned from Arima, Monya begged that he be taken to the Kantō. His father, however, said: 'As long as Lord Daisaku hasn't taken a position on the plans of Ōboshi and his group, I cannot decide what to do.[1] Let's wait a little longer; it won't be too late.'

Powerless and already sensing that he had missed the opportunity, Monya received the news of the loyal men and their realization of their ambitions at the end of the year with deep sadness. With clear resolve untinged with self-pity, he took his own life.

He died in place of his father, and in doing so atoned for his father's shame. His faith and his sense of duty are worthy of sympathy. They can also be seen in the story of Myōkai (cloister name of the wife of Horibe Yasubei), another unusual exploit in the annals of mankind, filled with endless sadness.[2, 3]

1. Brother of Takasada, who had petitioned the shogunate for restoration of the estates.

2. See II.3, I.21, and I.34. The name of the husband given here is the real historical name.

3. See I.21 and I.34, which spell the surname differently.

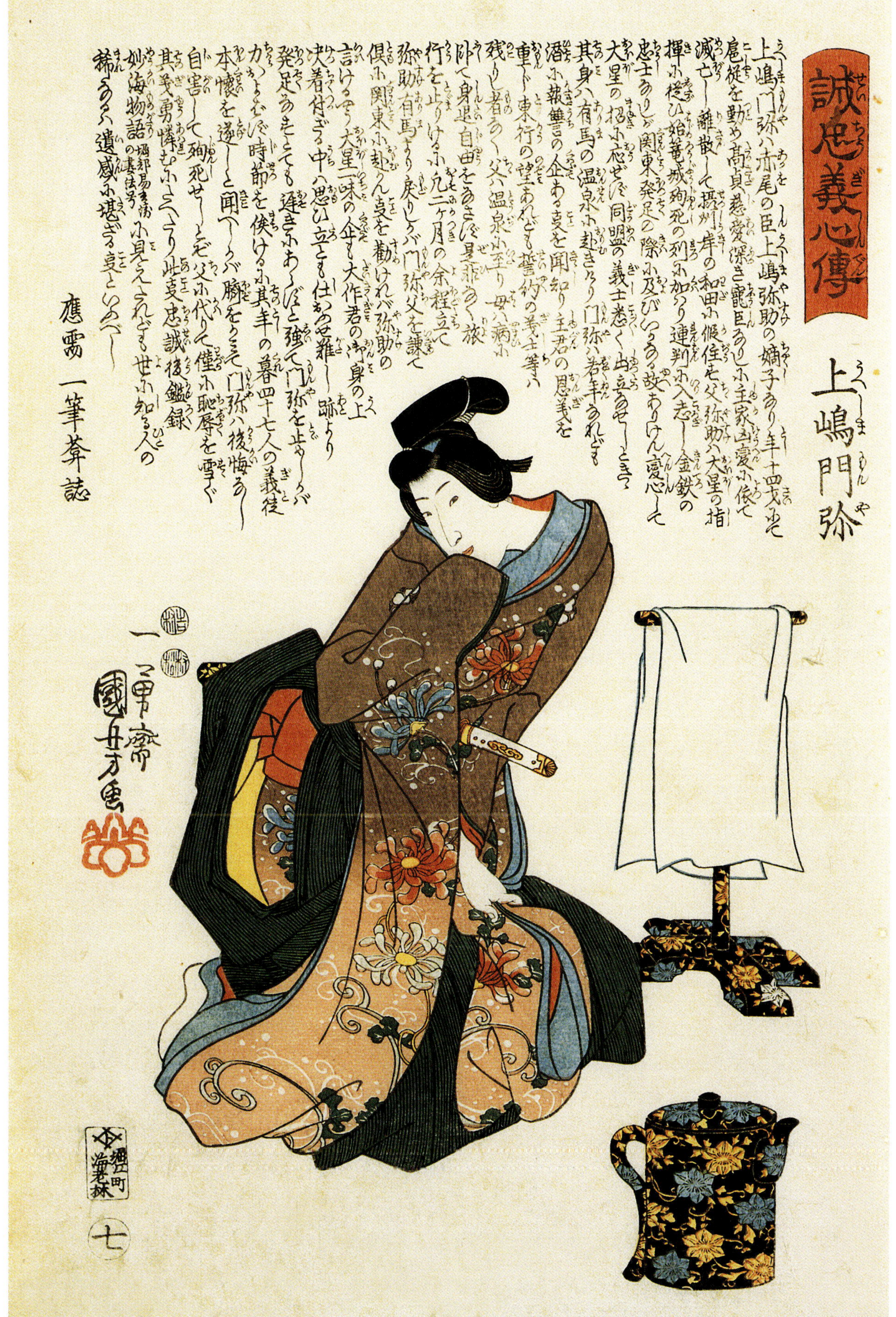

II.8

The widow Yōshin-in-ni beside a painted screen

The widow Yōshin-in-ni

After the completely unexpected execution of her husband and the confiscation of the family estates, En'ya Hangan's widow mourned without let-up. Her sleeves were not yet dry when she cut her jet-black hair.[1]

She composed the poem:

My black hair may grow
out of the thousand sinews
of my heart's desire,
but how sad I have become
since cutting one sinew of it.

And thus she became a nun, under the name of Yōshin-in-ni, and there in the mansion in Aoyama she said masses for her husband's soul and prayed to Buddha.[2]

One day Ōboshi Yoshio came by to wish her well. 'It's been a long time since we last saw each other,' he said, and they talked long about the past and shed copious tears. 'Since your obedient servant is going to depart for his home province in a few days, I have come to bid you goodbye. It has been such a long time since I have been able to see you in your lovely home and to inquire about your health. All living things must die, and death gives old age no respite; we never know what parting will be the last,' he said. Tearful as she was, the nun could not speak at times, but she managed words like: 'Since I am only a woman and what I say is not important, as long as my lord's enemy, Moronao, is alive I find my indignation at being under the same sky with him quite frustrating. These things go beyond human understanding. If I had the faith, surely I might see a way. Every day I go on thinking that at the end of some long journey there is a prospect that what I desire will be granted [...]'. Thus she went on, and Ōboshi, for all his words, was filled with shame at himself as he departed.[3]

Three days later, the message was brought by Teraoka. She was surprised and pleased and sent a waiting woman to Sengakuji.[4] That lady thanked the men and then gave Ōboshi her lady's apologies for her rudeness.

She was a truly virtuous, noble woman.

1. Meaning that she was still weeping uncontrollably.

2. The *in* in her name signifies her dowager status, and the *ni* shows that she is a nun.

3. He felt shame because her words seemed to rebuke him. She apologizes because she was not told of his secret plans.

4. The 'waiting woman' Yōshin-in-ni sent with the message to Sengakuji was Toda no Tsubone. See II.5.

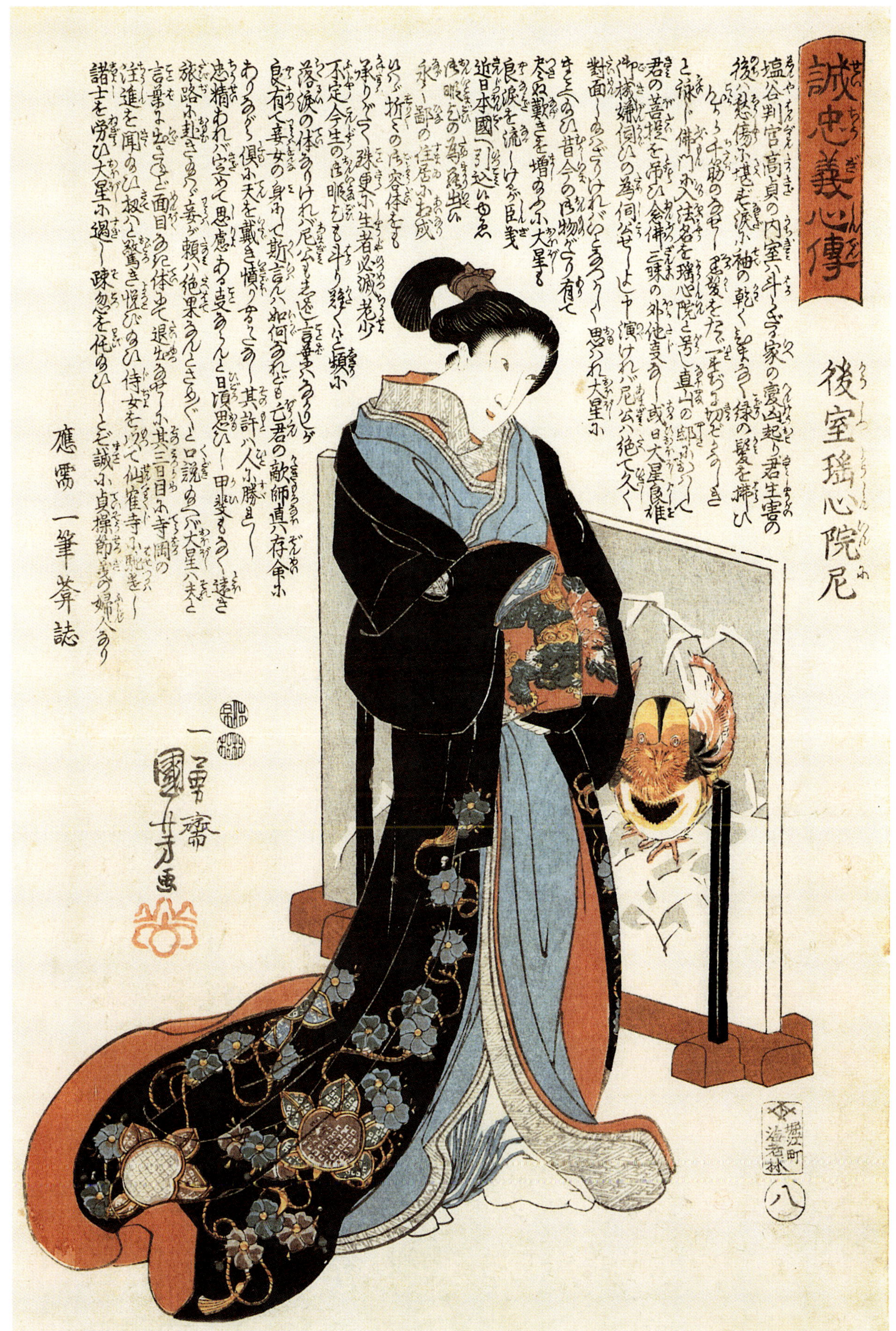
誠忠義心傳
後室瑶心院尼
應需 一筆菴誌
一勇齋國芳画
八

Mother of Tominomori Suke-emon

11.9

Mother of Tominomori Suke-emon with long letter

After the night attack, Tominomori Suke-emon was remanded into the custody of Mononoi Wakanosuke.[1] Then he, like all of the loyal samurai, was given clean clothing to replace those he had bloodied in the attack. When Suke-emon took off his clothes, however, the official noticed that he was wearing a woman's white underkimono.[2]

Suke-emon was embarrassed and said: 'This garment is not mine. I have an old mother, and she thinks about me day and night. When I was about to leave my home province and went to tell her about the vendetta, I felt sorry for her and told her simply that I was going with some other members of the clan to the Kantō on a pilgrimage to our departed master's grave and was saying good-bye before I left. My mother must have suspected what was going on for some time, and she told me that your skin gets cold while you are walking on the road. She then brought out this garment. In other words, I have just engaged in a vendetta wearing women's underwear. It's really not the thing to say at this time, but she is my mother, who doesn't have long to live, and I have great affection for her'. He went on, holding back tears: 'Talking about private things in this way is not at all befitting for a samurai, and I fear I have lost face'. The men listening to him wept in sympathy. Surely all who hear this story would have to agree that Tominomori was a truly faithful samurai.

After the loyal band carried out *seppuku*, a poem card bearing his last poem was sent to his mother.[3] She was pleased that he had shown himself to be a samurai without a stain, and showed not a sign of grief as she pronounced the name of the Buddha and carried out Buddhist ceremonies.

Tominomori's wife was at that time thirty years old. They had a son named Chōsaburō, whom she brought up well, while at the same time lavishing care on her aged mother.

1. This man will presumably take charge of Tominomori until he is executed. See Seward, p. 52 ff.

2. Wearing a beloved person's clothing close to the skin, perhaps even sleeping with it on, is a familiar action in Japanese literature. It is reported, incidentally, that Japanese soldiers in World War II died not with the name of the Emperor on their lips, but the word for mother: *okaasan*.

3. She seems to be writing her son a long letter. The heap of cloth in front of her may be a blanket she is sending with the letter - something else to swaddle him in her love.

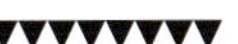

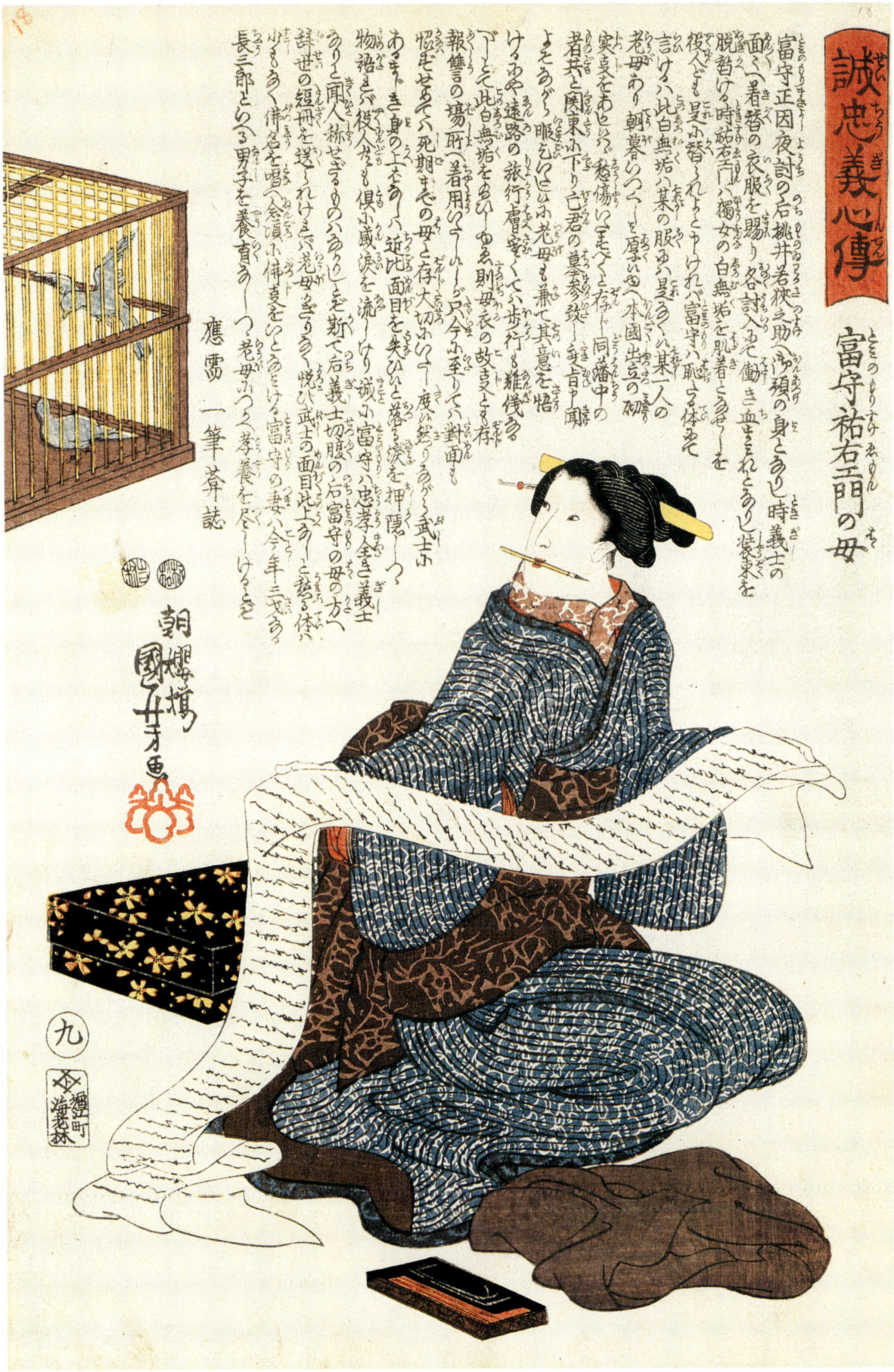

誠忠義心傳

富守祐右エ門の母

應需 一筆菴誌

朝櫻樓國芳画

九

Mother of Takebayashi Sadashichi

Takebayashi Sadashichi's mother was Takasada's wet-nurse, making Sadashichi his milk-brother. After the death of that lord and the delivery of his body to the temple, she became wild with grief and even lost touch with reality and said to Sadashichi:

'I raised our young lord strong and healthy in my bosom, and now suddenly he is a suicide.[1] But his enemy is all right. That's terrible. I'm only an old woman, and heaven won't give me the opportunity to avenge our lord and father, but you, a bow-and-arrow-bearing man born in his house, can do it for me. You can show your filial piety to lord and parent. You can kill Moronao and offer him at your lord's grave and ease his suffering under the sod. It would be just like being wounded or dying on the battlefield. It isn't any different; it's the same idea. By throwing away one life you pay for many years of loving kindness.'

Thus she went on pleading with him, and Sadashichi, restraining his tears, said: 'Although I am unworthy, I swear to heaven that I shall bring vengeance to our lord and set his heart at rest.'

Thus his mother was consoled and went to bed that night with joy, but the next morning, when the sun was already high, she was still not stirring, and Sadashichi went to her bed and found that she had committed suicide. She left a note reading:

I have given my life for our lord. I pass a duty to my son:

After I am gone
think of this last remembrance:
the dew on my sleeve,
the moon on a cloudy night
covered by a mist of tears.

Shocked and aggrieved but indignant to the core, Sadashichi was from this time forth a man fired with an unceasing lust for vengeance. He was truly a samurai, but also a faithful son who knew he had not yet carried out his mother's wishes.

People who heard this story wept.

II.10

Mother of Takebayashi Sadashichi amid cherry blossoms

1. This grief-stricken mother of Takebayashi Sadashichi in lovely kimono indeed appears distracted. Falling cherry blossoms intensify the sombre mood of this print.

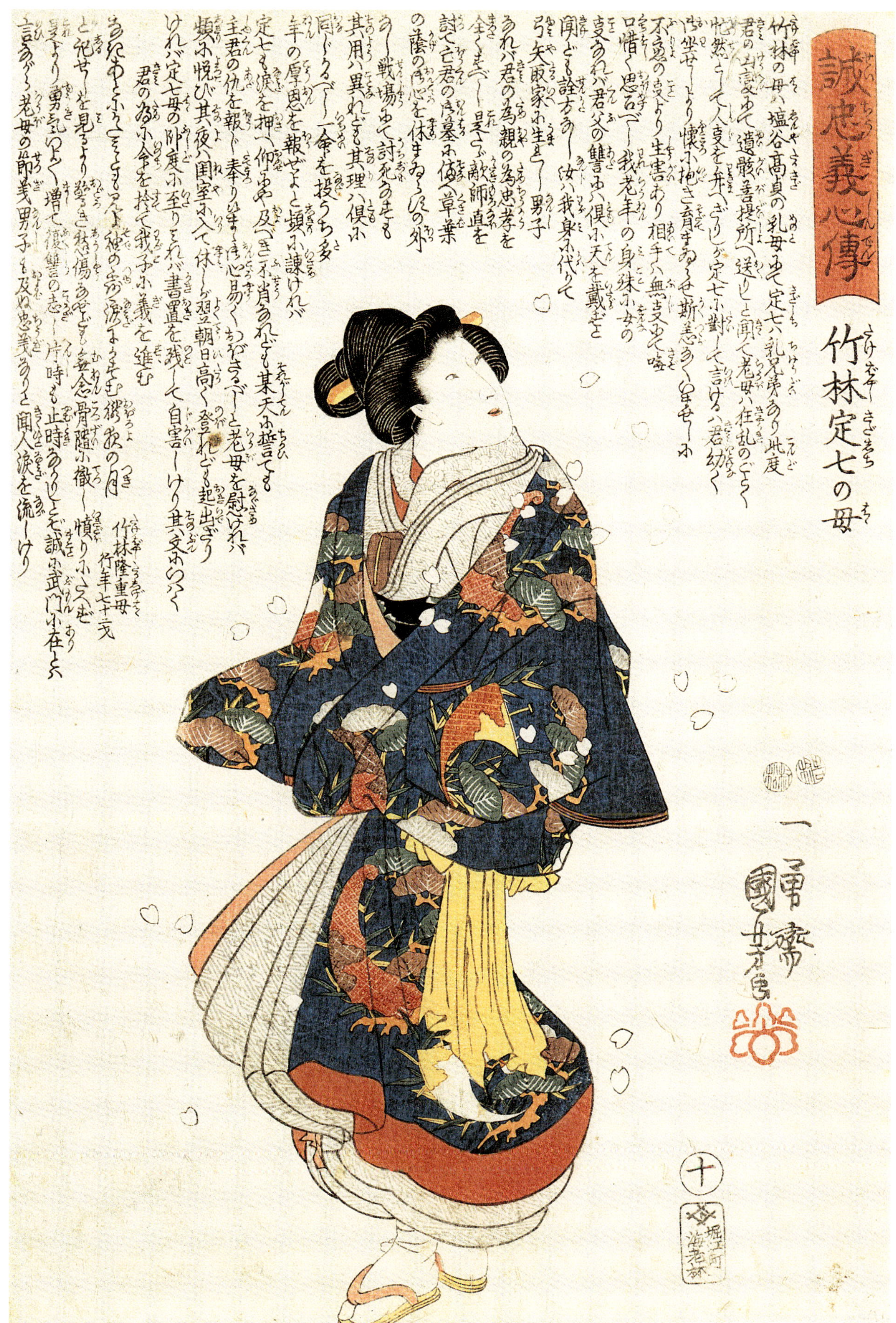
誠忠義心傳
竹林定七の母
一勇齋國芳画
十

Sister of Aihara Esuke Munefusa

11.11

Sister of Aihara Esuke Munefusa gazing at birds fluttering overhead

After the dissolution of the Akao estates, Aihara Munefusa wandered about the Naniwa area for a time and then changed his name, moved to the Kantō district, and took up residence in Aoichō, in Honjō. He had one younger sister, who was staying with relatives in Ono, in Banshū.

She was aware that Munefusa and his devoted companions were undergoing travail in order to carry out their plan of vengeance and that before long they would attain their heart's desire. Out of a wish to preserve the fame of these men for future generations, she started to write, on the first day of December, a short biography about the forty-some men bound by their oath. It was entitled *The chronicle of the Red Castle league (Akaki meiden)*.[1]

When Senzaki Yagorō saw it, he said: 'It's nicely written, but some will have difficulty understanding its way of putting things. I'm not very talented, but I think if I write some notes for it, people will understand it better.' Munefusa was pleased and asked him to help.

Munefusa then wrote a text that was detailed and dense but described the Akao adherents one by one - who was loyal, who was disloyal; who was courageous, who was cowardly - and named names. He sent this to his sister, accompanied by a poem that would make their names live after they were gone:

Worlds that have not seen
or felt the depth to which
these snows have fallen
will find their spirits darken
with the ink laid by this brush.

Thus, after her brother Esuke had carried through his plans, the sister penned the *League chronicle* in scores of copies and sent it to interested parties. Later, people came to realize how extraordinary the exploits of these men were, chronicled before them in such complete detail. By her actions in passing on so faithfully the record of Munefusa's determination, his sister's devotion became an everlasting model to military families.

1. The character for 'red' is the first character of 'Akao.'

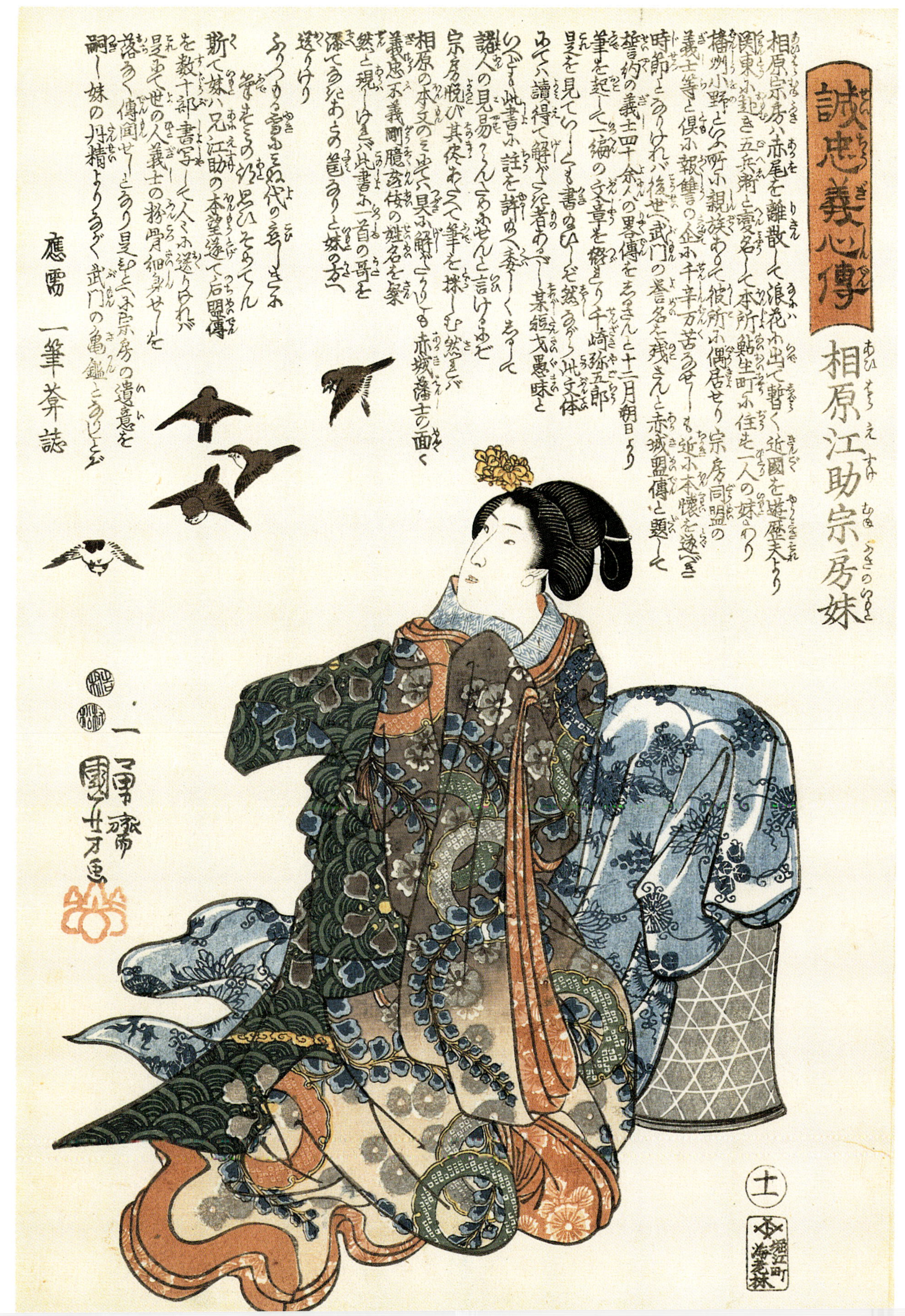
誠忠義心傳
相原江助宗房妹
十

Shimabara courtesan Kashiwagi-Daiyū

II.12

Shimabara courtesan Kashiwagi-Daiyū in flowing kimono

After Ōboshi departed from Akao, he lived an idle life in Yamashina, in Kyoto, and spent his days and nights in dissolute enjoyment in Shimabara, in Gion-chō.[1] On the anniversary of his late lord's death, he attracted the wrong kind of attention by having fish and poultry brought into his residence, soon filled with geishas and dancing girls, dancing drunkenly about.[2]

He saw much of the Shimabara courtesan named Kashiwagi-Daiyū, with whom he indulged in drink and debauchery for days on end on the second floor of the Kikyōya.[3] He called in comedians with names like Itchū and Shisei and threw money around to worthless individuals. In the end he sold the weapons he had brought with him to pay off the debts he had incurred for red-light district excesses.

Then he took off into the cold for the Kantō, without informing even his neighbours. His wife, O-ishi, paid off all his debts, down to the last penny.

For Kashiwagi, he left various small gifts, including cash. These she divided these among the girls in the establishment in recompense for many sleepless nights.

Then, later, after Ōboshi had carried out his mission, Kashiwagi was assailed by many concerns that she may have been ill-used, but when she thought of the sense of duty that he had maintained through it all, she placed a monument in his memory and prayed for his salvation on the anniversaries of his death.

Those who heard of her faithfulness admired Kashiwagi, and countless numbers came to the gay quarters and proposed to her. The house did a thriving business.

On the first anniversary of his death, Kashiwagi wrote this remembrance:

As the spring passes
and thoughts of you come again,
my sleeves become damp,
and I find the words we spoke
all bursting into blossom.

1. The Gion district of Kyoto is still one of the best known geisha districts in Japan. Few festivals are so publicized as that known as the Gion Matsuri, held each year in July.

2. Eating meat or fish on an anniversary was considered a sign of disrespect.

3. *Daiyū*, or *Taiyū*, was a title for high-ranked courtesans or geisha.

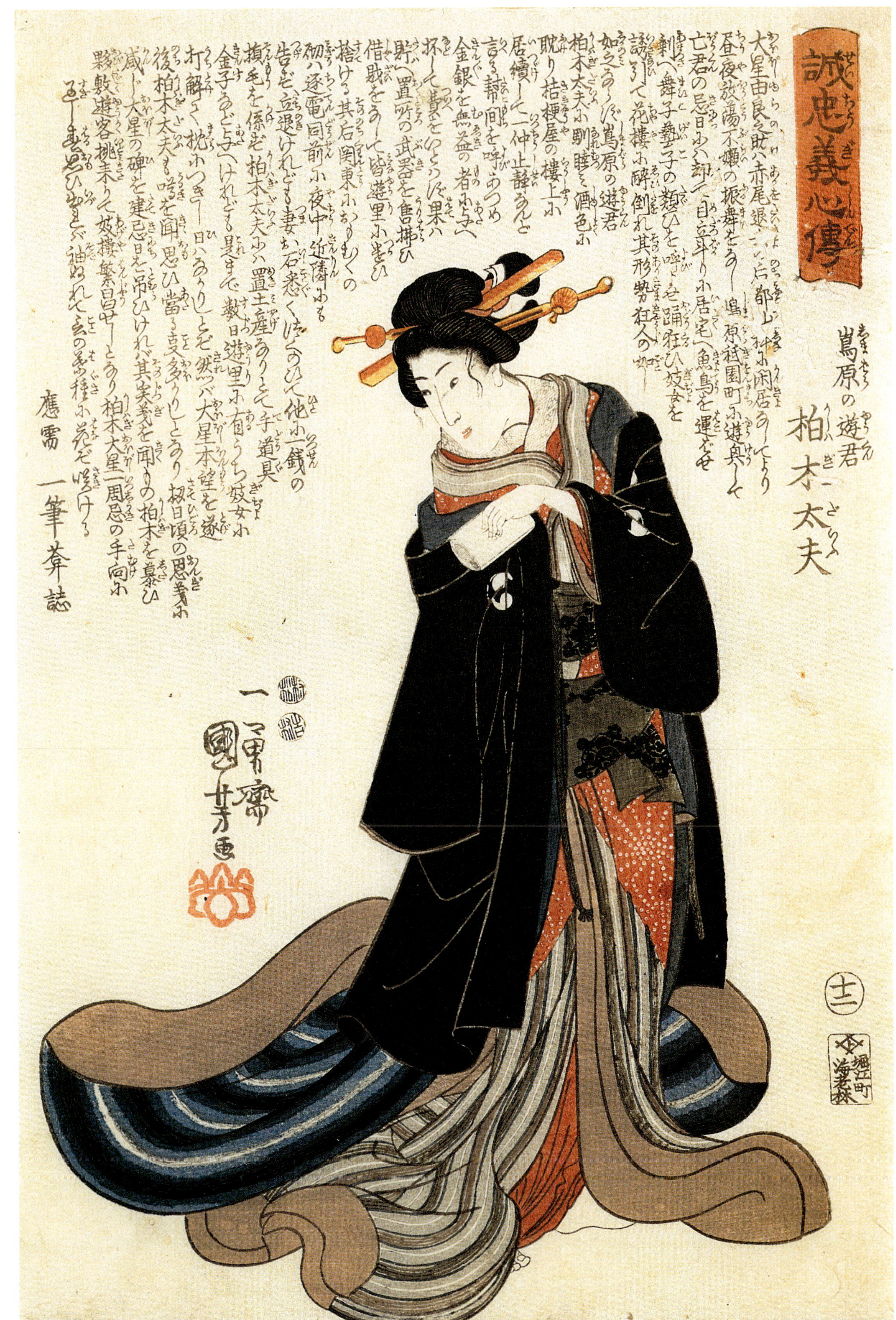
誠忠義心傳
嶌原の遊君
柏木太夫
應需 一筆菴誌
一勇斎國芳画
堀江町 海老林

Wife of Uramatsu Handayū

II.13

Wife of Uramatsu Handayū tying up a thief

Uramatsu Gihei was a hereditary retainer of the Akao clan who had two sons. The elder was named Handayū and the younger Masaemon. That younger son, however, had been adopted by Gihei with the permission of his natural parents. All of them were living in the Kantō area when the lord of the clan met his end, and there they received word that men were coming in from all points to die defending the castle.

Gihei was an old man, but he felt that as long as he lived what had occurred would be a blot on his honour as a samurai. He therefore got ready to go to Akao. Handayū followed his father's lead, and the two of them got their weapons in order and set out.

Even though the head of the house was away, the edict came down that his mansion was to be vacated, and Masaemon went to assist his mother and Handayū's wife in moving the household furnishings to a rented house in Jigokudani, in Kōjimachi.

At this time the *rōnin* from the Akao family were scattered about everywhere. It was a very confusing time, and many men took advantage of the occasion to commit mischief. In fact, one night someone who was aware that the Uramatsu household was made up only of women made his way in.

Handayū's wife was lying awake, but she did not panic. She quietly tied her sash and hid behind a screen when, unaware of her presence, a burglar started prying at the lock of a dresser. The wife jumped out, grabbed him and tied him up.[1]

'You're lucky that it was a woman's house you sneaked into to burgle. I was awake fearing something like this. Now I'm going to set you to guard our gate, and I'll get a good night's rest.' With that she took that big man, as if he were a little child, and tied him to a gate pillar. Then she closed the door, quietly went to her bedroom and slept.

The next morning the terrified thief apologized, and, since nothing was taken, she let him go. Word of this event got around in the neighborhood and let people know that, though the Uramatsu family members were not all home, none of them were people to be trifled with.

1. The scene is filled with womanly gear: a high pillow, a pipe, teacups, and the broomstick with which she seems to have brought this intruder down.

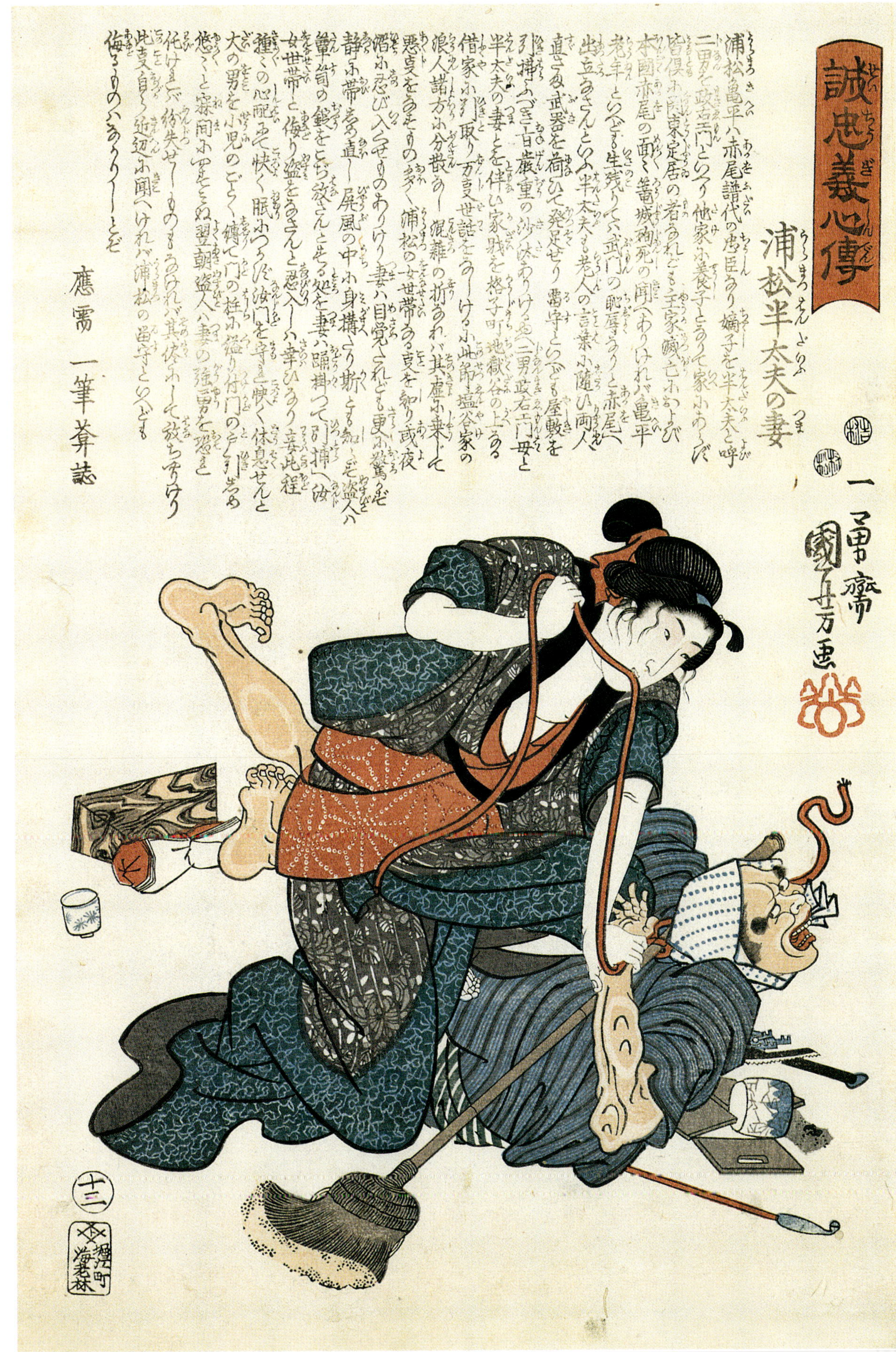
誠忠義心傳
浦松半太夫の妻
一勇斎國芳画
應需 一筆菴誌
十二

Wife of Okano Gin-emon

II.14

Wife of Okano Gin-emon clutching clothing to her breast

In Senzaki Yagorō's store, Gin-emon met a woman who had been a wet-nurse for a Kōno retainer, and after a time they became engaged. He had learned that her father had been a carpenter in charge of maintenance at the Kōno mansion for some years.

Through Yagorō, arrangements were completed to have Gin-emon adopted into the family as the prospective husband. To begin with, they announced his honoured status. Then she asked for leave from the Kōno family and returned with him to her home to take their vows as man and wife.

Gin-emon was a fine craftsman, skilled and versatile and eminently suitable to his new father, who felt him to be an incomparable person. He was introduced to the other men in charge of construction and, early in the spring, was declared his father-in-law's heir.

Gin-emon was delighted when he was shown the drawings of the mansion's features, and when he felt his plans had come to fruition, he immediately communicated with Ōboshi, and the enemy's terrain was completely scrutinized. Then, when the time for the attack had come, he told his wife that he had to go to the mountains for lumber.

The next day the news got to her that the husband who had left her the day before, Gin-emon, was one of the band that had wreaked vengeance on the Kōno family. She and her parents were dumbfounded. It occurred to them that this man had married into the family in order to study the enemy turf and had taken the marriage vows to suit the occasion. All they could do was await what fate had in store for him.[1]

Then, the year after the loyal retainers had committed *seppuku*, Gin-emon's wife shaved her hair and became a nun in order to pray for her husband's salvation.

1. This print is filled with tragic pathos. The garment the woman is embracing is, of course, Gin-emon's, as is the one she is wearing, while others are strewn about her. The cloth in her mouth is there to hold back her sobs. Her grief is complicated by the realization that her husband betrayed her for a cause. Loyalty to one's wife, in fact, romantic love in general, is not an important virtue in the Confucian code.

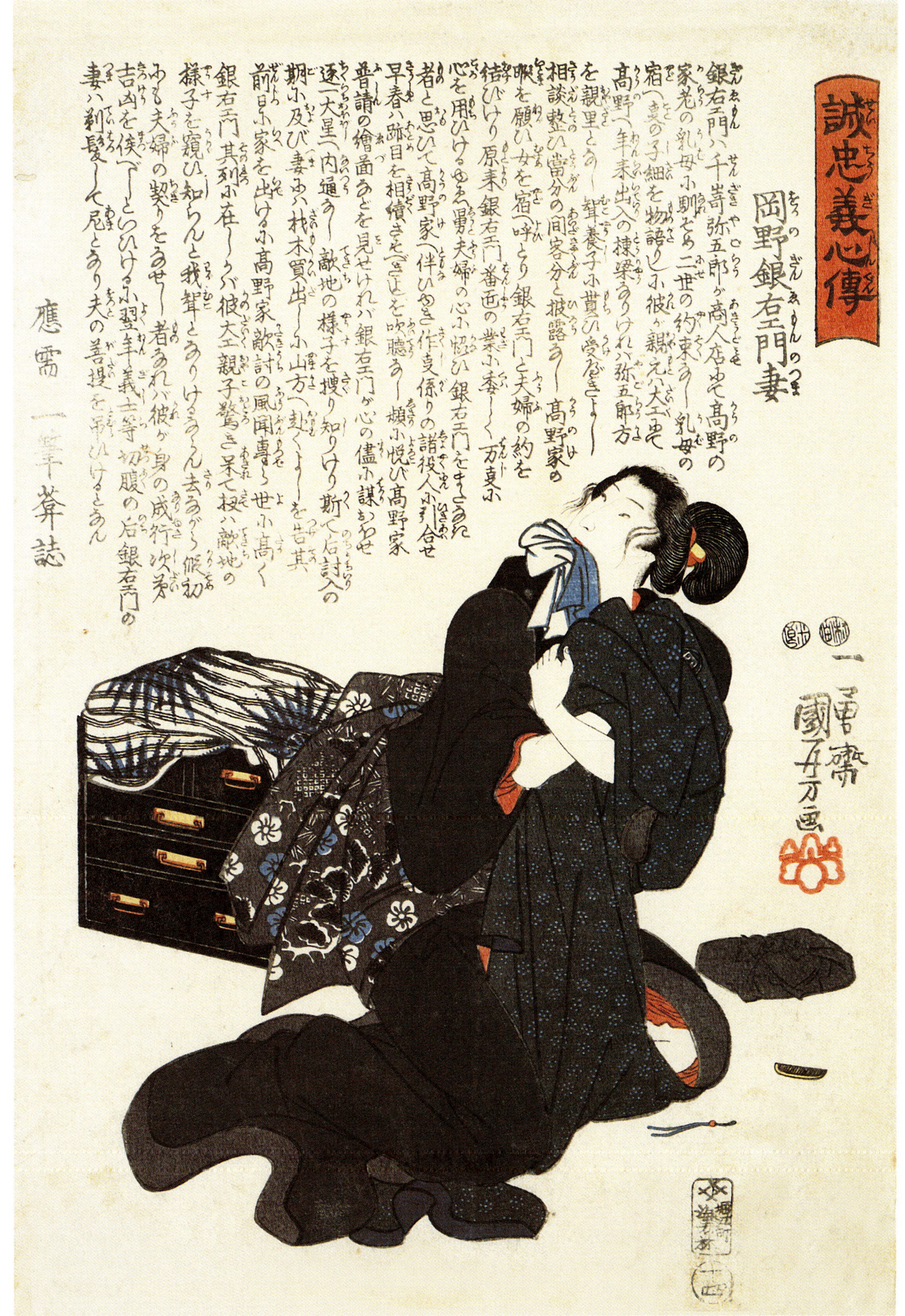
誠忠義心傳
岡野銀右衛門妻
應需 一筆菴誌
一勇齋國芳画

The swordsmith Tazaemon

Tazaemon was a swordsmith of great repute, with whom the Akao *rōnin* Uramatsu Handayū left a sword to be sharpened, a job which seemed never to be completed.[1] Tazaemon kept saying it was very difficult.

Handayū was quite upset and asked that the sword be returned as it was, because he was going on a trip soon. Tazaemon simply laughed and said that giving a master weapon of this kind a quick sharpening would be an insult to it. Then he said: 'Come back the day after tomorrow. I think I will have it for you then.' Like the dyer who is always putting his customer off, Tazaemon kept saying, 'Day after tomorrow,' and Handayū kept returning day after tomorrow and day after tomorrow until he decided he had taken all he could stand.

The time had come, in fact, for the band to take action, and Handayū was overjoyed when he came on the morning of the 13th to find the sword ready. He paid Tazaemon his fee and threw in a tip of one *bu*, in gold. Tazaemon brought out a repast of sake and seafood. 'It's so beautifully done, I would like to try it out on something,' Handayū said. Tazaemon said: 'The verandah pillar should work.'

So Handayū went out in the garden and took one great swing. Now, the sword was made by Osafune Sukesada. That first swipe cut halfway through the pillar. Handayū was very pleased with the marvelous cutting power it showed in the test. When he showed it to his comrades they said, 'You're mad.'

On the morning of the 15th, stories of the vendetta were already rampant. Crowds of people who had heard about Handayū were reported as having come to see that pillar. In fact Tazaemon's pillar became one of the wonders of Kanda Koyanagi-machi. Nobody knows exactly where it is now.

II.15

The swordsmith Tazaemon pointing from lotus position

1. The long boxes behind Tazaemon contain swords, with the name Kunimitsu on one and Munesada on the other. The large stone in the tub is his whetstone. The master craftsman has assumed the lotus position as he points to the pillar over his sake dispenser and tiny cup.

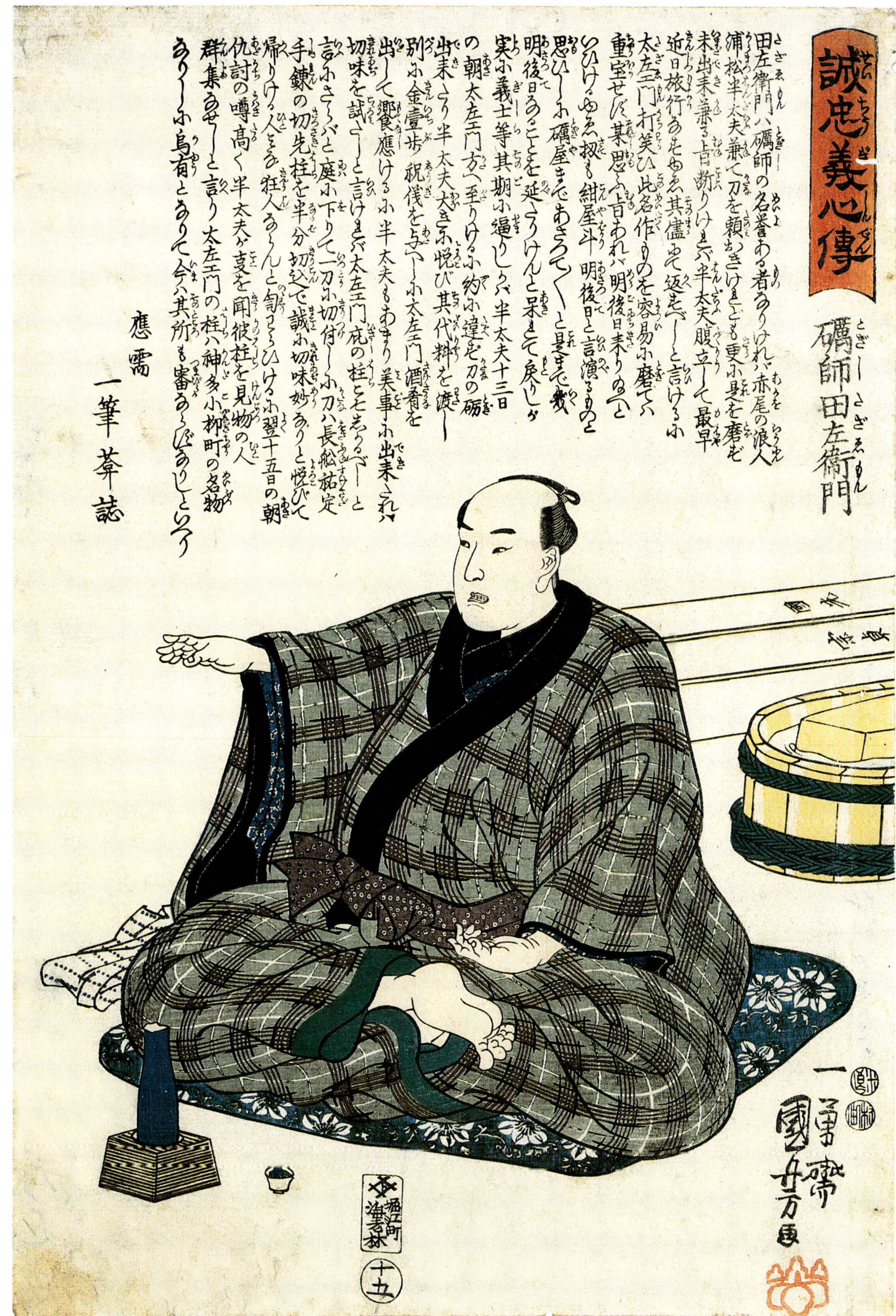
誠忠義心傳
礪師田左衛門
應需 一筆菴誌
一勇齋國芳画
十五

Ōboshi Sampei Nobutomo

II.17[1]

Ōboshi Sampei Nobutomo waiting by a palanquin

Sampei was a *rōnin* related to Ōboshi Yoshio through Ōboshi Shōji, a native of Tsugaru. He had been aware for some time of his cousin's plans and wanted to join the group and take part in the attack. On the fateful night, therefore, he waited by the side of the road as the advance on the Kōno mansion approached and pleaded with Yoshio to be taken along.

The older Ōboshi appreciated his loyalty but was fearful of having the vendetta look like a feud between their family and the Kōno. Sampei, however, was not daunted and, along with his friends Horii Kujūrō and Itō Asa-emon and students of Horiuchi Genzaemon, stood guard outside the Kōno mansion and held off any who attempted to come to the rescue of the Kōno clan. Along with Ikeda Gemba and his men, they kept the area around the enemy mansion secure.

As the attackers withdrew from the mansion, their mission accomplished, Sampei stood outside the Munenji gate by a palanquin he had hired for someone who might be wounded, holding Yasubei's forgotten spear.

There were many people like this who kept the faith with Ōboshi and his loyal comrades, helping them and knowing joy as well as relief in their success. All are pilgrims of the martial spirit, devotees of loyalty, and habitués of the realm of heroism.

1. Print no. 16 is listed by Robinson as 'not seen.'

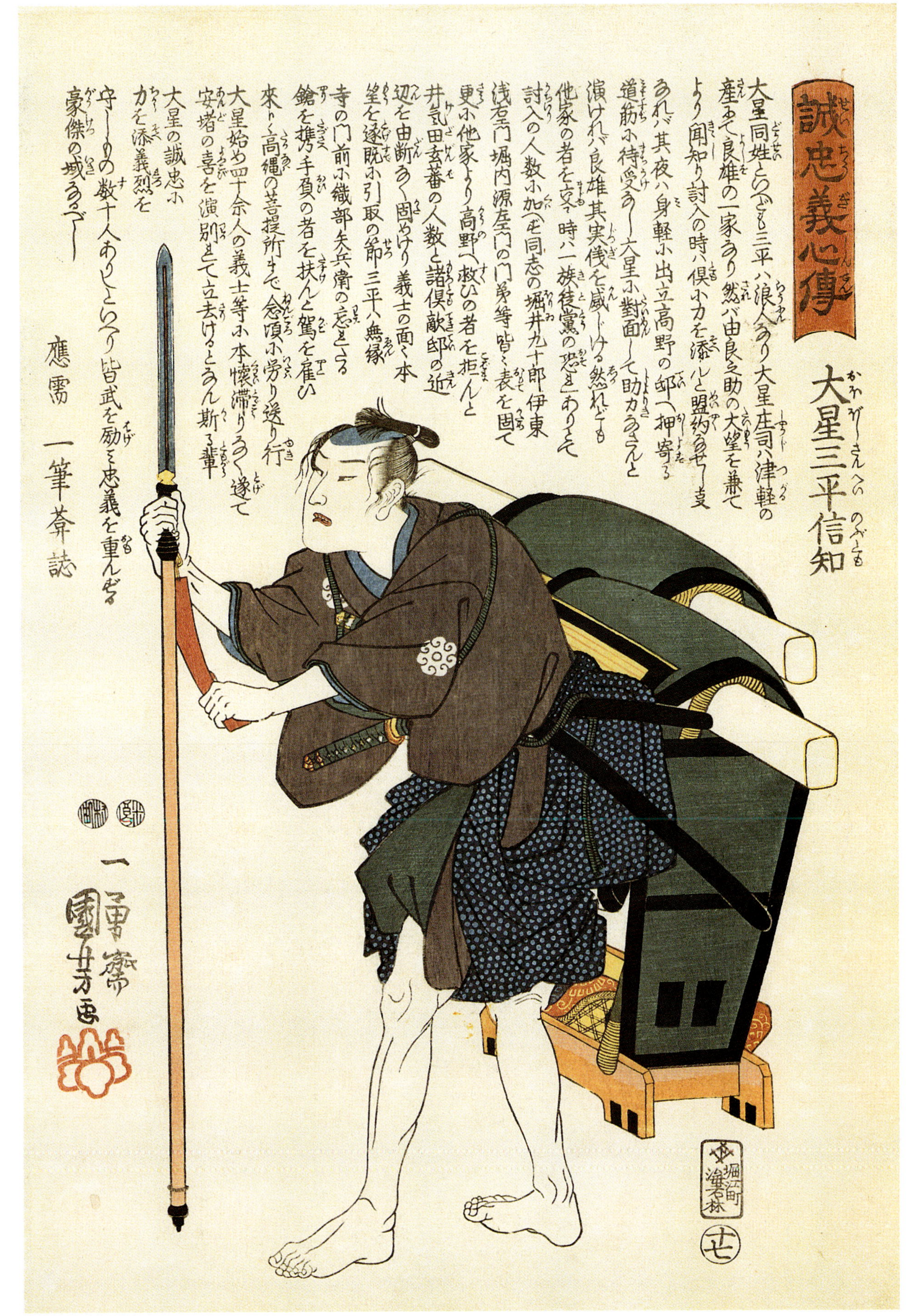
誠忠義心傳
大星三平信知
應需 一筆菴誌
一勇斎國芳画
堀江町 海老林
廿七

Old servant Katsusuke

11.18

Old servant Katsusuke holding forth a keepsake

After the abolition of the fief, Ōboshi held a number of meetings in the castle which arrived at a resolution to hold the castle and die fighting. Then, however, the Ono group was driven out, and a select group of determined men made a secret agreement and turned over the castle. The legation from Kamakura was welcomed, and the clan's samurai were dispersed.

As Ōboshi bided time near the castle, preparing to depart, an old man named Katsusuke, who had served with him for a long time, came to his dwelling and said: 'I have received the warmth of your bounty for many years, and I would like to go with you wherever you go, but I am old and not very useful and have come to say goodbye.'

Ōboshi nodded and rummaged around in his sleeve to find something he could give as a remembrance, and then, in a box of writing utensils that had not yet been packed to go on the boat, he found fourteen or fifteen *ryō* of coins. He took these and proffered them as a parting gift, but Katsusuke bristled and gave the money back, saying: 'I am an indigent old man who looks like he needs money, but now, having come here to say such a painful farewell, being given money is heartless.'

Ōboshi burst out laughing and said, 'There must be something you would like to have,' and walked about in puzzlement for a time, talking to himself. Then he took out his inkstone and drew a picture of a samurai and his servant on their way to the pleasure quarters.

'Here you are,' he said, 'going down with me to the teahouses. Take this as a keepsake.' With that he gave the drawing to the old man.

Katsusuke wept. 'There is nothing you could have given me that could please me more,' he said, and talked a little about the terrible events going on around them. Then, weeping profusely, he said goodbye and departed.

Ōboshi was impressed by Katsusuke's sincerity and sent the money to the man's home without telling him. The drawing can still be seen in the Akao Kagakuji.[1]

1. Mentioned in I.2 and I.5 as the temple where the compact was signed.

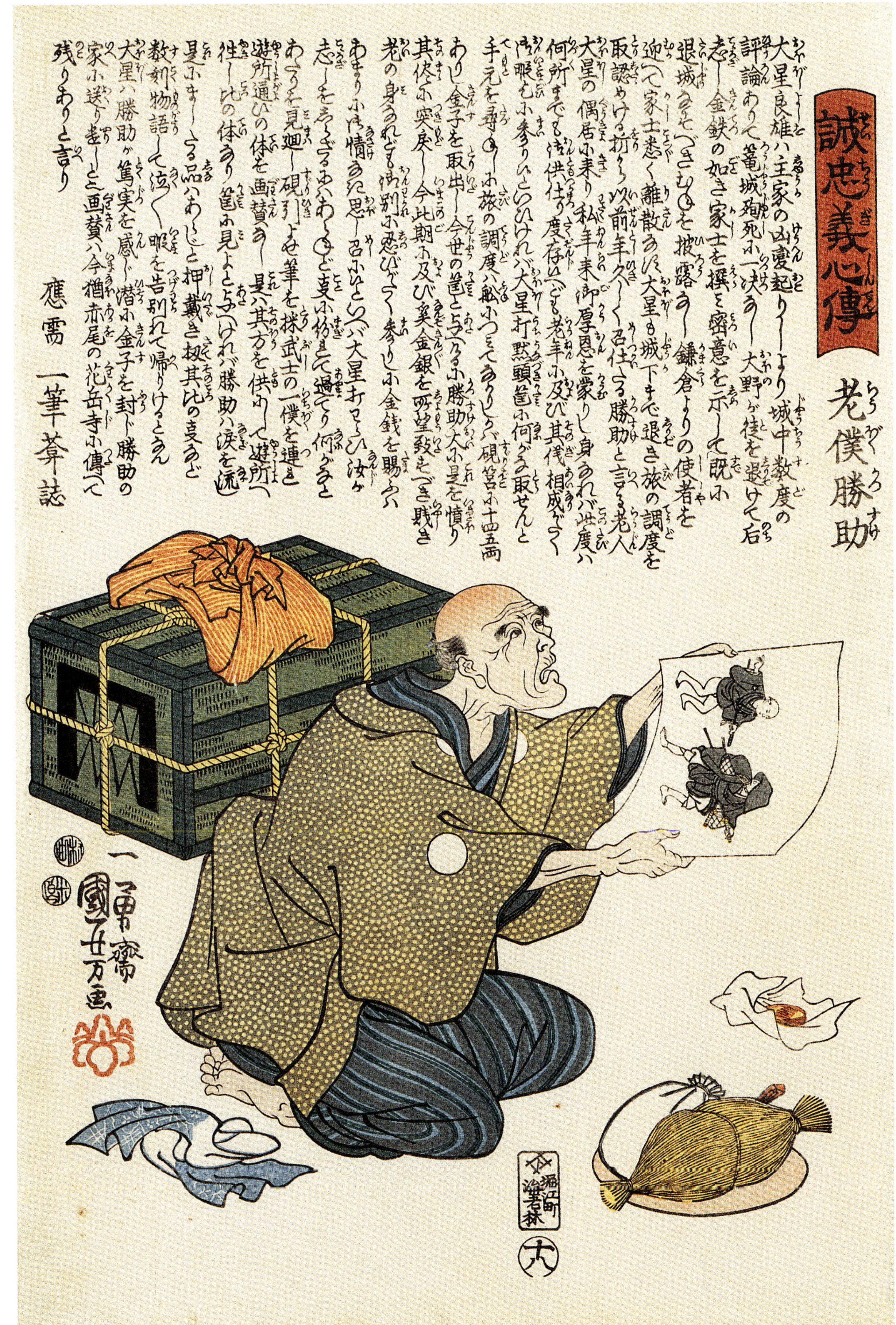
誠忠義心傳
老僕勝助
應需 一筆葊誌
一勇斎國芳画

Appendices

a. Romanizing Japanese

Romanization of names in the translations in this book will follow this table for sounds based on the aboriginal Japanese, meaning sounds other than those in Chinese loan-words:

a	ka	sa	ta	na	ha	ma	ya	ra	wa	
i	ki	shi	chi	ni	hi	mi	(y)i	ri	(w)i	
u	ku	su	tsu	nu	fu	mu	yu	ru	(w)u	
e	ke	se	te	ne	he	me	(y)e	re	(w)e	
o	ko	so	to	no	ho	mo	yo	ro	(w)o	-n

The vowels are pronounced as in Italian, or as in the English sounds *ah, ee, oo, eh, oh.*

It should be noted that the initial *s* consonant sound becomes an *sh* before an *i* sound; the initial *t* consonant becomes a *ch-* before a *u* sound and a *ts-* before a *u* sound; the initial *h* consonant is pronounced like an *f* before a *u* sound; the initial *y* consonant is silent before the vowel sounds for *i* and *e;* and the initial *w* consonant is silent before the vowels *i, u, e,* and *o.* The *-n* is the only consonant sound that can come at the end of a word.

Combinations of sounds other than those in the table, as with sounds beginning *hy-* and *ry-* and *ch-* with vowels other than *i,* as well as vowels written *ō* and *ū*, are part of Chinese loan-words. The *ō* and *ū* are given twice the normal duration.

b. Combined index of names on plates

Almost all of the translations of the texts on the individual plates begin with the complete name of the person pictured, expressed in three parts: first the surname, then two given names. Although we have attempted to keep variation to a minimum, occasionally one or another of the names is used in isolation.

The following list has been prepared to assist the reader in identifying the person referred to, as well as the print on which he, or she, is pictured, and given any part of the full name.

c. Notes on suffixes

The following suffixes appear on names with such regularity that explanation of them might be helpful:

-emon
(in some translations, rendered as *-yemon*) meaning 'guard at right gate' when not immediately preceded by *za*

-gorō
name suffix for fifth son

-jirō
name suffiix for second son

-rokurō
name suffix for sixth son

-saburō
name suffix for third son

-shichirō
name suffix for seventh son

-shirō
name suffix for fourth son

-suke
name suffix meaning 'assistant'

-tarō
name suffix for first son

-zaemon
meaning 'guard at the left gate'

d. On the currency

Currency values mentioned in the *Seichū gishi den* are difficult to analyse because they changed so much in different periods of Japanese history, and it is often impossible to know exactly what period Kuniyoshi's author Ippitsuan used for the setting. We don't know whether he used the values of his own late-Edo period of the 1840's or the Genroku period of 1702, in which the original events occurred.

Currency took many forms: gold, silver, copper, bronze, and rice. Comparative values shifted with different governments as the values of commodities, including the precious metals, fluctuated. The samurai, along with the *daimyō* and even the shogun, were paid in rice, the unit of which was the *koku* - 4.9629 bushels - called a *hyō* when it was bagged. The historical Ōishi Kuranosuke Yukitaka, for instance, (called by Ippitsuan Ōboshi Yuranosuke Yoshio) received a hereditary allowance of 1,500 *koku* a year. The samurai in the *Seichū gishi den* named Tokuda Sadaemon Yukitaka (I.20) received 9 *koku* plus support for three dependents. Hayano Wasuke Tsunenari (I.35) received his stipend not in *koku* but in 5 *ryō*, which may and may not mean that the *ryō* was roughly equivalent to the *koku* at that time.

According to Reischauer and Fairbank (*East Asia: the great tradition*, p. 606) 'It was roughly estimated that five *hyō* of stipend were sufficient to provide all the needs of one person for a year.' Sorai Ōgyū (1666-1728) a contemporary of the historical *rōnin*, said that his grandfather had bought a house in the commercial section of Edo for 50 *ryō* which was valued at 2,000 *ryō* in his father's time. (Yosoburo Takekoshi, *The economic aspects of the history of the civilization of Japan*, 1967, II, p. 135.)

The *Kōjien* dictionary (1955), gives the value of the *ryō* in gold as equal to 4 *bu* and in silver as 3 *bu* plus 4 *momme*. Takekoshi (III. 34) gives the value of the *ryō* in 1700 - the time of the *rōnin* - as 1 *ryō* in gold to 3.8 *kan* of copper.

Glossary

bijin-e
pictures of beautiful women

biwa
Japanese lute

biwa hōshi
storytellers, usually blind, who sang their narrations to the accompaniment of a lute

bu
monetary unit

Bunraku
puppet theater

Bushido
the code of the samurai

chū
loyalty, devotion

Chūshingura
Kabuki play about the forty-seven *rōnin*

daikon
giant white radish

daimon
wide-sleeved top garment with prominent crests worn on very formal occasions

daimyō
feudal lord

daiyū
title for a high ranking geisha

furigana
kana characters written beside Chinese characters to show how the writer wants them pronounced

futon
quilt mattress

giri
debt of loyalty that must be repaid in kind

gishi
faithful warriors

go
a game of checkers

gyōsho
cursive style of handwriting

hachimaki
headband

haikai
poem series formed of alternation of 17 and 14 syllable stanzas

haiku
verse of 17 syllables divided into 3 lines of 5, 7 and 5 syllables

hanshita
final tracing for the blockcutter

hara-kiri
a form of suicide by belly-cutting

hata-sashimono
war ornaments

hibachi
small Japanese charcoal brazier

hiragana
phonetic characters formed from the *sōsho*, or 'grass-writing' form of a Chinese character with a similar sound

hyō
measure of rice or grain

idō
floor fireplace

jin-sen
battle fan

Kabuki
the popular drama of Japan

kaishaku
seppuku assistant having the duty of beheading the suicide

kaisho
square, printed style of Chinese writing

kan
monetary unit

kana
Japanese phonetic (see *katakana* and *hiragana*)

Kanadehon Chūshingura
title of best known Kabuki play based on the *rōnin* story

kanamajiri
'mixture of kana and Chinese characters,' the basic form of written communication in Japanese

Kantō
generally refers to Edo, literally 'East of the barrier' (of Hakone)

katakana
phonetic character formed from a part of a Chinese character with similar sound

Kiri
imperial seal adopted and adapted by Kuniyoshi

koku
unit of measure equal to 4.9629 bushels

konbu
kelp, an edible seaweed

koto
a stringed Japanese musical instrument

kusudama
a suspended scented ball of artificial flowers with coloured streamers

kyōgen
literally 'mad speech,' comic drama usually presented alternately with Noh plays

Lao Tzu
best known Taoist philosopher

mie
an exaggerated theatrical pose used to mark moments of emotional climax

mitate
parody print

miyakodori
'capital bird'

momme
a unit of weight equal to 3.75 grams

mon
feudal badge

naga-bakama
long cumbersome trousers

naga-gamishimo
broad-shouldered ceremonial garment

naginata
long-handled sword or glaive

Noh
the classic drama of Japan

ōban
standard print size of approximately 38 x 25 cm.

obi
sash for Japanese kimono

on
obligation to Emperor, lord, parent or teacher

ri
approximately 2.5 miles

rōnin
a masterless samurai

ryō
monetary unit

samurai
a member of the warrior class in the Feudal period

sankin kōtai
'alternating attendance' required by shoguns for political control

sei (makoto)
truth, sincerity

seppuku
an alternate term for *hara-kiri*. A form of suicide

shi (samurai)
samurai

shin (kokoro)
heart, deep feeling

shoji
sliding panels of translucent paper used as doors and windows in traditional Japanese buildings

sho tokuri
1.8 litre bottle

soba
buckwheat noodles

sōsho
'grass writing,' most cursive style of writing

suemono-giri
'trial cutting,' or swordsman's skill of cutting a stationary object

sumo
Japanese style wrestling

tachi
long sword

taibi
'the end'

tameshi-giri
see *suemono-giri*

tanka
31-syllable poem

tanzaku
a narrow strip of writing paper for poems or names

Taoism
form of Chinese religion

tatami
woven straw mat

tokonoma
a shallow alcove, central devotional place in the Japanese home or banquet room

tokuri
small sake pitcher

tomo-e
crest design

ukiyo-e
woodblock prints of the 'floating world'

utai
Kabuki or Bunraku narrators

waka
a poem of five lines in a pattern of 7, 5, 7 and 7 syllables per line

waraji
straw sandals

yukata
dressing gown or robe

Select bibliography

Allen, Jeanne. *The designer's guide to samurai patterns*. London: Thames and Hudson Ltd., 1990.

Allyn, John. *The forty-seven rōnin story*. Rutland, Vermont & Tokyo, Japan: Charles E. Tuttle Company, Inc., 1981.

Benedict, Ruth. *The chrysanthemum and the sword: patterns of Japanese culture*. Boston: Houghton Mifflin Company, 1946.

Brandon, James R. *Chūshingura: studies in Kabuki and the puppet theater*. Honolulu: University of Hawaii Press, 1982.

Buck, Pearl S., trans. *All men are brothers*. New York: John Day, 1937.

Chamberlain, Basil Hall. *Japanese things*. Rutland, Vermont & Tokyo, Japan: Charles E. Tuttle Company, 1981.

Clark, Timothy T. '*Mitate-e*: some thoughts, and a summary of recent writings.' In *Impressions, The journal of the Ukiyo-e Society of America, Inc.*, no. 19, 1997.

[Dailey, Merlin C.]. *The Raymond A. Bidwell collection of prints by Utagawa Kuniyoshi*. Springfield, Massachusetts: The Raymond A. and Bertha U. Bidwell Fund for the Museum of Fine Arts, 1968.

[Dailey, Merlin C.]. *Raymond A. Bidwell collection: Utagawa Kuniyoshi*. Springfield, Massachusetts: Springfield Museum of Fine Arts, 1980.

Dickins, Frederick V. *Chiushingura; or, the loyal league*. London: Allen, & Co., Waterloo Place, 1880.

Dunn, Charles, J. *Everyday life in traditional Japan*. 1969. Reprint, Rutland, Vermont & Tokyo, Japan: Charles E. Tuttle Company, Inc., 1985.

Edmunds, Will H. *Pointers and clues to the subjects of Chinese and Japanese art*. London: Sampson, Low, Marston & Co., Ltd., 1934. Reprint, includes index, Geneva: Minkoff, 1974.

Forrer, Matthi. *Drawings by Utagawa Kuniyoshi*. The Hague: SDU Publishers, 1988.

Frederic, Louis. *Daily life in Japan at the time of the samurai, 1185-1603*. New York: Praeger Publishers, 1972.

Gunji, Masakatsu. *Kabuki*. Tokyo: Kodansha, 1969.

Halford, Aubrey S. & Giovanna M. Halford. *The Kabuki handbook*. 1974. Reprint, Rutland, Vermont & Tokyo, Japan: Charles E. Tuttle Company, Inc., 1979.

Hane, Mikiso. *Peasants, rebels and outcasts: the underside of modern Japan*. New York: Pantheon, 1982.

Hearn, Lafcadio. *Japan: an interpretation*. 1904. Reprint, Rutland, Vermont & Tokyo, Japan: Charles E. Tuttle Company, 1981.

Hepburn, James Curtis. *A Japanese and English dictionary with an English and Japanese index*. Rutland, Vermont & Tokyo, Japan: Charles E. Tuttle Company, 1990.

Jackson, J.H., trans. *Water margin*. Hong Kong: Commercial Press, 1963.

Japan National Tourist Organization. *The new*

official guide: Japan. Japan Travel Bureau, Inc., 1975.

Joly, Henri L. *Legend in Japanese art.* 1908. Reprint, Rutland, Vermont & Tokyo, Japan: Charles E. Tuttle Co. Inc., 1979.

Klompmakers, Inge. *Of brigands and bravery. Kuniyoshi's heroes of the* Suikoden. Leiden: Hotei Publishing, 1998.

Keene, Donald., trans. *Chūshingura (The treasury of loyal retainers). A puppet play by Takeda Izumo, Miyoshi Shōraku and Namiki Senryū.* New York: Columbia University Press, 1971.

Maslow, A.H. 'Cognition of being in the peak experiences.' In *The journal of genetic psychology,* 94, 1959.

Michener, James A. *Japanese prints from the early masters to the modern.* Rutland, Vermont & Tokyo, Japan: Charles E. Tuttle Co., 1959.

Mitford, A. B. (Lord Redesdale). *Tales of old Japan.* 1871. Reprint, Rutland, Vermont & Tokyo, Japan: Charles E. Tuttle Company, Inc., 1982.

Nakau, Ei. *Chūshingura ukiyoe.* Tokyo, 1988.

O'Neill, P.G. *Japanese names.* New York & Tokyo: Weatherhill, Inc., 1989.

Reischauer, Edwin O. and John K. Fairbank. *East Asia: the great tradition.* Boston: Houghton Mifflin, 1962.

Robinson, B.W. *Summary catalogue of drawings by Utagawa Kuniyoshi in the collection of Ferd. Lieftinck of Haren (Groningen) Holland.* Privately published, 1953.

Robinson, B.W. *Kuniyoshi.* London: Her Majesty's Stationery Office, 1961.

Robinson, B.W. *Kuniyoshi: the warrior prints.* New York: Cornell University Press, 1982.

Robinson, B.W. *Supplement to Kuniyoshi: the warrior prints.* 1996. Unpublished.

Saito, Shiuichiro and Edward Greey. *The loyal ronins.* New York: G.P. Putman's Sons, 1880.

Sansom, G.B. *Japan: a short cultural history.* New York: The Cresset Press, Ltd., 1952.

Schaap, Robert. *Heroes & Ghosts. Japanese prints by Kuniyoshi 1797-1861.* Leiden: Hotei Publishing, 1998.

Schmorleitz, Morton S. *Castles in Japan.* Rutland, Vermont & Tokyo, Japan: Charles E. Tuttle Co., 1974.

Seward, Jack. *Hara-kiri: Japanese ritual suicide.* Rutland, Vermont: Charles E. Tuttle Co., 1968.

Shaver, Ruth M. *Kabuki costume.* Rutland, Vermont & Tokyo, Japan: Charles E. Tuttle Co., 1990.

Shinmura, Izuru., ed. *Kojien.* Tokyo: Iwanami Shoten, 1955.

Shioya, Sakae. *Chūshingura: an exposition.* Tokyo: The Hokuseido Press, 1956.

Shively, Donald H. 'Tokugawa plays on forbidden topics.' In James R. Brandon, *Chūshingura: studies in Kabuki and the puppet theatre.* Honolulu: University of Hawaii Press, 1982.

Stewart, Basil. *Subjects portrayed in Japanese colour-prints*. London: Kegan Paul, Trench, Trubner & Co., Ltd., 1922. Reprint, *A guide to Japanese prints and their subject matter*. New York: Dover Publications, Inc., 1979.

Storry, Richard. *The way of the samurai.* London: Orbis Publishing Limited, 1978.

Takekoshi, Yosoburo. *The economic aspects of the history of the civilization of Japan*. London: Dawson's of Pall Mall, 1967.

Theatre Museum of the Waseda University. *Vol. 2 from the theatre prints from the Theatre Museum, Waseda University*. Tokyo, Waseda University Press, 1992.

Uspenskij, M.V. *The samurai of the Eastern capital or the forty-seven faithful samurai. In prints by Ichiyusai Kuniyoshi and in biographies by Ippitsuan*. Kaliningrad: Jantarnijj Skaz, 1997.